D0922926

SENATOR GERALD P. NYE
AND AMERICAN FOREIGN RELATIONS

Wayne S. Cole, a professor of history at Iowa State University, is the author of a related book, *America First: The Battle Against Intervention, 1940–41*.

Senator Gerald P. Nye and American Foreign Relations

Wayne S. Cole

THE UNIVERSITY OF MINNESOTA PRESS
Minneapolis

LIBRARY
JAN 8 1963
UNIVERSITY OF THE PACIFIC
114455

© Copyright 1962 by the University of Minnesota

ALL RIGHTS RESERVED

Printed in the United States of America at the
North Central Publishing Company, St. Paul

Library of Congress Catalog Card Number: 62-21813

PUBLISHED IN GREAT BRITAIN, INDIA, AND PAKISTAN BY THE OXFORD UNIVERSITY PRESS, LONDON, BOMBAY, AND KARACHI, AND IN CANADA BY THOMAS ALLEN, LTD., TORONTO

To

MY MOTHER, FATHER, AND SISTER

Contents

Battle against Intervention

Epilogue

Illustrations *between pages 72 and 73*

AGRARIANS AND AMERICAN FOREIGN POLICY

1

Agrarians and American Foreign Policy

THE two world wars in the first half of the twentieth century aroused Americans to earnest and passionate debate on the proper role for the United States in world affairs. During this heated controversy American "isolationists" battled furiously, almost desperately, to make their views prevail, and they won transient victories in the two decades between the wars. By mid-century, however, proponents of "internationalism" and collective security had triumphed, and "isolationism" was beaten, discredited, and generally rejected.

Gerald P. Nye of North Dakota was one of the more colorful and controversial leaders of this "lost cause." In 1934–36 he led the Senate Committee Investigating the Munitions Industry that was both an expression of and a force for isolationism. He was a key figure in the enactment of the neutrality laws in the 1930's, helping in hundreds of speeches throughout the country to publicize and popularize noninterventionist views. He provided powerful leadership for opponents of the increasingly internationalist policies of President Franklin D. Roosevelt. And Nye was a tireless spokesman in 1941 for the America First Committee in its fight against intervention in World War II.

Nye's career is particularly significant for an understanding of the role of agrarianism in the rise and fall of American isolationism. The central hypothesis of this study is that important roots of isolationism may be traced to needs, desires, and value systems of major segments of the American agricultural society. Agrarian radicalism of the Great

Plains and Middle West exerted fundamental influences on Nye's foreign policy views.

This study of Senator Nye also analyzes the transition of American isolationism from liberalism to conservatism. In the 1920's and early 1930's most leading isolationists on foreign affairs were liberals or progressives on domestic issues. By the time the Japanese attacked Pearl Harbor, however, noninterventionists were commonly associated with conservatism, and most of their successors since World War II have been thoroughgoing conservatives. This shift also occurred in Nye's views. In his career it resulted partly from changes in the political bases from which he operated – changes necessitated by his growing opposition to President Roosevelt on the national scene and to William Langer in North Dakota. These political changes were accompanied by Nye's increasing opposition, in principle and in practice, to great presidential power. His agrarian orientation was also a factor. Crusades for the farmer against "Wall Street" and "big business" had aligned him with liberals. But when the urban masses and their liberal spokesmen began to play larger roles in the dominant political coalitions, Nye's continuing sympathy for the farmer moved him into accord with conservatives.

The terms "isolationist," "continentalist," and "noninterventionist" are used to cover a major pattern of American reactions to changing world conditions. They are also used to identify one of several theories concerning the role the United States should play in international affairs. The term "isolationist," though almost universally used, is misleading. Most of those to whom the label was applied did not wish literally to isolate the United States from the rest of the world. Central themes in isolationist attitudes were "unilateralism" and "noninterventionism." As unilateralists these people did not believe that the United States could prevent wars through cooperation with European states. They feared that international commitments would simply involve the United States in the wars that inevitably swept other parts of the world. They were determined to maintain a maximum degree of sovereignty and freedom of action for the United States in world affairs. Most of them opposed American membership in the League of Nations and in the Permanent Court of International Justice. In this connection, many isolationists (including Nye) had faith in the "power of example" – they believed that the United States could do more for the world by building and maintaining American prosperity and freedom under democracy than it could through internationalism and military force. As noninterventionists they believed that it had been a tragic mistake for the United States to enter World War I and that the United States could and should have stayed out of that conflagration. They took the same attitude toward World War II. Their noninterventionist attitudes toward European wars, however, were not necessarily extended to developments in Latin America, the Pacific, or the Far East. It was sometimes (though not always) possible to find isolationism and imperialism combined in the views of a single individual. Some pacifists supported the noninterventionist position before Pearl Harbor, but most noninterventionists were not pacifists. Isolationism also included a powerful strain of nationalism – though nationalism generally affected spokesmen for other points of view as well.[1]

Either explicitly or by implication, scholars have advanced varied theories attempting to explain why many Americans embraced isolationism. Most of these theories have, in effect, found explanations in conditions or developments within the United States. Most theories on the subject do not pretend to exclusiveness.

It is commonly assumed that the geographic remoteness of the Middle West, where isolationism traditionally has won particularly strong support, is of key importance in explaining the attitudes of middle westerners toward foreign policy. This theory may have much validity, but it should be remembered that isolationism received powerful backing in the Northeast and the Far West as well.[2] Several studies have demonstrated that Republicans have tended to endorse the noninterventionist position in greater numbers than Democrats. Undoubtedly political partisanship contributes to the explanation but many Republicans have been prominent in opposition to the isolationists, and some Democrats have been as convinced of the soundness of the noninterventionist approach as any Republican.[3] There is evidence suggesting that religious affiliations and attitudes have made some individuals particularly receptive to noninterventionist appeals. Roman Catholics and Lutherans, for example, appear to have been more isolationist than the population as a whole. Religious influences by themselves, however, probably account for only a small part of isolationist strength.[4]

Emotional and psychological bases for isolationism have been emphasized in a study by Bernard Fensterwald, Jr.[5]

A theory that has attracted particularly great attention is the one that finds ethnic roots for American isolationism. Samuel Lubell, after careful investigation, concluded that the most important stronghold for American isolationism was to be found among the German-American ethnic groups. While not emphasized by Lubell, the Irish-Americans (and perhaps Italian-Americans) may also have had significant influence.[6]

Some suggest that isolationism arises out of ignorance or disinterest concerning international affairs. Thomas A. Bailey showed that "graders"—those who never went beyond the eighth grade in school—were more likely to react in isolationist terms than those with more formal education. This was, however, only a difference in degree, and most graders held foreign policy views similar to those of most high school and college graduates.[7] If ignorance, by itself, were an adequate explanation, one could reasonably expect that the South (with the poorest educational and informational facilities) would have been the leading isolationist section of the country before Pearl Harbor. In fact, the South was easily the most enthusiastically interventionist of the nation's regions before the United States formally entered World War II.[8] Furthermore, many isolationists were tremendously interested in world affairs and were often as well informed on international developments as the persons who disagreed with them.

Probably no single hypothesis explaining American isolationism is sufficient. The causes of isolationism are varied and diverse. Given the inevitable limitations of human knowledge and the inadequacy of available facilities for measuring and testing causal forces in human history, it is reasonable to suppose that scholars will in the future continue to disagree on the relative weight to be assigned the various factors.

There is, however, one other extremely important part of the explanation that should not be overlooked. This may be found in the fortunes and misfortunes of American agriculture.[9]

Gerald P. Nye was a particularly striking representative of agrarian-based isolationism. Throughout his entire public career (both as a small-town newspaper editor and as a United States senator from North Dakota) Nye's views were molded by the mores and interests of the agricultural society of the upper Missouri-Mississippi Valley. As the twenty-two-year-old editor of the *Creston Daily Plain Dealer* in Iowa in 1915 Nye wrote that "The farmer today is the backbone of the land."[10] He never abandoned this belief. And his attitudes on foreign policy were constructed from exactly the same fabric as his economic, social, and political views.

Nye did not use "agrarian" in a precise, restricted, or fixed way. Sometimes he spoke in terms of social and economic groups; other times he referred to geographical sections made up of diverse groups. Though he never explicitly reduced his analysis to this format, Nye's conception of agrarian interests may be described graphically as a series of concentric half-circles.

The inner core, of course, was the dirt-farmer himself—particularly the Great Plains wheat and livestock farmer. Then came a half-circle comprising the townspeople and the small businessmen who served the needs of farmers and whose economic prosperity was directly dependent upon the farmer. Nye was part of this group. In Iowa, in 1915, he wrote: "There is much in common between the farmer and us 'city guys.' When the farmer suffers then the rest of us suffer."[11] Five years later in an editorial he told his readers in Cooperstown, North Dakota, that the "interests of the city and town . . . in large measure, have much the same complaint against 'Big Business' and profiteers as have the farmers."[12] The next half-circle that may be identified encompassed the major sections of the country (South and West) whose economies were predominantly agricultural and which felt conflicts of interest when dealing with the Northeast, with Britain, and with Western Europe. Nye's sectional view was broad enough to include, at least by implication, major cities such as Chicago, and major businesses and businessmen whose interests were closely linked to agriculture. At certain stages in his thinking Nye even welcomed the big industrialist Henry Ford as an ally in the battle against "Wall Street."[13] In this context, it is not surprising to find so many middle western big businessmen among the leading noninterventionists before Pearl Harbor. The wealth of some of these, including Jay C. Hormel, Philip T. Swift, and John Cudahy, had been acquired in the processing and distribution of agricultural products. Still others, like George N. Peek of the Moline Plow Company and General Robert E. Wood of Sears Roebuck and Company, profited from purchases by farmers.[14] Finally, Nye also saw a bond between the farmer and the "common man" everywhere in the United States — though his empathy with urban workers was very tenuous. The outer half-circle, then, was made up of these common folk.

Nye's conception of agrarian interests becomes additionally meaningful when considered in terms of those he battled against. His adversaries were largely urban: business, industry, finance, and (late in his career) labor. Again, these may be visualized in a series of concentric half-circles, in part overlapping those composed of the groups Nye defended.

Despite his emphasis upon the community of interest between the farmer and townspeople, his editorial crusades for the Nonpartisan League included criticisms of the businessmen in cities of eastern North Dakota. They may be placed in the first half-circle of adversaries. Second, Nye and his colleagues in the Nonpartisan League found villains among the financial and business leaders of Minneapolis and St. Paul, Minnesota, who, he said, exploited North Dakota as if it were a colonial area. In 1919 Nye wrote: "For thirty years the people of North Dakota have been exploited by the millers, the manufacturers, the money loaners, and the railroads centering in the Twin Cities. They bought our goods at unreasonably low figures and sold us back the manufactured product at inflated prices, after we had paid the freight both ways. Even farm mortgages drew a higher rate in North Dakota than on the same class of land in Minnesota. As a consequence North Dakota has not prospered as it should."[15] Third, Nye's blasts were directed against the urban Northeast. "Wall Street" in particular was the target for Nye's wrath on both domestic and international issues. In 1928 the senator wrote: "Ever since the first pioneer fought his way through the lonely trails across the Alleghenies and began the development of that part of the continent west of the Atlantic seaboard, there has been growing up a theory and practice that the resources of the United States were created by the Almighty for the benefit and profit of those who live in the great cities of the East. . . . Only a cursory knowledge of present-day conditions is required for a realization that the entire economic structure, the entire financial system, indeed, the whole philosophy of government as manifest in its practical applications, is designed for the benefit of that group of States which lie east of the Mississippi and north of the Ohio and Potomac Rivers."[16] Fourth, Nye found enemies of agriculture in the vast industrial and financial metropolis bounding the North Atlantic — including the eastern seaboard of the United States as well as Great Britain and Western Europe. In this sense, Nye's criticisms of Great Britain and his noninterventionism were integral parts of his agrarian crusade against the growing dominance by urban financial and industrial power, a dominance that he blamed for many of the agricultural (and national and international) difficulties plaguing the times.

It is easy to illustrate how Senator Nye's foreign policy attitudes fell within the framework of agrarian interests. For example, his noninterventionism grew in part out of disillusionment regarding the effects of American involvement in World War I. For one thing, of course, the hoped-for peace and democracy all over the world had not resulted; instead, dictatorships and new conflicts emerged from the ruins left by that war. In addition, however, Nye blamed American participation in World War I for many of the farmers' economic difficulties in the 1920's and 1930's, and he saw no reason to believe that American involvement in a second world war would have any better effects on the farmers' lot.[17] Although in 1929 Nye favored a large appropriation to finance shipments of surplus American wheat to the starving millions in China, he later vigorously opposed foreign aid programs (such as Lend-Lease and post-World War II aid programs) that, in effect, subsidized industrial exports more than agricultural exports.[18]

The Nye munitions investigation of 1934-36 was a logical extension in the realm of foreign affairs, of Nye's long crusade against big business, international bankers, and Wall Street. Initially, the munitions investigation was at least as anti-business as it was anti-war. Later the investigation broadened its attack so that the executive branch of the government as well as big business came under fire. This development too was logical in terms of agrarian interests. The President was more dependent upon the growing urban constituency for his political sustenance than he was upon the shrinking rural voting population. In Congress, however, and in state legislatures farming areas were overrepresented. If Nye's efforts to restrict presidential powers and to increase congressional authority in foreign affairs had prevailed, the effects generally would have been more welcome to rural America than to its cities.[19]

The Neutrality acts supported by Senator Nye imposed no significant limitations on agriculture since the self-denying provisions in the legislation applied primarily to the urban segments of the economy. For example, the arms embargo that Nye supported prohibited the export of certain types of industrial products, but placed no comparable restraints on the export of agricultural and mineral products. The bans on loans and the cash-and-carry provisions inhibited urban financiers and shippers, but the effects on the farmer were indirect at most.[20] Nye opposed large naval appropriations, and thus would have restricted government "pump priming" in urban shipbuilding and steel manufacturing centers of the East. Since North Dakota got very few war contracts, limiting military appropriations might have been to its economic advantage; in effect, this would have reduced federal subsidies to eastern urban areas and made tax increases for North Dakota less necessary.[21]

Not everything in Nye's foreign policy views fits into an agrarian frame of reference. Even those of his views that may be explained in agrarian terms can also be explained partly in other ways. Nevertheless, the senator's approach to American foreign relations becomes much more meaningful in the light of the agricultural value systems and interests that he represented.

In this sense, Gerald P. Nye was in the same tradition as Thomas Jefferson and William Jennings Bryan. There were differences and variations among the three, of course. Of them, only Jefferson was actually a farmer. The social and economic origins of both Bryan and Nye were more modest than Jefferson's. Neither Bryan nor Nye possessed the great intellectual and scholarly talents of Jefferson. Bryan and Nye were more doctrinaire than the pragmatic Jefferson. Both of them tended to personalize and simplify their analyses, while Jefferson was more alert to complexities and subtleties. Jefferson lacked the powerful oratorical abilities of Bryan and Nye. Their religious views differed, each from the others. Neither Bryan nor Nye was born early enough to be the spokesman for continental territorial expansion that Jefferson was. In contrast to Jefferson and Bryan, Nye won no significant political support in the South. Furthermore, each of these three men was confronted with different conditions in international affairs.[22]

Nevertheless, these and other differences should not obscure fundamental similarities — similarities that were rooted in the agricultural interests they all admired and represented. Jefferson, Bryan, and Nye all emerged from farming regions and their views and values were shaped in essentially agricultural environments. All three glorified the farmer and the rural way of life. Jefferson wrote that "Those who labor in the earth are the chosen people of God, if ever He had a chosen people, whose breasts He has made his peculiar deposit for substantial and genuine virtue." In his "Cross of Gold" oration Bryan exclaimed that "the great cities rest upon our broad and fertile prairies. Burn down your cities and leave our farms, and your cities will spring up again as if by magic; but destroy our farms and the grass will grow in the streets of every city in the country." On this subject of farmers and farming Nye spoke the language of Jefferson and Bryan with vigor and conviction. Each of these men rose to political prominence in a period of agricultural ferment. They provided leadership for the farmer at moments when agricultural difficulties and urban political dominance invited farmer protest and "revolt." Jefferson, Bryan, and Nye shared an antipathy for moneylenders and creditors, and blamed those who controlled such sources of wealth for the farmer's difficulties. They opposed the use of government machinery for the special advantage of the financier, the manufacturer, and the trader. All three were considered radicals in their day, and each urged political and economic reforms, but in spite of inconsistencies in the views of each of them, none really wanted a "planned economy" or continuous positive participation by the federal government in the economy. Each sought, rather, to abolish the "special privileges" of the urban capitalists, in the confident belief that the farmer could take care of himself if he were in a "fair fight" with other economic groups. In this sense, all three sought, ideally, a laissez-faire economy with a minimum of government intervention in economic affairs. Though their emphases varied in different situations, each feared "big government" just as each feared "big business." In varying degree, each was skeptical of the political responsibility and judgment of urban workers.[23] But Jefferson, Bryan, and Nye shared a faith in the capacity of political democracy – particularly democracy rooted in American agriculture – to cope with the problems of human society.

Jefferson, Bryan, and Nye also held similar attitudes on foreign affairs, attitudes that were as securely linked to agriculture as were their views on domestic issues. Like many of the farmers they represented, Jefferson, Bryan, and Nye were "continentalists." All three served in public offices while major wars were raging in Europe. And all three opposed United States intervention in those European wars. Each was critical of Great Britain. Although there were exceptions (like Bryan's support for the treaty annexing the Philippine Islands), all three tended to oppose American imperialism outside the Western Hemisphere. Each endorsed the maintenance of military defense forces for the United States, but none of them believed that national security required very large military establishments. Each generally opposed major naval building programs. All denounced "militarism," and were generally skeptical of the wisdom and effectiveness of military solutions to international problems. The same agrarian attitudes that led these three men to oppose domestic policies favoring financiers, manufacturers, and traders also encouraged them to oppose large military preparedness programs, overseas imperialism, and involvement in European controversies. They believed such programs and policies primarily benefited urban business groups at the expense of the farmer, the worker, and the small businessman. Their hostility to creditors probably accounted for part of their lack of enthusiasm for Great Britain. None of them favored commercial or financial isolation for the United States, but generally they were not willing to go so far as their political opponents in providing governmental protection for American business and investments in other parts of the world. Jefferson and Nye both supported trade embargoes and self-denying economic restrictions in an effort to prevent the United States from entering European wars. Their faith in democracy helped lead both Bryan and Nye to favor popular referendums on the issue of peace and war. None of the three was wholly consistent through the years, but in spite of specific exceptions and deviations most of the foreign policy views of Jefferson, Bryan, and Nye were extensions of their views on domestic issues. And their views on both domestic and international affairs grew out of their understanding of the interests, needs, and desires of important segments of American agriculture.

None of these men, however, believed he was putting group interests above "national interests," nor did they generally couch their foreign policy proposals in terms of group interests. Jefferson, Bryan, and Nye were nationalistic and patriotic citizens. Like everyone else then and now, however, their evaluations of "national interests" were conditioned by the value systems of the groups in which they moved and with which they sympathized. And their points of view were products largely of an agricultural society. Without denying the importance of power, national security, and other noneconomic considerations in international affairs, Jefferson, Bryan, and Nye sincerely believed that what was good for agriculture was good for the country. Their conceptions of "national interests" were influenced by the groups and interests with which they were most closely associated.

Thomas Jefferson, in an age when most Americans were farmers, was twice elected President of the United States. He became the revered symbol of an era and of a way of life and thought. Even William Jennings Bryan a century later could win nomination to the presidency three times on the Democratic party ticket. But the shattering of the old agrarian sectional alliance, the growth of cities, and a revival of farm prosperity (and complacency) combined to assure Bryan's defeat. Gerald P. Nye could and did win political victories in the agricultural state of North Dakota. Exceptional circumstances plus his own considerable political abilities enabled him to win some skirmishes on the national scene. He was even mentioned as a dark-horse possibility for the Republican party presidential nomination. But his efforts to restore the farmer to the political dominance he had known in the age of Jefferson were doomed to defeat in the twentieth century by the changed nature of the American economy and by changed world conditions.

Nye's views and crusades on foreign policy were extensions of his views and efforts on behalf of agriculture—and they failed. The results of the agrarian challenge led by Nye and his colleagues might have been foreseen by more perceptive and careful observers. Nye and his fellow agrarians, however, were by no means prepared to concede defeat before the battle.

AGRARIAN CRUSADE

2

The Oldest Nye Boy

GERALD P. NYE was reared in the agricultural state of Wisconsin during the Populist-Progressive eras, and he was guided to manhood by the example of his newspaperman father. The future senator was born in the small town of Hortonville, Wisconsin, just after ten o'clock on the night of December 19, 1892, the first of Ella and Irwin Nye's four children.[1]

His maternal grandparents had come to Wisconsin from New York State. Ella Prentice Nye had grown up on a farm near Dale, Wisconsin. Always rather frail, she died two months before Gerald's fourteenth birthday in 1906. Two and one-half years later, when Gerald was a high school sophomore, his widower father married Annie Semple, for whom the boy developed a warm affection that lasted throughout his stepmother's life.[2]

Irwin Raymond Nye exerted a tremendous influence upon his eldest son. Irwin, born and reared on a farm near Hortonville, traced his ancestry back to Benjamin Nye who had migrated to Massachusetts from England in 1635. (The Nyes had gone to England from Denmark over a century earlier.) Gerald's ancestors served in America's military forces during the American Revolution and the War of 1812, and both of his grandfathers were in the Union army during the Civil War.[3] Irwin obtained only limited formal education but he had a good mind, an active temperament, and a keen sense of public responsibility. He taught school for two or three years, but as a very young man entered the newspaper business. When Gerald was born Irwin was editor of a weekly newspaper at Hortonville. He soon expanded his operations and in November 1893 moved with his wife and baby to Wittenberg, Wisconsin, where he edited the weekly *Enterprise*.[4]

Wittenberg was in a farming and timber region populated largely by German and Norwegian settlers. The community had been established only about a dozen years earlier and it was incorporated as a village just a few months before the Nyes arrived.[5]

Irwin Nye was never a financial success. He became, however, a dedicated and responsible crusader for reform causes through his newspapers. He was village president for a time, was once elected to the Shawano County board of supervisors, and served as Wittenberg postmaster for a dozen years.[6] A staunch Republican, he denounced William Jennings Bryan's silver Democrats as vigorously as he had earlier criticized Grover Cleveland's Democratic administration. He enthusiastically supported "Billy" McKinley and even found words of praise for Mark Hanna. Irwin became an early and devoted supporter of Robert M. LaFollette of Wisconsin. Like LaFollette, he was skeptical of the Democratic and Populist claims to represent farmers and backed McKinley for President against Bryan in 1896 and again in 1900. Under the influence of LaFollette and Theodore Roosevelt, Irwin Nye became increasingly independent and progressive, denouncing political corruption and "the greedy grasp of the corporations which have for years been dictators of Wisconsin legislation."[7] It was an important event in 1905 when Irwin and twelve-year-old Gerald traveled the thirty miles to Shawano, Wisconsin, to hear an address by LaFollette, then reform governor of the state. After the speech Irwin proudly took his son to the speaker's platform to shake hands with "Fighting Bob." At the same time Gerald also met the governor's son, Bob, who was a few months younger than the oldest Nye boy.[8] More than twenty years later Gerald and "young Bob" were to share the distinction of being the youngest members of the United States Senate. As Gerald grew up he was immersed in the mores and values of the protest and reform movements that enlivened the western political scene during those years. When Gerald later took up the cudgels against big business, Wall Street, and special interests on behalf of the common man and the farmer, he was in a real sense continuing his father's earlier crusades.

Gerald (pronounced with a hard G) demonstrated little enthusiasm for his studies in Wittenberg High School. He was on the honor roll only once in four years and had to take algebra a second time after failing it. He was, however, an energetic participant and leader in extracurricular activities. Regularly elected manager of high school athletic teams, he played forward and center in basketball, quarterback on the football team, and a variety of positions on the baseball squad. The Wisconsin lakes and streams provided him with early opportunities for fishing—a recreation he continued to enjoy throughout his life. Gerald was elected president of the high school Literary Society in his junior year, and he took an active part in organized high school debates. Earnest discussion of political affairs and public issues was an accepted part of the daily diet in the Nye household. His hands sometimes showed the stains of printer's ink as he learned the printing and newspaper business by helping with the *Enterprise.* In his senior year he was president of the high school athletic association, captain of the basketball team, and class president. In a class of eleven, however, he was neither valedictorian nor salutatorian when he graduated from Wittenberg High in 1911.[9]

After graduation Gerald wanted to attend Marquette University to prepare for a career as a dentist but lacked sufficient funds. Although he at first planned to work only long enough to earn the needed money, financial reverses beset him and he never attended college. When in July 1911, he assumed the editorial responsibilities for the *Weekly Review* in Hortonville, Wisconsin, it was the beginning of a fifteen-year career as a newspaperman in Wisconsin, Iowa, and North Dakota.[10]

The energetic eighteen-year-old editor—five feet, ten and one-half inches tall, with a lean and wiry build—had many of the same traits he displayed later, in more polished form, in his political career. Gerald was loyal to his family and friends—some later said he was too trusting. Generous with both his funds and his energies, he, like his father, was not skilled in hanging onto money that came his way. He found it difficult to say "no" to a challenge. Then and later, Nye enjoyed controversies and had a remarkable talent for becoming involved in them. "There is a plain dividing line between right and wrong," he wrote in an early editorial, and Nye was ever eager to crusade in the name of righteousness against what he considered evil.[11] Intense, aggressive, vigorous, and outspoken, he enjoyed a good battle and he fought to win. In his journalistic sallies he generally lacked his father's lighter, more subtle touch, and though he learned from experience, the son's standard strategy as a newspaperman was figuratively to put his head down and flail away with both fists. He wanted a fair fight, but in the fury of the melee it was difficult to tell where the blows might land.

In his first editorial job young Nye campaigned for "clean government" in the village of Hortonville. The ten or eleven saloons operating in the little community of about eight hundred people were his particular target, for he considered liquor "worse than the devil ever thot of being." He also opposed the village president and village board who, he wrote, were controlled by the saloon element and ignored violations of local liquor regulations.[12]

With the paper's enthusiastic support, the anti-saloon group was able to win control of the local Republican party caucus in 1913 and nominate its own slate of candidates for village offices. The night before the election on April 1, 1913, Nye teamed with the Catholic priest and a local banker to distribute an extra edition of the *Review*, which vigorously urged support for the "Progressives" running in the Republican column against the saloon candidates. Their nominees won every contest in the election.[13]

A limited success as a force in civic affairs, the *Weekly Review* floundered as a business venture. Nye, who had bought the paper in 1912, spent money more freely than his income justified. He spent it for living expenses, for lavish Christmas gifts for his family, and for a power press to replace his old hand press. By the end of September 1914 he found himself nearly $2,500 in debt. A large part of this debt was secured by his parents and maternal grandfather, who could not afford such a strain on their resources. To compound the financial difficulties, his anti-saloon crusade lost him advertising, job printing, and subscriptions that might have come his way if he had been more "judicious." In 1914 Nye confessed that, despite some supporters, he "had more enemies in Hortonville than any other ten men put together." He rejected bankruptcy and promised to pay all his creditors, but his newspaper was losing money with every passing day. It ceased publication under his editorship on October 8, 1914. The young journalist undoubtedly learned from this fiasco in business, but it was a disturbing experience for both Nye and his parents.[14]

Gerald's next venture in journalism was with the *Creston Daily Plain Dealer* in Iowa. Creston was a busy shopping and business center for a fertile farming area in the southwestern part of the state. The *Plain*

Dealer—one of three newspapers serving the city of seven thousand people—had been established in 1912 by a group of doctors and others to stimulate "civic and moral" reform. When twenty-two-year-old Nye became editor and manager of the *Plain Dealer* in February 1915, the newspaper was impressive in format, news coverage, advertising, and editorials. This eight-page daily was a big responsibility for the young man, but he demonstrated greater restraint and judgment than he had in Hortonville. In his first editorial on February 23, he promised that the *Plain Dealer* would "be found on the good side of every question. We shall straddle the fence in no event for there is always a better side to any question which may come up for consideration."[15] During his entire newspaper career Nye was a prolific editorial writer. He wrote two, three, or even four editorials nearly every day on local, state, national, and international topics.

In news coverage and in his editorials Nye stressed some of the same themes he had emphasized earlier at Hortonville. He, of course, became involved in a variety of local issues. He also continued to excoriate demon rum. No week (almost no day) passed without editorials and articles attacking saloons and appealing for temperance and prohibition.[16] The temperance movement was by no means exclusively rural in origin, but Nye's early opposition to saloons (like Bryan's views on the subject) was well within the framework of agrarian reform movements.

Nye's editorials in Iowa sang the praises of the farmer and emphasized his importance to townspeople and businessmen. "We who are not 'tillers of the soil,'" Nye insisted, "don't amount to much more than a row of pins when compared to our farmers." When rain and bad roads kept farmers at home, the editor reminded local merchants how dependent they were for their prosperity upon purchases by farmers.[17] These paeans were probably good business in that agricultural area, but in the light of Nye's background there is no reason to doubt his sincerity.

The *Plain Dealer* also carried much news and many editorials on state and national matters. Later as a Republican senator he became critical of Woodrow Wilson, but the young Gerald Nye warmly and enthusiastically supported the Democratic President on practically every major issue (domestic and foreign) during his two terms: the Federal Reserve Act, the income tax law, the Federal Trade Commission Act, the Clayton Act, the Smith-Lever Agricultural Extension Act, for instance. In 1915 "the liquor question" was the only domestic issue on which Nye found fault with the Wilson administration. As he did many times later, Nye warned that the Republican party faced defeat if it nominated a reactionary for President. He urged the party to choose "progressive candidates" and recommended Iowa's progressive senator, Albert B. Cummins, for the 1916 G.O.P. presidential nomination.[18]

Under Nye's management, the news columns and headlines of the *Creston Daily Plain Dealer* gave much coverage on world affairs and the diplomatic and military events in World War I. In his editorials in 1915 Nye devoted more attention to foreign affairs than he did at any time again until he became head of the Senate munitions investigation nearly twenty years later.

Some of Nye's editorials in 1915 contained germs of the views on foreign policy he later expressed in the United States Senate. For example, he wrote of "the absolute futility of war" and insisted that wars require men to "Give all to get nothing." Nye commended President Wilson's efforts to maintain American neutrality despite provocations from both Great Britain and Germany. In March 1915, he urged the government not to protect shippers that were trading with belligerents: by supplying munitions and food to belligerents, he believed, the United States was helping to prolong the European war.[19] In that same month he advised the United States to set an example by disarming, for other countries would then "respect us rather than take advantage of us."[20] These views were similar to those voiced by Nye as a senator two decades later.

Gradually, however, particularly after the sinking of the *Lusitania* on May 7, 1915, Nye assumed a more truculent attitude toward Germany. The dominant tone in his editorials became quite different from the position he took before World War II. The day after the *Lusitania* disaster Nye advised Americans not to "suffer unlimited abuse and insult"; America should keep out of the war as long as possible but should be "ready to fight when disrespect and insult grows to a degree that is shameful."[21] Nye was highly critical of Secretary of State William Jennings Bryan for resigning from Wilson's cabinet because of the harshness of the second note to Germany protesting the sinking. In his view it contained nothing to which the secretary should have objected.[22] After his resignation Bryan conducted a vigorous campaign opposing intervention and Wilson's foreign policies, speaking and acting much like Senator Nye before Pearl Harbor. But in 1915 Nye denounced Bryan—a "great leader but a poor follower," the young editor called him [23]—for playing politics with foreign policy and urged him to support the President.[24] Nye's attacks on Bryan were almost identical to charges repeatedly leveled against his own noninterventionist efforts a quarter of a century later.

Nye also lauded Secretary of State Robert Lansing for protesting against British violations of American rights as a neutral. The United States, he believed, had a responsibility to lead in such protests.[25] He urged hyphenated Americans (including German-Americans) to place their Americanism above their Old World connections.[26]

By the end of August 1915 Nye was writing that Germany had gone so far that the United States no longer owed it diplomatic friendship. He urged the American people to "leave the whole thing to President Wilson and be ready to act when he thinks the time comes, if it ever does come."[27] This admonition to trust and follow the President was exactly the attitude that Nye warned *against* before the United States entered World War II. Years later Senator Nye freely confessed and publicly regretted the "interventionist" views he had expressed before World War I.[28]

One of the owners of the *Plain Dealer* later wrote that Nye was "a good ways above the average as a prospect for a really successful newspaperman."[29] After nearly a year with the *Plain Dealer*, however, Nye took a position with the *Des Moines Register and Leader* as circulation manager for the southern half of Iowa. He did not hold this job long. The work was not congenial and he was not well fitted for it.[30] In May 1916 he left Iowa to seek his fortune as owner and editor of a small weekly newspaper in turbulent western North Dakota.[31]

In the farming states of Wisconsin and Iowa the bases were laid for Nye's future development. But it was on the semiarid, windswept plains of North Dakota and in the Nonpartisan League that Nye's agrarian radicalism took form. And Nye's foreign policy views as a United States senator emerged directly out of this agrarian radicalism.

3

North Dakota Newspaperman

NORTH DAKOTA has correctly been called "the most isolationist state in the nation."[1] Each of the major theories on the origins of isolationism leads the researcher to North Dakota sooner or later. Geographic remoteness – North Dakota is located at the geographic center of the North American continent, approximately fifteen hundred miles from the oceans in almost any direction. Except for Canada on its border, North Dakota is as remote from foreign countries as any state in the union. Political affiliations – in the first half of the twentieth century most North Dakotans viewed the Democratic party with about the same enthusiasm that most southerners reserved for the Republican party. If Republican political affiliations help to account for isolationism, North Dakota could reasonably be expected to be isolationist. Religious affiliations – approximately seventy-five per cent of all church members in North Dakota belonged to either the Lutheran Church or the Roman Catholic Church. Methodists were far behind in third place. If there was a tendency for Lutherans and Catholics to be more isolationist than members of other denominations, North Dakota had a balance in religious affiliations favoring isolationism. Ethnic origins – although there were more North Dakotans of Norwegian and Russian descent than of any other national stock, most of the Russians were originally from Germany, and those who traced their ancestry directly to Germany were fourth (after Norwegians, Russians, and Canadians) among the many ethnic groups in North Dakota. In some areas of the state the concentration of people of German or German-Russian descent was very great.

If German-Americans were inclined toward isolationism, important parts of North Dakota could be expected to be isolationist strongholds.[2]

In addition, however, no state in the twentieth century has been more completely agricultural than North Dakota, and its isolationism grew directly out of its agricultural economy and out of the protest and reform agitation that economy spawned.

When Gerald Nye reached North Dakota in 1916 nearly ninety per cent of the 600,000 people there were classified as rural (farm and small-town population), nearly as high a percentage of rural population as there was in the United States when Thomas Jefferson became President in 1801. Not until the 1950 census did the actual farm residents (not counting townspeople) constitute less than half the state's total population. Most of the wealth and income of the state derives from agriculture. Wheat is the most important product, North Dakota generally ranking second only to Kansas in its production. Cattle production also is important, particularly in western parts of the state.[3]

North Dakota's cities are small. Fargo, the largest city, had only about 20,000 people in 1916, and Bismarck, the capital, approximately 6,000. The cities and towns, largely marketing and distributing centers, were almost as dependent upon agriculture for their well-being as the farmers were themselves. North Dakota ranks near the bottom among states in industrial production. And its limited industrial development in the first half of the century involved for the most part the processing of agricultural commodities.[4]

Though North Dakota is predominantly agricultural, the shortage of rain in many years makes it extremely difficult for farmers in central and western North Dakota to thrive (or even survive) economically. During the early years of the century, in addition to the acute difficulties imposed by nature the North Dakota farmer's economic health was threatened by the fact that the state government was regularly controlled by non-farm (and even non-Dakota) forces, and credit, transportation, industrial goods, and agricultural markets were controlled largely by urban groups outside the state. The hard-pressed farmers were in a highly receptive mood in 1915 when Arthur C. Townley, an organizer of considerable skill, began to marshal agrarian protest sentiment through the Nonpartisan League. Townley aimed his attacks against big business, and proposed to improve the farmer's lot through political action to break the hold by outside railroad and financial interests over the state's economy and government. He advocated state ownership of terminal elevators, flour mills, and packing houses, and wanted state grain inspection, exemption of farm improvements from taxation, state hail insurance, and rural credit banks operated at cost. The movement was influenced by the state's socialists, but appealed to many thousands who were never socialists. By the time Nye arrived in North Dakota the Nonpartisan League had approximately thirty or forty thousand members and was becoming a formidable political force in the state.[5]

No part of North Dakota was less suited by nature for farming than the western slope area where Gerald Nye first located. In May 1916 the twenty-three-year-old newspaperman bought and assumed management and editorial responsibilities for the *Fryburg Pioneer* in Billings County.[6] That area in the North Dakota Badlands had been primarily cattle country in the last third of the nineteenth century (young Theodore Roosevelt had established a ranch there but most of his cattle died in the devastating winter of 1886–87).[7] Then in the first decade of the twentieth century the farmers' frontier began to penetrate the region—encouraged by better-than-usual rainfall and by relatively high prices for agricultural products. Nye's newspaper, the *Pioneer*, was well named, for Fryburg had been founded only about three years before he arrived. In a very real sense Fryburg was a response to the needs of the new farmers in the area. In 1916 the tiny community of approximately sixty people boasted "two grain elevators, a restaurant and hotel, a pool hall, two stores, a bank, a newspaper, two farm implement dealers, an auto livery, a feed barn, as completely stocked and equipped a lumber yard as there is in this part of the state, and a blacksmith shop."[8]

Nye and his neighbors had high hopes for Fryburg, but most of the land in Billings County never should have been plowed. The acute shortage of rain in the area (less than fifteen inches per year in the three and one-fourth years Nye was there) made the lot of farmers and townspeople extremely difficult.[9] Those lands that were so unsuited for the production of wheat were ideal for the production of the agrarian radicalism that Nye soon embraced.

Despite his later prominence in the Nonpartisan League, Nye did not actively support that organization or its principles for many months after he arrived in Fryburg. The new editor did, however, become involved immediately in Billings County politics. In particular, he led a campaign to move the county seat from Medora to Fryburg, a campaign obviously designed to "boost" his new home. Medora was an older town established by the Marquis de Mores in the 1880's as a part of his brief but unsuccessful cattle operations there.[10] Just as Fryburg was a product of expanded farming activity in the county, Medora had grown out of the cattle industry. The heated debate over the location of the Billings County seat in the fall of 1916 was partly a struggle between farmers and cattlemen for control in the county. Nye was with the farmers.

Nye promised that his newspaper and Fryburg would conduct a clean and honest campaign for the county seat, but in the fury of the battle, he was soon charging the "Medora gang" with using "Dirt, Greed, Selfishness, LIES, Misstatements, Booze, Bribery, Sneak Methods and Everything that is Unfair and Not Honorable." The violence of this language repelled even some who approved of his objective, and in the final week of the campaign he was more restrained.[11]

The election of 1916 was, of course, important on the state and national levels. In state politics, the Nonpartisan League entered the Republican primaries and successfully won party nominations for all its choices for state offices, including Lynn J. Frazier for governor. In the fall the League campaigned vigorously for the Republican state ticket.[12] In the national campaign it was Woodrow Wilson against Charles Evans Hughes. Nye supported the Democratic candidate. With an eye to his predominantly Republican readers the *Pioneer's* editor emphasized that his newspaper was "inclined to Republican ideas" but he insisted that "Political Parties too often appear as the mere profitable plaything of a comparatively few men to cause the Pioneer to stumble to its knees in worship of any one party as a nation's one hope." Though Nye considered Wilson "as able an executive as ever this country had,"[13] and urged his re-election, national politics got little attention in his editorials in 1916. And in spite of Nye's later activity in the Nonpartisan League, he published no editorials on the state political campaigns, and his newspaper did not actively support the Nonpartisan League before the election. Instead, the *Fryburg Pioneer* focused almost exclusively on the county seat battle.

The Democratic presidential candidate carried the Republican state of North Dakota in November 1916, just as he had four years before. At the same time, the Nonpartisan League candidates for state offices, running on the Republican ticket, were uniformly successful—a striking victory for the new agrarian protest organization. The battle to which Nye had devoted his energies was, however, lost: the proposal to make Fryburg the county seat was decisively defeated at the polls.[14]

In 1917–18 Nye published fewer editorials than in any other years during his newspaper career. Those he did write in 1917 and many in 1918 concerned foreign affairs and the war effort. At Fryburg, as he had earlier in Creston, he wholeheartedly supported President Wilson's foreign policies, his conduct of the war, and his peace negotiations. Furthermore, as a civilian Nye actively contributed to the war effort on the home front.

In February 1917, after Germany began its unrestricted submarine warfare, Nye lauded President Wilson for breaking diplomatic relations with Germany: any other course "would have been cowardly and to the discredit of the U.S." He did not believe the United States should keep its ships and citizens off the seas to avoid incidents with Germany in 1917, contending that the United States would have to go to war with that nation if "Germany disregards our protest and the carrying out of her programs works to the loss of American property or American lives." When war was declared early in April 1917, the *Fryburg Pioneer* carried the news in a small article on the front page without big headlines. Nye did not publish an editorial on the subject until three weeks after war was declared; then his front-page comments urged every person to support the war effort and asked farmers to "farm more intensely."[15]

In later front-page editorials he urged Americans to "be pro-American, first, last and all the time" in supporting the war effort. Despite his earlier and later enthusiasm for Robert M. LaFollette of Wisconsin, Nye in 1917 vehemently denounced the senator for his address before a Nonpartisan League meeting in St. Paul, Minnesota. In his speech LaFollette had been critical of American entry into World War I, but the press generally misquoted him in such a way as to make him appear positively disloyal. Nye, joining in the general clamor against LaFollete, insisted that most Nonpartisans were "ace high in patriotism," but he considered LaFollette "prejudiced, unpatriotic and dangerous" because of his St. Paul speech. Nye wrote that LaFollette had made himself "the most thorough anti-American on American shores and the most thorough ass of his time, Kaiser Willhelm excluded perhaps."[16] This pattern of associating LaFollette with the hated enemy was exactly the method that would be used repeatedly to discredit Nye when he opposed American involvement in World War II more than twenty years later.

Nye registered for the draft in 1917 but, with a wife and baby as dependents, he was not called and he did not serve in the armed forces. (In his first year in North Dakota, Nye had married Anna Margaret Munch on July 22, 1916, at his parents' home in Bayfield, Wisconsin, where his father was editing a newspaper. Anna was a nurse from St. Joseph, Missouri, whom he had met in Creston. This marriage lasted nearly twenty-four years and produced three children: Marjorie, Robert, and James.[17]) Probably no one in Billings County was more active in home front activities. As Billings County food administrator, county director of Liberty Loan and War Savings drives, member of the county executive committee to get Red Cross donations, and county director of the United War Work Drive, he neglected his newspaper business to travel about the county and state attending meetings and conferences. When in 1918 there was an acute agricultural labor shortage because of the war, he even helped farmers with harvest work in the fields.[18]

Nye continued to support President Wilson during the negotiation of the armistice and peace treaty ending World War I. He warmly commended Wilson for his handling of the German armistice proposals in October 1918, urged continuing the war until Germany offered "to unconditionally surrender," and lauded Wilson's decision to head the American peace delegation.[19] Wilson's critics were denounced by Nye for weakening the President's influence at the peace conference. In March 1919 he charged that Republican opposition to the League of Nations was "politics, plain politics."[20] In commenting on the League of Nations in April 1919, Nye wrote: "A peace loving nation need have no fear of the working of the League,—it could hardly be other than beneficial regardless of how secure and lasting it might or might not be."[21] Nye also approved the reparations imposed on Germany. "When Germany gets thru paying her war debt it is not likely that any material number of people in that country will desire to get back into a work meant to out-do the entire world. The demanding of payment of this debt will do more for World Peace than will a thousand League of Nations."[22]

Not until the middle of 1919 did the rationale of the Nonpartisan

League's agrarian radicalism begin, significantly, to color Nye's attitudes toward peace. In July 1919, not long before he left Fryburg, he loosed this blast: "The big capitalist groups will always pursue immediate profits and pay little attention to laws, treaties and gentlemen's agreements except to use them as pawns. . . . there are two possible ways of preserving world peace. One is to unite world capital under one dominant power as our capital has been united under a few Wall street financiers. The other is to bring in industrial democracy which will end the national business rivalry. When farmers and workers get practically all they produce the need of seized foreign markets and bullet-defended foreign investments will cease. The first solution, financial slavery of the world to a few, is more intolerable perhaps than war. The second means a strenuous fight against our home exploiters, but it is necessary to honorable, lasting peace."[23] This editorial did not mean that Nye was abandoning his support for Wilson's peace treaty and the League of Nations. It does suggest the shift of emphasis in his attitudes that accompanied his growing association with the agrarian protests of the Nonpartisan League in 1918–19. His years in Wisconsin and Iowa had given Nye a general agrarian point of view, but the exposure to the Nonpartisan League provided him with a more fully developed and precisely defined agrarian philosophy. During World War I Nonpartisan leaders had extended the implications of their domestic views into the realm of foreign affairs.[24] As Nye became active in the League he refocused his own foreign policy views.

During Nye's first year and a half in North Dakota his *Fryburg Pioneer* gave the Nonpartisan League little attention. Not until March 1918 did the *Pioneer* begin to be vigorous and continuous in its support of the League and its program, which had two broad aims: "(1) To restore the government of the state of North Dakota to the people of the state; (2) To use the power of state government to aid in developing the state for the benefit of its citizens and to prevent its exploitation for the benefit of out-siders and to the injury of the people of the state."[25] The election of 1916 had come close to accomplishing the first objective, but the League did not control the state senate, which blocked major parts of its program. Nonpartisan leaders were determined to correct this situation in the primaries and the general election of 1918. On March 1, 1918, in a front-page editorial, Nye heartily endorsed the activity of the League in Billings County. He backed the Nonpartisan candidates in the Republican primary in June 1918, and portrayed the Billings County primary as a struggle between "prairie farmers" and the League on the one hand and the "Medora interests" on the other. The farmers and the League won sweeping victories in the primary.[26]

When Nye received an unsigned "valentine" warning him to "Cut out your nonpartisan stuff or we'll cut you and your paper," his response was to publish it in the *Pioneer*, re-emphasize his support for the League, and defy his critics to do their worst.[27] The League, in August 1918, considered organizing a Nonpartisan newspaper in Billings County, but the project was postponed because of the satisfactory support the League was already receiving from Nye's *Pioneer*.[28]

Serious attacks of influenza suffered by Nye, his wife, and his daughter in the flu epidemic of October and November 1918 prevented the young editor from being active in the final stages of the political campaign. He found enough energy, however, for an editorial urging his readers to support the Nonpartisan League candidates running on the Republican ticket on both the county and state levels. The national significance of the congressional elections was given no attention in the *Pioneer* in the fall of 1918.[29]

Nye, of course, was delighted when League candidates were uniformly successful in winning state offices and huge majorities in both houses of the state legislature. He urged the new legislature to rise to its opportunities by enacting the entire Nonpartisan "industrial program,"[30] which included a Bank of North Dakota, a Mill and Elevator Association to develop a state system of mills and elevators, compulsory state hail insurance, a state Home Building Association, an Industrial Commission to manage these new state enterprises, and exemption of farm improvements from taxation. When the League program was quickly passed by the legislature, Nye urged voters to approve the seven key measures submitted to them by referendum in June 1919. "The time has come," he wrote, "for the people of North Dakota to sign a declaration of industrial independence. It is time that they developed North Dakota instead of allowing the Twin Cities to skim the cream off our agricultural and industrial resources. This is exactly what the Nonpartisan legislation does. It keeps North Dakota money at home by preventing the exploitation of our producers by outside monopolies."[31] A few days before the referendum a front-page editorial in Nye's *Pioneer* proclaimed that it was "a battle between popular rule and industrial autocracy."[32] To Nye's considerable satisfaction the voters approved each of the items referred to them.

The political successes of the Nonpartisan League, however, could not save farmers (and Nye) from acute difficulties in the arid Badlands. Drought hit Billings County in each of the years Nye lived there. In 1919, when there was less than ten inches of rainfall in the entire year, farmers suffered "drought, grasshoppers and the worst crop failure in years."[33]

People were leaving the parched region almost every week, and Nye himself was trying to get out. Several months earlier he had taken the first steps to sell the *Pioneer* to the Publishers' National Service Bureau, a department of the Nonpartisan League. When Nye's paper was designated the official newspaper of Billings County by the State Printing Commission, the Medora *Billings County Herald* was obliged to sell out to the Service Bureau as well. In August the two papers merged as the *Billings County Pioneer* with Nye retained as manager and editor. In the meantime Nye was actively seeking more promising opportunities elsewhere and in September 1919 he assumed editorial management of the farmer-owned *Griggs County Sentinel-Courier*, at Cooperstown, North Dakota.[34]

Cooperstown, in the eastern part of the state, the county seat of Griggs County, was founded in the 1880's when the colorful bonanza farms dominated the county. Even after that era passed, more abundant rainfall and better soil helped to make it much more prosperous than Billings County. The principal agricultural product, of course, was wheat. In 1919 Cooperstown had a population of around eleven hundred people, most of them of Norwegian descent.[35]

This community was a center for opposition and hostility to the Nonpartisan League. The powerful Independent Voters' Association (I.V.A.), organized to counter the League, originated partly in Cooperstown in 1918–19. Townspeople and businessmen were intensely hostile toward farmers in general and Nonpartisans in particular. Solid citizens of the community often viewed Nonpartisans as "socialists," "freelovers," and "atheists." Nonpartisans generally were not welcome in their homes, and some townspeople even preferred not to sit next to them in church.[36]

Nevertheless, the Nonpartisan League was well organized in the county. With encouragement and assistance from the Publishers' National Service Bureau, some two hundred farmers in the county organized a stock company that bought the *Griggs County Sentinel-Courier* and employed Nye, not quite twenty-seven years old, to manage and edit the weekly. It soon became one of the leading Nonpartisan newspapers in the state, and its aggressive young editor acquired growing power in Nonpartisan politics. He found his six years at Cooperstown exciting and interesting.[37]

As he promised in his first editorial, the *Sentinel-Courier* under his management was "a constant fighter" for the interests of Griggs County farmers. At the same time, Nye tried earnestly to make the newspaper "a medium of understanding between the farmer and the business man" in the county, repeatedly emphasizing the common interests of farmers and businessmen in combating "big business" and "the Eastern power." He did not eliminate town-farm friction, but he believed that his efforts helped improve relations.[38]

The *Sentinel-Courier* had unequivocally supported the Versailles Treaty and the League of Nations, but Nye never worked up any enthusiasm for either party or candidate on the national level in 1920.[39] He devoted his energies instead to the state campaigns—backing the Nonpartisans with tremendous vigor. In the June primaries in 1920 the League candidates for Republican nomination included Lynn J. Frazier for governor and Dr. Edwin F. Ladd for United States senator. Nye vehemently and repeatedly attacked William Langer, who had broken with the League and was running for governor with I.V.A. support against Frazier.[40] After their nomination in the Republican primaries, Nye was equally vigorous in urging election of the Nonpartisan candidates. Their victory in the November general election was satisfying, but the growing power demonstrated by the I.V.A. disturbed Nye.[41]

In 1920–21 the postwar depression hit North Dakota severely. A farmer complained that he could not "get enough out of my crop to buy clothe and fuel fore my family to keep from freezing this winter." The *Sentinel-Courier* carried accounts of numerous bank failures and acute deflation and credit shortage. In this situation a Cooperstown bank refused to lend money to the newspaper "at present; and not later on, unless the policy of the 'Sentinel-Courier' be materially changed." But Nye continued to state his position forthrightly. In an editorial he told of a farmer who paid forty cents for a plate of lamb chops in Chicago – seven cents more than he had cleared in the sale of a whole lamb. Nye emphasized that farm debts had more than doubled in the preceding decade. He concluded: "Conditions of this sort are making what in North Dakota are called 'Socialists' and 'Free-lovers' faster and in greater numbers than all the orators and agitators in the country could produce in a lifetime." He blamed the economic crisis on big business and big financial institutions in the East: "Big Business is a peril to the farmer, to labor and to small business men."[42] The depression did not last long on the national level, but in North Dakota (and among farmers in general) it did not end for more than twenty years.

In spite of the economic situation, the Nonpartisan League lost support at the polls in the unprecedented recall election in October 1921. In this heated controversy Nye's *Sentinel-Courier* gave all-out backing to the League's industrial program and to state officials who had been elected with League endorsement. The people of North Dakota voted to retain the state enterprises included in the League's industrial program. But at the same time, ironically, they voted to remove Nonpartisan Governor Frazier, Attorney General William Lemke, and Commissioner of Agriculture and Labor John N. Hagan from office and to place administration of the program in the hands of men backed by the I.V.A. Nye was hurt and discouraged by the League reverses, but promised to help the new state officers "in the conduct of the League program."[43]

The year 1922 was a difficult one for Nye. In January the *Sentinel-Courier* office was looted of its files and records, and critics suggested that Nye might have done it himself to cover possible wrongdoings. The stockholders and directors of the company, however, cleared Nye of all responsibility and refused to accept his tendered resignation.[44] In March, he suffered a serious attack of bronchitis and influenza. After an ear operation in Minneapolis, he resumed his newspaper duties, but in July, he had to return to Minneapolis for a mastoid operation. His recovery was slow and very painful. While in the hospital he had regular visits and dental care from an acquaintance, Dr. Henrik Shipstead, a Minneapolis dentist active in Farmer-Labor politics. In less than four years Nye and Shipstead were to work together as colleagues in the "western insurgent bloc" in the United States Senate. Not until the middle of August, after an absence of six weeks, did Nye return to Cooperstown. During both of his absences in 1922 the *Sentinel-Courier* carried only occasional "canned" editorials from other publications. Nye clearly set the tenor of the newspapers he edited.[45]

The Nonpartisan League did not show great strength in either the primaries or the general election of 1922, although with League support Frazier won nomination and election to join Dr. Ladd as North Dakota's spokesmen in the Senate.[46]

At least as early as September 1923, some of Nye's admirers began to discuss the possibility of offering him as a candidate for United States representative from the second congressional district. Nye protested that he was not an office-seeker and that there were others in the district better qualified for the position. But he obviously was pleased by the support developing for him. To George Heinze, an early and vigorous "tub-thumper" for his candidacy, Nye wrote: "I like politics. I've known politicians of real worth and merit, clean and able men who rose above the type ordinarily spoken of as politicians. Knowing such men I do not feel that one need be ashamed of being called a politician or playing the game of politics, for not all politicians are rotten, nor are politics necessarily unclean in their entirety. Likewise, I do not look with scorn upon the honest politician who goes after honors in which he hopes to serve an honest purpose in a statesman-like way. . . . Yet, were I today to go fishing for anything in the way of political favor I am afraid I would lose what I feel to be the greatest asset in any work I might undertake politically, namely, that record of playing an honest and unselfish hand in the political controversies."[47] Still, Nye did not close the door. And early in November 1923 a "Nye for Congress Club" was organized in Griggs County.[48]

Early in February 1924 the Nonpartisan League held its state convention in Bismarck to select candidates for the Republican primary in June. Nye's name was placed in nomination at the convention, along with several others, for congressman from the second district, but the choice went to John C. Sherman, a "dirt farmer." A. G. Sorlie, a Grand Forks businessman, was designated the League's candidate for Republican nomination for governor. It was hoped that Sorlie, a middle-of-the-roader, might win additional support from Republicans who were not Leaguers. The convention voted to stay out of national politics, but considerable enthusiasm was expressed for Robert M. LaFollette, a possible presidential candidate on a third-party ticket. The League considered the third-party idea but decided to remain in the Republican column at least until after the state primary. Nye was disappointed over his failure to win League endorsement, but he promised to support the entire League ticket, including Sherman, and he and his newspaper lived up to that promise.[49] In the June Republican primary League candidates, including Sorlie, won nominations in eight of the eleven contests for state offices. Sherman, however, was defeated by Thomas Hall in his bid for nomination to the position Nye had wanted. Nye denounced Hall and said he was not "the kind of man North Dakota believes in as a public servant today."[50]

The Nonpartisan League in North Dakota generally had tried to accomplish its goals politically by working through the Republican party. As long as the League controlled Republican nominations and policies this method was effective. But as the I.V.A. gained more power in the party many Leaguers, including Nye, began to look more favorably on third-party activity in the state. This speculation coincided with moves by LaFollette and others toward a national third party.

In the middle of 1923 Nye had hinted at the possibility of a third party. Repeatedly denouncing both major parties on the national scene, he insisted that they "give protection, grant subsidy and in general privilege practically every industry in the nation excepting the basic industry, agriculture."[51] Late in 1923 Nye wrote: "The Republican party can stave off a third party by naming LaFollette or another of his kind as the party standard bearer in the next campaign. The Democrats can stave off a third party by naming Ford or Bryan as their candidate for President of the United States. . . . If the Republicans and Democrats run true to their form of the past and the nominations are dictated by the few who have absolute control of the nominations through the convention system, then most assuredly there will be a third party."[52]

Calvin Coolidge and Hiram Johnson had been the only candidates whose names were printed on the ballots in the Republican presidential primary in North Dakota in March 1924. Nye greatly preferred Johnson over Coolidge, but he was sorry that LaFollette had not permitted his name to be entered and supported a write-in campaign for the Wisconsin senator. Nye wrote that "LaFollette's very name breathes the spirit of protest which exists in the West." LaFollette, though beaten by Coolidge in the primary, ran well ahead of Johnson. After the presidential primary the *Sentinel-Courier* urged the state to "hop onto the third party wagon" without waiting for developments at the Republican and Democratic national conventions.[53]

Late in July 1924, after the party primaries, the Nonpartisan League held an advisory conference in Bismarck. The conference unanimously endorsed LaFollette for President and Burton K. Wheeler as his running mate. It also decided that the League candidates who had been defeated in the primaries (including Sherman) should run in the independent column in the general election. As the hours dragged on, however, fear grew that Sherman could not win. He eventually agreed to withdraw, and Gerald P. Nye was chosen by the conference to run for Congress in the independent column with LaFollette.[54]

As might have been expected, Nye campaigned energetically in the fall of 1924 and went into debt to help finance his campaign. He corresponded widely, used his own printing presses to turn out campaign literature, and spoke in every county in the district. Congressman Edward Voigt of Wisconsin, who spoke German, urged support for Nye in German-American parts of the district. Senator Ladd campaigned with Nye for three weeks. A "LaFollette-Nye Club of Griggs County" worked for his election. Nye was not only endorsed by LaFollette's Progressives and the Nonpartisan League, but also by labor groups.[55]

Nye's campaign literature summarized his platform in these words: "Make government responsive to the will of the people, who pay the bill for being governed. Give equal privileges to all; or take them away from those specially privileged now." Nye insisted that the "all important issue in this day and age is that concerning the abandonment of privilege under this government of ours." In developing his views Nye editorialized: "This government of ours, if unwilling to protect the farmer with new legislation, must sooner or later kill the vast amount of legislation which protects other interests, at the expense of agriculture."[56]

In the election in November 1924 candidates running on the Republican ticket in North Dakota (including both League and I.V.A. candidates) were uniformly victorious. Sorlie was elected governor and the state's electoral votes went to Calvin Coolidge. In this clean sweep, Nye went down to defeat at the hands of Republican Thomas Hall by a margin of more than three thousand votes, although he carried ten of the nineteen counties in his district. LaFollette ran second in the state in the presidential race — well ahead of the Democratic candidate. Nye was disappointed, naturally, both for himself and for LaFollette.[57] Nevertheless, his vigorous campaign and his strong showing in the election increased his prominence in the League and in the state. Despite his defeat, he was in an improved position to capitalize on future political opportunities.

A major opportunity emerged unexpectedly late in June 1925 with the death of Senator Ladd, whose term did not expire until March 1927. The selection of Ladd's successor could be accomplished either by a special election or by gubernatorial appointment. League leaders opposed holding a special election and strongly urged Governor Sorlie to appoint a progressive to the post.[58] In letters, personal conferences, and editorials, Nye repeatedly urged the governor to appoint a progressive. He hinted that if Sorlie did not make an appointment satisfactory to progressives, the governor could lose the League's political support but if he acted properly he could "get 'right' with the progressives." Although Nye did not endorse any particular person for the position, he did describe the qualities he thought the appointee should have: "A man who knows North Dakota and has deep appreciation of her economic needs; a man with the spunk needed to overcome the 'salving' of political and social leaders; a man of determination and fight, one with the courage of his convictions so pronounced as to command respect from even those who do not easily agree with him; a man who is politically progressive and who has gone through the fire of time in the progressive fight to prove his metal; a man who will stand with his political party in every act that helps to make it the 'party of the people,' but who will never acknowledge his party as his master." However others may have viewed him, Nye probably was describing what he saw in his own mirror.[59]

Late in July 1925 the Nonpartisan League held a convention in Bismarck to consider the matter of Ladd's replacement. Governor Sorlie urged the delegates not to endorse any particular candidate but to leave it to him. While acceding to his request, the convention did adopt a resolution urging the appointment of a true progressive who would work with Senator Frazier.[60]

Sorlie wanted to be senator himself. He even considered the possibility of resigning as governor and having his successor appoint him to the Senate. This, however, might have been considered a breach of faith with the voters who had elected him governor.[61] Furthermore, there was considerable uncertainty about whether the governor under North Dakota laws had the legal authority to make an interim appointment. Conservative Republicans in the Senate expressed doubt that such an appointee would be seated. In any event, Sorlie decided against offering himself for the post at this time. Nye insisted that it really did not matter whether the Senate seated the man appointed or not – the publicity gained by the appointee would greatly enhance his chances for success in the general election of 1926.[62]

Early in November 1925 Sorlie finally announced his decision. A special election to replace Senator Ladd would be held in June 1926, at the same time as the primary elections. This decision did not rule out the possibility of an interim appointment to last until the special election, but it made such an appointment less likely.[63]

Sorlie's announcement caused an uproar among Nonpartisan leaders. Nye published a severe editorial in the *Sentinel-Courier* on November 12, criticizing the governor's decision.[64] Even before Sorlie's announcement, Nye and other Nonpartisan leaders had planned a meeting for Friday, November 13, in Bismarck, to discuss the issue. This meeting was held as planned in Nye's hotel room, and the League leaders present agreed to urge the governor to make an appointment. As a result, later in the afternoon the governor met with them. Not only did the group urge Sorlie to appoint a progressive, but it became apparent that if he failed to do so his political future would be seriously jeopardized insofar as League support was concerned. The governor protested that even those in the room could not agree on who should be appointed. He asked the Leaguers to write their first, second, and third choices for the appointment on slips of paper and give them to him personally. He did not announce the results of the poll, but it apparently revealed the diversity that he expected. No one obtained a majority of the votes, but Nye was among those who received support. The governor then asked Judge F. J. Graham and Charles Talbott of the Farmers Union to come to his office at nine o'clock the next morning. As Sorlie left the hotel room, apparently as an afterthought, he asked Nye to accompany Graham and Talbott the next day.[65]

As the three waited upon the governor Saturday morning, they expected the appointment to go to Judge Graham. When the governor received them he obtained assurances that the three would all support whichever one of them he appointed. When he said, "Now I'll tell you why I decided to appoint Jerry," young Nye was probably the most surprised—and certainly the most delighted—person in the room. He was to hold office as the appointee until after the special election in June 1926. The appointment on November 14, 1925, preceded Nye's thirty-third birthday by more than a month.[66]

Some of the reasons for Sorlie's decision to appoint Nye may be surmised. Despite Nye's influence in the League, there were others of greater prominence and maturity available who wanted the appointment—including Judge Graham. The choice of Nye disappointed and even displeased many Leaguers. But by appointing Nye, whom Sorlie called "a clean cut young fellow" and "a true progressive Republican," the governor was doing what the League had demanded, thus laying claim to continued political support from the League. At the same time, Sorlie probably considered Nye the weakest of the several Leaguers seriously considered for the appointment and believed he would be easier to defeat than other potential appointees if the governor ran for the Senate later.[67] But Sorlie underestimated his man.

Nye quickly arranged his affairs in Cooperstown, assigning the editorial responsibilities for the *Sentinel-Courier* to another man. A week after his appointment Nye left for Washington—literally the first time he had ever gone east of Chicago. In addressing a farewell gathering in Cooperstown Nye promised that he would make "a constant endeavor to secure for agriculture, our basic industry, the equality in legislation to which it is entitled. My entire life has been spent in agricultural states. Born in Wisconsin, where I was raised in the atmosphere of my father's print-shop, I early became interested in the problems of agriculture and politics. After leaving Wisconsin I continued my newspaper work in what is perhaps the greatest of all agricultural states,—Iowa—following which I came to North Dakota. In all of these states I have observed the handicaps with which the farmer is beset."[68]

Nye lived up to his promise to battle for the farmer in Washington. But during his nearly twenty years in the United States Senate he became still more prominent and active in foreign policy controversies. His efforts in foreign affairs were, as has already been indicated, logical extensions of his agrarian economic and political views. Even in

Cooperstown, where he had expended most of his energies on local and state affairs, the agrarian radicalism of the Nonpartisan League left its fundamental imprint on his views concerning foreign policy. As a Nonpartisan Nye had blamed big business and Wall Street for many of the farmer's difficulties. He complained that the eastern capitalists controlled the government and used political power to gain unfair "special privileges" that worked to their advantage and against the farmer. There was no reason, in Nye's opinion, to suppose that these "selfish" interests and their political lackeys restricted their activities to the three-mile limit. Just as Nye found them responsible for domestic evils, so he found them responsible for international difficulties, militarism, and war.

In his *Sentinel-Courier* editorials Nye had criticized munitions makers, international bankers, and militarists. He favored conscripting wealth in wartime as a way of preventing war. He favored prohibiting loans to governments using those funds for armaments. He believed that disarmament conferences (including the Washington Conference of 1921–22) were undermined by munitions makers who feared that disarmament would reduce their profits. And he believed that more democratic control of foreign policies would weaken the influence of "special interests" thereby making world peace more likely.[69] These views that he advanced as a North Dakota newspaperman were almost identical to those he later expounded in more detailed form in hundreds of addresses as a United States senator. And the philosophy his attitudes on foreign policy reflect was nurtured on the plains of North Dakota in the agrarian protest movement.

❧ 4 ❧

Young Senator Nye

FOR NINETEEN YEARS as a United States senator, Gerald P. Nye crusaded for the farmers just as aggressively and as consistently (on both domestic and international issues) as he had as a Nonpartisan newspaperman. At the time he first arrived in Washington, however, there was serious question whether the boyish appearing westerner would even be seated in the Senate. His credentials were presented on December 7, 1925, but the Senate did not permit him to take his place as a member of that body until January 12, 1926. And even then it was accomplished by a margin of only two votes.

The controversy over seating Nye was not concerned with his personal qualifications. The formal issue was whether the governor had the legal authority to make the appointment, the North Dakota legislature having neglected to empower its chief executive to make temporary appointments to fill vacancies in the Senate, as provided in the seventeenth amendment to the Constitution. A law of 1917 did authorize the governor to make appointments to fill vacancies in state offices, but those opposed to seating Nye contended that a senator was not a state officer and that the governor therefore did not have the authority to make the appointment. Others insisted that a United States senator was a state officer and that the state legislature had intended its 1917 act to apply to United States senators; some took the position that failure to seat Nye would, contrary to the Constitution, deprive North Dakota without its consent of equal representation in the Senate.

Political considerations were probably more decisive than the legal issue in the controversy over seating Nye. Though he was a Republican, Nye was also a progressive, and he was expected to join the "insurgent" bloc that regularly voted with the Democrats against Coolidge Republicans. "Old Guard" Republicans feared for their already weak hold on the Senate. Nye and his friends assured majority leaders that he would vote Republican in organizing the chamber. He promised to "go along with the Administration" as far as his principles would permit. Despite his previous (and later) denunciation of the administration, en route to Washington Nye had even credited President Coolidge with "a sincere effort to improve conditions." But conservative eastern Republicans, pressed by conservative Republicans in North Dakota, opposed seating a "radical."

The majority report of the Senate Committee on Privileges and Elections opposed, but a minority report favored, seating him. The Senate deferred action until after the holidays, during which time Nye returned briefly to Cooperstown. There friends were raising funds through small contributions to tide him over financially until the issue was resolved.

In January senators debated for five days before finally voting to seat the young man. Twenty-six Democrats, fourteen Republicans, and the one Farmer-Labor senator (Shipstead of Minnesota) provided the forty-one necessary votes. The Republicans were largely western insurgents including William E. Borah of Idaho, Smith Brookhart of Iowa, Arthur Capper of Kansas, James Couzens of Michigan, Lynn J. Frazier of North Dakota, Hiram Johnson of California, Robert M. LaFollette, Jr., of Wisconsin, Charles McNary of Oregon, and George Norris of Nebraska. Thirty-one Republicans and eight Democrats—largely from the East and Southeast—voted in opposition. Several western Republicans who generally voted with the administration were conveniently absent when the vote was taken.

Immediately after the vote, Senator Frazier escorted the thirty-three-year-old Nye down the aisle of the Senate chamber to take the oath of office. Because the Republican side was filled, he had to take a seat in the back row on the Democratic side of the aisle. Excepting only "young Bob" LaFollette, Nye was the youngest member of the Senate at that time.[1]

When he first entered the Senate Nye was almost callow and shy toward his colleagues. As a small-town boy, he was (and remained) awed by the august body to which he had been elevated. While he positively enjoyed his committee work as a senator and obtained great satisfaction from addressing public groups, he had a diffidence in speaking on the floor of the Senate that he never overcame completely. A veneration of the great men who served in the upper house was combined with sensitivity about inadequacies in his own background and abilities. Though he spoke countless times on the Senate floor, and developed even in the early years considerable talent as a public speaker, he lamented many years later that his feelings of inferiority there had made him less effective than he might have been in accomplishing positive legislative goals.[2]

Perhaps partly because of his feelings of inadequacy, Nye was serious, earnest, and tireless in the performance of his senatorial responsibilities. He had a sense of humor, but his mien was generally serious and he rarely laughed aloud. He spoke in a quiet, low-pitched voice. He was, then and later, conscientious, friendly, considerate, and a good listener.

Nye also brought to the Senate driving ambition, a sense of public responsibility, tremendous energy, great physical endurance, and courage. He had acquired more polish, subtlety, and restraint since his early days as an editor, but he was still a rugged and aggressive adversary in political controversies. With his more cautious colleagues often urging him on from the safety of the sidelines, Nye spoke out candidly on explosive issues. His frankness made him good copy for newsmen. The former newspaperman recognized the value of publicity and knew how to get it; even as a "baby senator" he won more than his share of the headlines.

He did not look the part of a senator and he always appeared younger than he was. In a group with more than its share of paunches and bald heads, Nye was trim and lean, generally weighing around 155 to 160 pounds. He kept his brown hair smoothly combed. For relaxation Nye enjoyed watching the Washington Senator baseball games in the summer and wrestling matches in the winter, and welcomed rare opportunities to get away to western lakes and streams for fishing. He developed into a good golfer, played bridge, and was a heavy smoker. When he first arrived in Washington he wore "yellow shoes, a gaudy tie, and a high-water haircut," but he became one of the better dressed men in the Senate, tending toward dark suits and colorful ties. He was not particularly active in Washington social life.[3]

During his first eight years in office the senator turned most of his attention to domestic political and economic matters rather than to foreign relations. Before he could even complete Senator Ladd's term, however, he had to win the special election in June 1926. And in order to remain in the Senate after March 1927 he had to win the primary nomination and the general election in 1926. Although many in the Nonpartisan League were not enthusiastic about him and there were active rivals for the office, Nye had a considerable number of supporters, and the statewide publicity accorded his appointment and his first speech in the Senate, in which he opposed the World Court, gave him a head start that adversaries in the League could not overcome. The Nonpartisan state convention in February 1926 denounced the World Court as a tool of international bankers, commended Nye for opposing it, and unanimously nominated him as its choice for the United States Senate.[4] In both the special election and the Republican primary Nye was opposed by the conservative Coolidge Republican L. B. Hanna, a prosperous banker, landowner, and former state governor, backed by the I.V.A. "Regular Republicans."[5]

Nye's vigorous campaign to beat Hanna really began on the floor of the Senate. In March he fervently defended North Dakota and its industrial program against charges of "socialism" and "bolshevism."[6] In April he introduced a resolution urging that the same settlement of war debts that was extended to European governments be arranged for American debtors (including farmers).[7] Late in May on the Senate floor he denounced government favoritism to wealthy business interests and its failure to help farmers. The Mellon tax revision legislation, he asserted, "provides great reductions in taxes to those who can best afford to pay taxes and causes the masses of the people to pay a greater proportion of the whole tax to be collected than was the case under the old bill." He insisted that the income tax reductions in the legislation saved the entire North Dakota population one-twentieth the amount it saved John D. Rockefeller, Jr., and concluded that "Favors have been granted by Congress to the railroads, the bankers, and great industries time and again. Congress considers what it has done for them 'good business'; but when the same measure of aid is asked for the farmer, it immediately becomes paternalism and class legislation." He hoped that the government would "come to the rescue of the farmer before it is too late to save our entire economic structure in America."[8] In these addresses Nye expressed views that he felt intensely and sincerely. But he was also concerned with the coming elections, and his Senate speeches gained wide publicity in North Dakota.

In June he energetically campaigned throughout the state on national issues. He denounced the Coolidge administration while Hanna defended it. He opposed the World Court while Hanna supported it. Nye promised to serve faithfully the farmer's interests in Washington and pointed to his efforts on the farmer's behalf during the few months he had been in office. In addition to League endorsement, Nye also won support from the Standard Railroad Labor Organization's publication, *Labor*. The "business administration" of Calvin Coolidge would have been a heavy cross for any candidate to bear in the depression-plagued farming country of North Dakota. And it proved to be a crushing load for Hanna. On June 30, 1926, Nye won both the special election for the short term and the Republican nomination for the regular term by margins of more than 20,000 votes over his opponent. In the later stages of the campaign a few League leaders in Griggs County came out against Nye, calling him "a double-crosser," "a character assassin," and a few other choice names. But Nye carried Griggs County by a margin of three to one. In the November 1926 election he won an even more decisive victory, carrying every county in the state and receiving more than twice as many votes as the combined total obtained by the four men who ran against him.[9]

Assured by the elections of a longer stay in the Senate, Nye returned to Washington and again took up the standard for the farmer. In Senate speeches, in committees, in public addresses, and to the press Nye hammered consistently on his theme: stop giving special government assistance to large urban business and financial groups, or start giving comparable assistance to farmers. Over and over again in different ways Nye emphasized: "The time has not come and will never come when the farm people of the northwest will ask for anything more from their government than is accorded to other people. . . . our real purpose in the west with relation to government is only one of insuring that government shall shower its favors alike upon all sections of the United States." In his view America could not remain prosperous long "with our basic industry, agriculture, in a state of decay." Although in repeatedly stressing the seriousness of the farmer's plight he hinted at the possibility of revolutionary developments,[10] Nye was never fundamentally a radical. He wanted the farmers' status within the total economy improved to help preserve the system against revolutionary challenges that economic frustrations and desperation might arouse.

Senator Nye supported the McNary-Haugen farm bills, which were designed to do for farmers what protective tariffs did for manufacturers. Since there were exportable surpluses, the prices for major American agricultural commodities were set on the world market and were not benefited by tariffs. By separating the domestic and foreign markets the McNary-Haugen bills aimed to protect the domestic price of farm products while disposing of surpluses at lower prices on the world market. The costs of the program were to be financed by an equalization fee levied on the farmers who produced the commodities. These bills represented efforts to help farmers through government action, rather than by removing special privileges of business and finance. Nye was not particularly sanguine about the contributions these or comparable proposals might make to farm prosperity. He believed that "If the law of supply and demand were permitted to operate unhampered by more modern economic processes, there would be far less ground for such demand of help as the farmer is now asking from government." He considered the bills "a step in the right direction," voted for them in 1927 and 1928, and denounced President Coolidge for vetoing them each year, but he never considered them a panacea that would solve all the farmers' problems.[11]

The senator believed that forces controlling money and credit (Wall Street and international bankers) were more responsible fundamentally for the farmers' difficulties than the market and price considerations with which the McNary-Haugen bills and the later Agricultural Adjustment acts were concerned. In contrast to his attitudes during the Wilson administration, Nye considered the federal reserve system responsible for deflation and the credit difficulties of farmers.[12] In September 1927 Senator Nye urged progressives in Congress to rally behind a whole battery of proposals: reducing the national debt, increasing income tax rates in the upper brackets, maintaining the inheritance tax, abolishing "lame duck" sessions of Congress, placing the Muscle Shoals facilities (including sale of power directly to consumers) under government operation, outlawing branch banking, curbing the power of the Federal Reserve Board, developing the Great Lakes–St. Lawrence waterway, abandoning protection of private loans abroad, adjusting pensions to meet increased living costs, studying "the public utility monopoly," and legislating against large campaign expenditures.[13]

Before the end of the Coolidge administration, the junior senator from North Dakota also was given the first of his several opportunities to direct a Senate investigating committee. In this instance (as in each of the major investigations he conducted), his search for corruption perpetrated by wealthy men for selfish interests was consistent with his agrarian radicalism. In December 1927 Nye was the lowest ranking Republican member of the Senate Committee on Public Lands and Surveys. But since the ranking Republicans were chairmen of other committees, Nye became chairman after less than two years in the Senate. His committee had responsibility for continuing its probe into facets of the Teapot Dome oil scandal that had been winning headlines for four years. In particular, the committee examined financial manipulations surrounding the Continental Trading Company, Ltd., and the handling of certain bonds by such people as Harry F. Sinclair of the Sinclair Oil Company and Robert W. Stewart, chairman of the board of Standard Oil of Indiana. The trail in the investigation led to high levels in both political parties. The explosive political implications of the inquiry may have been one reason why ranking Republicans did not seek the chairmanship that fell to young Nye.

The main responsibility for conducting the questioning was assumed by Senator Thomas J. Walsh, Democrat of Montana, who had directed the investigation from the beginning. Nye learned much about the conduct of an investigation from this old master of the art. They did not, however, always see eye-to-eye. Nye made his own contributions to the inquiry, and he asked key questions that helped lead to prosecutions following the investigation. Although he endorsed the committee's report, submitted to the Senate by Walsh on May 29, 1928, he also filed a scathing supplemental report. In his own report Nye charged that the oil scandals were "Conceived in darkness and selfishness and dedicated to the proposition that the cause of privilege and the privileged must be served." The other committee members did not endorse his report, Walsh complaining that Nye made statements that were not justified by the evidence. Nye won nationwide publicity for his role in the committee, and the inquiry further emphasized for him the corrupting influence of great wealth upon the government and political parties.[14]

Neither major political party in the first half of the twentieth century was constituted in such a way as to accommodate Gerald P. Nye conveniently on both the state and national levels at the same time. Since North Dakota was almost a one-party Republican state, and the Nonpartisan League worked through the Republican party, Nye *had* to be Republican on the state level if he expected to hold public office. His Republican affiliations obviously made it impossible for him to work within the Democratic party nationally. But Nye's progressivism and his agrarian values prevented him from feeling content or comfortable in the Republican party on the national level. And since both parties reflected the increasing urbanization of the United States in the twentieth century, Nye criticized both and charged that "selfish interests" and "money power" of the urban Northeast controlled them. He repeatedly warned that if one or the other of the parties did not become more responsive to the will of the people new political alliances and perhaps even a new party might emerge.[15]

The senator realized that the heritage of nineteenth-century sectional controversies made the re-creation of the agrarian alliance between South and West in a national political party unlikely at that time. Still, in 1926 southern Democrats and western Republicans had joined forces to back the McNary-Haugen bills. Nye wanted to keep this agrarian alliance intact to accomplish legislative goals. He also hoped to guide the Republican party in progressive directions, and with Borah, Norris, Johnson, LaFollette, and others, he played an active role in organizing and leading a bloc of progressive Republican senators. That group of ten or twelve from the West and Middle West controlled the balance of power in the Senate on many issues during the Coolidge and Hoover administrations.[16] Nye's periodic efforts to win the Republican party to progressivism, however, never really succeeded. Consequently, only twice in his public career did he campaign aggressively for the election of a Republican presidential candidate. And both times his efforts were based more on opposition to the Democratic nominee than on enthusiasm for the Republican candidate. The first of these two campaigns was for Iowa-born Herbert Hoover against New York City's Alfred E. Smith in 1928.

Nye would have preferred George W. Norris of Nebraska as the

Republican presidential nominee in 1928, but when Hoover of California and Senator Charles Curtis of Kansas won the Republican nominations, Nye gave them his support. The Republican candidate opposed the McNary-Haugen bills, but in 1928 he was not considered so conservative as his party. Smith's campaign was so moderate, even conservative, that many liberals (urban and rural) found it difficult to build up enthusiasm for him. Furthermore, Smith's equivocation on the McNary-Haugen farm bills did not provide much incentive for progressive Republicans to jump over the political fence to support him. From an agrarian point of view Hoover was not particularly satisfactory, but Smith was not significantly better and might be worse. Nye wrote that "the Republican party deserves a thorough whipping, but if I must help administer that whipping at the expense of rewarding Smith and Tammany I must postpone that whipping." Nye did not, however, oppose Smith on religious grounds. Shortly before the election, after conducting an active speaking campaign for Hoover in North Dakota, Nye, along with Senator Frazier and Representative J. H. Sinclair, issued an open letter urging North Dakota voters to support Hoover against Smith. They charged that "the influences behind Smith" were "privilege-hunters and favor-seekers." "The interests of our great agricultural state," they contended, "will be far better served by Mr. Hoover, who shows a keen grasp of the perplexing agricultural situation, than by Mr. Smith, who is acquainted only with city pavement farming, and who never in any of his elections has carried the agricultural counties of the State of New York." Despite the refusal of the Nonpartisan League to endorse Hoover, he carried North Dakota (as well as the nation) by a substantial margin over Smith. The President-elect assured Nye that his administration would act promptly to cope with the agricultural problem.[17]

In April 1929 President Hoover called a special session of Congress to provide farm relief. Farm bloc senators urged enactment of an export debenture plan. This proposal, tantamount to a government subsidy for agricultural exports, was roughly comparable to the McNary-Haugen bills except that the costs would be handled directly by the federal government rather than through equalization fees levied against farmers. Hoover opposed the debenture plan and personally urged the senators to vote against it. After a White House conference with the President, Nye said he was considering the possibility of voting against the debenture proposal on the ground that he had "always been opposed to a subsidy for farmers." The North Dakota reaction on the issue caused Nye to revise his thinking and he voted with the majority in the Senate to add the debenture plan to the farm bill. When the House of Representatives refused to act on the debenture plan, President Hoover helped to persuade Senator Nye to vote for the conference report which omitted it. Nye justified his vote on the ground that Senate insistence upon the debenture might have defeated the farm bill altogether. President Hoover signed this Agricultural Marketing Act into law on June 15, 1929.[18]

Nye's second opportunity to direct a Senate investigation came during the Hoover administration. He was appointed chairman of the Select Committee on Senatorial Campaign Expenditures in 1930. Four other senators served with him on this bipartisan committee, but Nye played the principal role and conducted hearings in several states. In Nebraska his committee probed the unsuccessful maneuver to block renomination of Senator George W. Norris in the Republican primary. Norris' opponents conspired to have a grocery clerk from Broken Bow, Nebraska, by the name of George W. Norris file papers at the last minute for the Republican senatorial nomination. They hoped in this way to divide Senator Norris' votes and permit a third man to win the primary election. The ruse failed when young Norris' name was kept off the ballot on the ground that his papers were filed too late. In Illinois Nye's committee and its staff examined the large expenditures (around $317,000) in Mrs. Ruth Hanna McCormick's campaign for the Senate in the Republican primary. Mrs. McCormick objected to the methods used by the committee's investigators, charging: "Prosecution became persecution. My offices were broken into and my personal and business correspondence files were rifled. Spies invaded my living headquarters. My residence and office telephone wires were tapped, and they are still under supervision." She employed private detectives to probe into Nye's background and activities, but they failed to reveal anything discrediting him. After winning the primary she was defeated by the Democratic candidate in the general election. Nye introduced legislation aimed at controlling the influence of great wealth upon democratic processes, but, as usual, he was less effective in accomplishing legislative goals than in revealing and publicizing evils. One of the factors that deterred him was the knowledge that southern congressmen would "fight strenuously against what will be considered encroachment upon a matter of states rights."[19]

The stock market crash in the fall of 1929 did not mark the beginning of the depression in North Dakota. It only intensified a depression that had already engulfed the state for nearly a decade. The nationwide economic crisis provided a climate in which Nye's cries would find a more receptive audience, outside of farming areas, than formerly. Late in October 1929 he introduced a resolution calling for a Senate investigation of speculation on the stock exchanges.[20] In June 1931 he blamed the economic crisis on the growing concentration of wealth in the hands of the few and an increasing selfishness of wealthy men. He said: "Before we can ever free the great masses of the American people from the fear of unemployment and starvation we must do something to revise our methods of wealth distribution. . . . I have no quarrel whatever with the man who becomes wealthy by the sweat of his own brow. I respect him, and he is entitled to his wealth. But the man who gathers millions and millions of dollars each year by the sweat of the brows of others does not deserve the respect of the American people. The right to wealth depends upon how much the man who has it is of service to society."[21]

In May 1932 Senator Nye said that the cause for the depression was "a lack of buying power, not a lack of confidence on the part of Americans in the future." Hence, the Hoover administration's remedies for the depression that were oriented toward maintaining higher prices or stimulating prosperity at the top — such as tariff protection or the Reconstruction Finance Corporation — did not appeal to Nye. He charged that the R.F.C. carried "water and food to the very oppressors of the common people through these many years." In his opinion if there was to be "pump priming" it should start with "the masses of the people" — including the American farmers. He did not embrace the "trickle-down" theory for ending the depression.[22]

Even before the national political conventions in 1932 Nye on the floor of the Senate asserted: "The greatest trouble with us, with Congress, with the Government, is that we fear new thoughts; we dread to depart from the beaten path; we withhold our support of things which are new and a departure from old ways. It is my hope that the next six months will have the effect of impressing upon Congress and the President the importance of accepting drastic means and new ways of righting wrongs of long standing."[23]

In the midst of the economic crisis and in the presidential election year of 1932, Nye faced the North Dakota voters in his bid for another term in the Senate. A full year before the Democratic national convention the senator was convinced that Governor Franklin D. Roosevelt of New York "would make a very strong candidate" for President on the Democratic ticket.[24] Long before the Republican national convention in 1932 Nye warned that in the campaign he would criticize the Hoover agricultural policies,[25] and he did so. His conservative Republican opponent in North Dakota, George F. Shafer, invited defeat by endorsing the Hoover administration's policies. Shafer was confronted by an impossible combination in the primary: a serious depression, an unpopular national administration, and a popular progressive adversary who was a master of the art of campaigning in North Dakota. The result was a clean sweep by Nonpartisan candidates in the Republican primary of June 29, 1932, with Nye leading the ticket. He obtained more votes than any other candidate for any office in the primaries. He carried every county in the state except two (Cass County, where Fargo is located, and Griggs County). He got more than twice as many votes as Shafer, and 40,000 more votes than William Langer who won the Republican nomination for governor.[26]

In the general election Nye was opposed by Democrat P. W. Lanier. Despite efforts to make him commit himself, Nye refused throughout the campaign to tell whether he favored Hoover or Roosevelt in the presidential race. He told voters that he had "had too much trouble making up my own mind who to vote for for president to seek now to inflict my choice upon the people of North Dakota." Nye said that if Republican candidates in North Dakota favored Roosevelt it would be "foolish . . . to so announce themselves, in a realization that once many voters start in a column they go straight down."[27]

If that possibility really concerned him, he could have saved his worries. For on November 8, 1932, most North Dakota voters voted for Franklin D. Roosevelt in the Democratic column, and then shifted to vote for Nye, Langer, and the other Nonpartisans in the Republican column. Both Roosevelt, a Democrat, and Nye, a Republican, got roughly two and one-half times as many votes as their leading opponents, Hoover and Lanier. Both Roosevelt and Nye carried every county in the state. Roosevelt won 178,350 votes, while Nye won 172,796. No other candidates for any office came close to equaling the totals accumulated by either of these two men in North Dakota. Langer was elected governor but he got the lowest popular vote of any of the elected state officials. Clearly, in 1932 the North Dakota people were not voting to defend the *status quo*.[28]

Senator Nye began to criticize the Roosevelt administration's New Deal before it was even a year old, but *not* as a conservative Republican who feared innovation. He did not share the views of the big businessmen who attacked the New Deal through the American Liberty League. In 1933–34 Nye was to the left of Franklin D. Roosevelt and the "First New Deal," and he criticized the President's program from the point of view of an agrarian liberal who thought it did not go far enough in grappling with the economic emergency. He denounced the New Deal for favoring big business and great wealth while neglecting small business, labor, farmers, and debtors. He was ahead of the Roosevelt administration in his views on many issues. On some of these (tax and labor policies, for example) the administration caught up with Nye when it moved further to the left in the "Second New Deal" era of 1935–38. On banking, credit, and antitrust policies, however, the administration never went so far as he would have preferred in 1933–34.[29]

Nye regretted that the Roosevelt administration did not handle the banking crisis of 1933 by going "into banking on its own account, including the issuance of its own money." In the fall of 1933 he suggested that the federal reserve system ("a bankers' system") be replaced by "a real government bank" that would "issue bonds equivalent to the total of our outstanding farm mortgages. These bonds would not be sold. They would be held as a basis for the currency issue to pay off the mortgages, the government taking over the mortgages and permitting their gradual liquidation on terms possible for the farmers to meet without loss of their acres or undue hardship. . . . From agriculture the system would be speedily extended to the financing of all industry. It would amount in fact to the establishment of a money based solely on government credit. Of course it would extinguish all gold based creditor values."[30]

As he had earlier, Nye emphasized credit and money policies, and the removal of special privileges of big business, more than he stressed direct government aid to farmers. In his opinion, North Dakota voters thought the Agricultural Adjustment Administration helped farmers in 1933–34 but they did not want to make it permanent. Nye was "skeptical of production restrictions" for agriculture and was convinced that "what the farmer most needs is a sympathetic banker." The A.A.A. was not the New Deal agency that won his greatest attention.[31]

He focused, instead, on the National Recovery Administration under General Hugh S. Johnson, and its government-enforced codes of fair competition. Nye gave qualified endorsement to the N.R.A. when it was created in 1933, but he said the results would depend upon how it was administered. He did not object to the codes of fair competition as such and, indeed, had earlier introduced legislation calling for comparable arrangements.[32] By the fall of 1933, however, the senator began to criticize the N.R.A. In a letter to General Johnson late in November he charged that the N.R.A. was encouraging monopolies at the expense of small businesses. Nye was not defending "the man who is a misfit in the business world," but he objected to "monopolists taking advantage of N.R.A. machinery and improving upon their chance to win a more complete concentration of industry, of wealth, and of the power that always goes with it." He charged that N.R.A. "fostered monopoly, giving every advantage to big business at the expense of little business. It has increased prices to the consumer without correspondingly increasing his income." The "real need," he said, "is for decentralization, more employment and tremendously increased buying power."[33]

Senator Nye's criticisms of the N.R.A. in particular and of the New Deal in general were in tune with his agrarian-based attacks on big business. They were consistent with his conviction that the depression was due to excessive concentration of wealth in the hands of a few. And they were logical corollaries of his belief that the solution for the depression was to be found in improved distribution of wealth and increased purchasing power among the masses. His appeals on behalf of small businessmen re-emphasized ideas he had often expressed before, both as a newspaperman and as a senator.

Nye's charges against the N.R.A. led him to a series of conferences with Senator Borah, General Johnson, and President Roosevelt in December 1933 and early in 1934. A direct result of these discussions was the creation of the National Recovery Review Board headed by the famed lawyer Clarence Darrow. Nye conceived the idea for the board and suggested some of the men appointed to it. In the weeks that followed the Darrow report of May 1934, which criticized the N.R.A. on essentially the same grounds that Nye had earlier, the senator attacked Johnson for not adequately, in his opinion, correcting the flaws in the operation of the N.R.A.[34]

In April 1933, long before the New Deal "Soak-the-Rich" tax law of 1935, Nye introduced an amendment to pending tax legislation that would have increased sharply the surtax on annual incomes of more than $100,000, to promote a redistribution of wealth, but his proposal was defeated.[35] Nye was also ahead of the Roosevelt administration in supporting more sweeping legislation to protect labor and labor organizations. Nye endorsed the Wagner labor bill in 1934 and regretted that President Roosevelt asked for its withdrawal from legislative consideration at that time. It was doubtful, he felt, that section 7(a) of the National Industrial Recovery Act would provide labor with the protection it deserved. In addition he endorsed "emergency relief" to cope with "widespread destitution."[36]

Nye did not lose hope for Roosevelt and the New Deal in 1933–34. But he complained that the President had "not swung far enough to the 'left' to please the nation's liberal element" – including Nye.[37] At about the same time, *Progressive* listed Gerald Nye as one of only eight senators who had voted in 1933 for the "public interest" on all of ten key issues dealing with labor, tax, veteran, and farm matters. All eight of these liberal senators were from the West and South: Shipstead of Minnesota, Frazier and Nye of North Dakota, LaFollette of Wisconsin, Cutting of New Mexico, Wheeler of Montana, Robinson of Indiana, and Long of Louisiana. None of these men, it should be noted, was an internationalist on foreign affairs. During the early New Deal Nye retained his agrarian viewpoint, but his compassion encompassed labor, small business, and consumers of the cities, as well as farmers.[38]

At the same time that the New Deal was the center of attention on the national scene, Nye was in the midst of the turmoil in North Dakota state politics. The political crises in North Dakota during 1934 centered around the antics of the state's unpredictable governor, William Langer. This colorful and controversial North Dakotan, a graduate of Columbia University law school, had been an early Nonpartisan, but he broke with the League in 1919. In 1932, however, he was elected governor with League support on the same ticket with Nye. Many believed that the senator's vote-getting ability had helped carry Langer to victory. In any event, Langer was the only Republican elected governor in any of the forty-two states won by Roosevelt in 1932. It was impossible for most North Dakotans to be neutral about Bill Langer. They either loved him or hated him. And he developed a remarkable talent for winning the adoration of the beset farmers of western North Dakota.[39]

Soon after Langer began to serve his term as governor, rumors of skulduggery began to seep out of the state. In February 1934 President Roosevelt's secretary of the interior, Harold L. Ickes, called Nye to his office and told the senator of evidence that Langer was pressing workers on federal relief to contribute to the Nonpartisan newspaper, *The Leader*. Senator Frazier and Harry L. Hopkins, federal relief administrator, were also brought into the discussions. As a result, on March 1, 1934, Hopkins relieved Langer of his authority to administer federal relief in North Dakota. On that same day Nye took the floor in the Senate and expressed "embarrassment" and "regret" that it was necessary to speak on such "distasteful practices" in his state. He found the evidence persuasive, however, and urged "that the departments concerned proceed with speed in actions against those alleged to be guilty of wrongdoing as a result of their urge for money to maintain newspapers and prepare for future election campaigns. Let the ax fall where it will, even though it shall involve indictment and trial of one rewarded by election to so high an office as that of Governor of the State." Senator Frazier seconded Nye's statement. Nye believed that he had no alternative. He could not in principle condone Langer's actions, and he believed that it was politically essential to disassociate himself, the League, and his party from responsibility for Langer's activities. Langer and his followers, on the other hand, charged Nye with betraying the Nonpartisan League and with attacking Langer simply for selfish political advantage.[40]

During the next dozen years the political feud between Nye and Langer overshadowed all other developments in North Dakota state politics. Nye won a temporary edge over his adversary in 1934, and a solid victory in 1938. Langer, however, was the ultimate victor in the long political war. Langer's success in converting the Nonpartisan League into his own personal political machine, while gradually maneuvering Nye into alliance with conservative forces in the state, was a major factor in Nye's eventual political downfall in 1944–46. It should be noted that their quarrel was limited to the domestic arena; there was no significant difference in the foreign policy views of the two men.

In 1934 it appeared for a time as though Langer might even win the initial engagement. In agricultural western Dakota he successfully portrayed himself as the persecuted friend of the oppressed farmers, assailed by villains from the outside, including the traitor Nye. Langer carried the main body of the Nonpartisan League with him and, despite a walk-out by anti-Langer Nonpartisans, won the League's endorsement for another term as governor at its convention early in March. The convention adopted a scathing denunciation of Nye.[41]

Before the primary election Langer was indicted and convicted of a felony in federal court on charges of securing political contributions from federal employees. At the same time Nye conducted a vociferous campaign against Langer on behalf of T. H. H. Thoresen for the Republican nomination for governor. Nevertheless, on June 27, 1934, Langer won nomination for another term as governor in the Republican primary election by a margin of nearly 30,000 votes over the total obtained by the two men running against him. Shortly after the primary Langer was sentenced to eighteen months in federal prison and a $10,000 fine. As a convicted felon with an appeal pending, he was removed from office by the North Dakota supreme court on July 18, 1934.[42]

With Langer temporarily out of the running, his wife, a former New York City socialite, ran for governor in her husband's place. Senator Nye, his own political future in jeopardy, campaigned actively against Mrs. Langer for Thomas H. Moodie, the Democratic gubernatorial candidate. Thus his feud with Langer backed Nye into an alliance with Democrats and conservative Republicans who had little in common except a determined desire to stop Langer. It was a rugged campaign with very few holds barred on either side. Nye leveled charges of graft and corruption against Langer. Langer's supporters began a drive for a recall election to remove Nye from office. Langer, however, stopped the move early in August—probably fearing that it would fail.[43] Even President Roosevelt got in on the excitement when he stopped for a few hours on August 7 at Devils Lake, North Dakota, on his way east across the country. Senator and Mrs. Nye joined the presidential party and, at Roosevelt's request, Nye personally introduced the President to the audience at Devils Lake. Roosevelt let it be known that he hoped for the election of the Democratic slate, including Moodie.[44]

Only one Democrat had ever been elected governor of North Dakota before 1934 – and that had been more than twenty years earlier. In November 1934, however, the Democratic Moodie, with Nye's support, won election as governor over Mrs. Langer by a margin of 17,000 votes. Moodie's success was short-lived. The state supreme court disqualified him on February 2, 1935, on grounds of insufficient residence in the state to be eligible for the office. The lieutenant governor became acting governor, and Langer prepared to do battle a later time.[45]

By 1934 Senator Gerald P. Nye had established himself as a leading spokesman for the progressive Republicans from the agrarian West. His place in history, however, was not destined to rest primarily upon his performance as a liberal crusader for domestic reforms. In 1934, while he was in the midst of his squabbles over the New Deal and while he was involved in the political brawl with Langer in North Dakota, Senator Nye faced the greatest opportunity of his Senate career – the chairmanship of the Senate Committee Investigating the Munitions Industry.

5

International Bankers and Munitions Makers

ON THE RELATIVELY FEW OCCASIONS when Senator Nye spoke on foreign policy issues during his first eight years in office, his views directly reflected his agrarian frame of reference. Repeatedly from 1926 through 1933 he opposed foreign policies that seemed oriented primarily to the advantage of urban groups (financiers, manufacturers, or traders) and favored actions in foreign affairs that might benefit the farmer. Then in 1934 the Senate Special Committee Investigating the Munitions Industry offered the perfect vehicle for carrying Nye's agrarian radicalism into the realm of foreign relations. From 1934 until the Japanese attacked Pearl Harbor on December 7, 1941, no one in either house of Congress played a more prominent and influential role in the debates and controversies over American foreign policy than Senator Gerald P. Nye.

Despite his initial preoccupation with domestic affairs, prophetically a foreign policy issue had been involved in the controversy over seating Nye in the Senate and was the subject for his first Senate speech on January 23, 1926. Nye, like other western insurgent Republicans, opposed American adherence to the protocol of the Permanent Court of International Justice, the World Court. Senators James A. Reed of Missouri and William E. Borah of Idaho both had serious doubts about the legality of Nye's appointment, but they voted to seat him—partly to strengthen the bloc opposed to the World Court. Advocates of the Court believed that the prolonged debate over seating Nye was an indirect filibuster against the Court.[1]

New senators are expected to be unobtrusive. But Nye was facing elections in June and had to provide North Dakota voters with evidence that he was worthy of their support. With the encouragement of Borah and Johnson, who promised to come to his assistance in the debate if he needed it, but with great trepidation, Nye made his first speech in the Senate only eleven days after he was sworn in.[2]

Though he spoke more effectively on many later occasions, Nye's speech against the World Court vividly illustrated how his agrarian radicalism meshed with his attitudes on foreign policy. Sounding like the Nonpartisan he was, Nye emphasized that "the World Court is being forced upon our Nation, not by the people who would provide against future wars, but by men who are the makers of war, the international bankers." He contended that it was "at least possible that the international bankers, having made vast and extensive investments in the Old World, might need now a world-wide collection agency, and would look to the World Court as affording just the agency needed." He traced the deflation and credit difficulties of farmers to the machinations of these bankers. He expressed the belief "that the money power reigns supreme, is now known as the international banker, has quite thoroughly conquered in America, has wealth aggregated in a few hands, and is now, perhaps, seeking new fields to invade and to mass the wealth, not of one lone nation, but the nations of all the world." Suspecting that international bankers were responsible for propaganda supporting the Court, Nye introduced a resolution that would have urged governors to put the question to a vote of the people in the states. Nye conceded that the United States owed "moral support to the nations of the world in the settlement of affairs which are of concern in the providing of peace and prosperity to the world." But he urged that Americans "first look to the welfare of our own household and see what we can do to place crippled agriculture, for example, in a position that will permit it to function to the advantage and prosperity of those engaged in the great agricultural industry."[3]

In his address Nye implied that his opposition to the World Court might endanger his political future. In fact, as he hoped it would, the speech probably strengthened his position with the voters in North Dakota. This does not mean that the views expressed in his speech were conditioned solely by political expediency. In this episode, as on most of the foreign policy issues he faced during his nineteen years in the Senate, Nye's personal convictions probably coincided with the views of most of his constituents. Nye could and did serve *both* principle and political advantage through the positions he took on foreign policy.

Despite the insurgents' opposition, the Senate on January 27, 1926, by a vote of 76 to 17 adopted the resolution favoring American adherence to the World Court protocol, Nye, of course, voting with the minority. As it turned out the final victory belonged to the minority, for the last of five reservations attached to the resolution, which would have barred the Court from giving advisory opinions without American consent in cases involving the United States, was not acceptable to other countries and no compromise was forthcoming from the United States.[4]

Nye's agrarian-based hostility to international bankers was also reflected in his attitudes toward the war debts owed by European states to the United States government. In the 1920's the United States negotiated agreements with most of the governments that owed war debts. These agreements greatly reduced the total amount ultimately to be paid. This was done, not by reducing the principal, but by lowering the interest rates. In the spring of 1926 when the Senate considered the agreement with Italy Nye insisted that if the United States reduced the financial obligations of foreign states it ought to show comparable generosity to Americans (including farmers) who had gone into debt in the name of the war effort. He introduced a joint resolution to this effect. When Secretary of the Treasury Andrew W. Mellon opposed it on the ground that it was not "sound," it died in committee.[5]

Nye's views on war debts remained unchanged at the time of President Herbert Hoover's moratorium in 1931–32 that relieved European governments from making payments on their debts to the United States for one year. The senator said that "if we are going to be a nice fellow to Europe we should also extend some hand of help to our own people" – including farmers. Since the moratorium applied only to intergovernmental debts, it would, he believed, protect international bankers by giving them "first access to whatever ability Europe might have to pay at this particular time." Instead, Nye wanted refinancing of both domestic and foreign loans to ease the burden of debtors in that deflationary era and force financiers to bear a more substantial part of the burden of the depression. Canceling all the war debts would have been one solution, but Nye opposed cancellation on the grounds that this would transfer the burden to American taxpayers and leave European governments free to spend more on armaments – armaments that Nye believed enriched munitions manufacturers and increased the dangers of war. To complete the cycle, Nye believed that war itself enriched industrialists and financiers but ultimately impoverished farmers.[6]

The senator's lack of sympathy for international bankers and his essentially economic analysis of international affairs were emphasized further when President Coolidge sent the Marines back into Nicaragua in 1927. Calling American policies in Nicaragua "financial imperialism," Nye insisted that the United States was "helping to crucify a people in Nicaragua merely because Americans have gone there with dollars to invest and we have made it our policy to give whatever protection is possible to those dollars." The United States, he said, was following this policy "in virtually every country of the world!" In January 1928, Nye introduced a Senate resolution urging "that it shall never be the policy of the United States to guarantee nor protect by force the investments and properties of its citizens in foreign countries."[7]

Nye's agrarian viewpoint was as readily apparent when foreign trade was the issue as it was when he discussed international finance. For example, he was alarmed by the decline of American agricultural exports relative to industrial exports in the 1920's and by the growing imports of raw materials – including agricultural products. Nye believed that these developments would "materially injure agriculture" and that "our present fiscal and foreign investment policies" may have been partly responsible.[8] Though Nye later opposed foreign aid programs, in May 1929 he introduced a bill "for the relief of the distressed and starving people of China and for the disposition of wheat surpluses in the United States." This bill which would have subsidized the export of American wheat and wheat products to China to the extent of $200,000,000, failed of passage. But two years later Nye saw a new opportunity to improve the export situation when the Grain Stabilization Corporation, created by the Farm Board established under the Agricultural Marketing Act, began to make large purchases of wheat in an attempt to buoy up prices. Nye then proposed that 100,000,000 bushels of this surplus wheat be disposed of through sale to China, and a large wheat loan actually was made by the United States to that country.[9]

In 1929–30 Senator Nye, Senator Borah, and their insurgent colleagues wanted tariff revision confined exclusively to agriculture. Nye believed that "a tariff bill in the interest of the agricultural industry alone can be accomplished without severely taxing the consuming public." Although the huge exportable surpluses made tariffs on wheat of questionable value to American farmers, tariffs on certain agricultural commodities might, Nye hoped, help farmers a little. If duties on nonfarm industrial products were substantially increased, however, the result would be a net loss for the farmer. He complained that the committees responsible for tariff matters in both houses of Congress were loaded with men from eastern industrial states, while leading farm states (including North Dakota) were not even represented on the Senate committee. Nye urged the Senate to "slash the industrial rates or kill the bill"; for "every dime of protection given agriculture this bill would make farmers pay a dollar in tolls on the things they buy." The Hawley-Smoot Tariff with its very high rates was adopted in 1930 over the opposition of Senator Nye. Later he also voted against the Reciprocal Trade Agreements Act of 1934.[10]

Logically enough, Senator Nye favored construction of the St. Lawrence Waterway, for such an outlet to the sea by way of the Great Lakes "would mean millions of dollars saved to North Dakota annually" in reduced transportation costs. He blamed New York and J. P. Morgan and Company for obstructing the project: New York because it would lose profits on shipments to and from the Middle West, and the House of Morgan because it feared competition for its utility enterprises from the public power projects that would be part of the waterway.[11]

Another issue in foreign relations on which Nye took a stand early in his Senate career was that of immigration. Conscious of his Scandinavian and German constituents, he objected to permitting the national-origins clause of the Immigration Act of 1924 to become effective in 1929 on the grounds that it "would decrease the number who would come from Norway, Sweden, Ireland, Germany, and Denmark." As he phrased it: "It has been the rugged, hardy, honest, and courageous people who have come to us from those northern European countries . . . who have paved the way to development of the western country."[12]

In January 1930, Senator Nye delivered a major address before the Conference on Causes and Cure of War, in Washington, D.C., in which he opposed "any program which offers the remotest chance of America being drawn into ties and alliances which would make us parties to the intense intrigue involved in Europe." His conclusions in this major speech conveniently summarize many of the foreign policy views Nye held during his early years in the Senate. He said he believed:

"That government must respond to the wishes and interests of the masses of its people;

"That there is need for world leadership and example;

"That back of any successful war-outlawry program there must be the motive looking to the well being of the people of every country instead of the motive to perpetuate the status quo . . . of an existing order;

"That in nearly every war it is the people who bear the burdens . . . and that it is not the people who cause wars bringing them no advantage, but that they are caused by fear and jealousy coupled with the purpose of men and interests who expect to profit by them;

"And finally, that more than we need any set-up of world machinery to judge and determine controversies, we need an abandonment of those causes which seek world control of money, of credit, and of trade, not in the name of a great people but in the name of selfish individuals and interests."[13]

In his early years in the Senate Nye also began to speak out on military defense policies. In March 1934 he said that he did not want to "do away altogether with preparation for war, because . . . civilization has not yet reached the stage where that drastic course could be permitted," but large naval construction programs were "occasioned not by a desire to defend ourselves against aggressors . . . but to go to all quarters of the earth, there to make war as we have made war in the times past, down in Nicaragua, for example." He emphatically denied that "the only way to maintain peace is to be prepared for war." He contended that disarmament conferences fail because of "lobbyists for the munition makers, who do not want, above all things else, anything resembling disarmament."[14]

Given Senator Nye's background and traits—his penchant for crusades against evil in the name of righteousness; his sympathy with the agrarian radicalism of the Nonpartisan League; his hostility to the powerful financial and industrial interests of urban America; his essentially economic conception of politics and foreign affairs; his experiences in earlier Senate investigations; and his ambition, energy, courage, and delight in a challenge – it was not necessary that he change his stride or direction when he moved into the national limelight as chairman of the Special Committee Investigating the Munitions Industry in 1934.

This does not mean that Nye alone was responsible for instituting the investigation, or that it was only a response to demands from American agriculture. The antecedents of the idea extended far back in European and American history, with organized agitation for such an inquiry and for the economic controls implicit in it dating from World War I and before. Furthermore, the groups and individuals in the United States endorsing the investigation were diverse and it won support from all sections of the country. If anything, the moving forces that led to the investigation were more urban than rural. It was embraced by Henry Luce's conservative *Fortune* magazine as well as by the leftist publications *Nation* and *New Republic*; it won enthusiastic support from pacifist organizations on the one hand and the American Legion on the other; the Senate investigation assumed "isolationist" patterns, but "internationalists" initially viewed the idea with favor; churches gave their active support, but so did atheistic Marxians; it was a legislative action, but the administration also said it favored an inquiry. Indeed, in the first eight months of 1934 enthusiasm for the general idea was so widespread that opposition was often cowed into silence.[15]

The munitions investigation was based on an economic and psychological interpretation of the causes for wars. It assumed that armament races, international friction, and wars themselves were encouraged by munitions manufacturers and financiers in their quest for profits. The investigation was clearly anti-war in intent. In 1934, however, it was as anti-business as it was anti-war. The stock market crash of 1929 and the collapse of the business prosperity of the Coolidge-Hoover "New Era" caused a general disillusionment about the virtues of unrestrained free enterprise. In the depression years of the 1930's criticisms of business and business ethics were popular, with the idea of government regulation of big business for public welfare gaining wide acceptance.

The anti-business character of the munitions inquiry was rooted in both rural and urban values and both liberal and radical patterns were present. Liberals generally hoped that the munitions inquiry would result in government control of munitions industries and big finance; radicals (both urban and rural) preferred nationalization of those industrial units required for national defense. Although Nye defended the property rights of farmers and small businessmen, he was inclined to prefer government ownership of munitions industries rather than rely only on regulation. The senator had been attacking big business for many years, but the anti-war and anti-business atmosphere of the depression ensured an unusual receptiveness for his views in cities and towns, as well as on farms.

There were many individuals, organizations, publications, and politicians that contributed to the movement culminating in the Senate munitions investigation. The key figure, however, was the keen-minded, dedicated young pacifist Dorothy Detzer, executive secretary of the Women's International League for Peace and Freedom. As early as World War I this organization had urged investigation and regulation of the international munitions traffic, and in 1932 and 1933 it adopted resolutions calling for a Senate investigation. Armed with those resolutions, and with considerable conviction and ability, Miss Detzer set out to persuade some senator to introduce the necessary resolution and push it through the upper chamber. Her initial efforts failed. Only Senators Norris and LaFollette were responsive. But Norris believed he was too old and LaFollette said he was already overburdened with legislative responsibilities. No one else was willing to take on the task — partly because it might be political suicide.[16]

Shortly before Christmas in 1933, Miss Detzer told Senator Norris of her failure and discouragement. The old gentleman then went over a list of the ninety-six senators with her, systematically crossing red lines through the names of his colleagues as he eliminated them from consideration. One by one he found individuals too lazy, moral cowards, too stupid, too close to the army, in poor health, overburdened with work, with too much copper in the home state, or faced with pending elections. When Norris finished, only one name remained, that of Senator Gerald P. Nye of North Dakota. Nye had favored Norris for President in 1928; his investigating committee had aided Norris in the elections of 1930; and the two men had worked together in the progressive bloc in the Senate. Nye had criticized the role of munitions makers in international relations at least as early as 1920, and he had repeated his criticisms in varied form many times in the ensuing years.[17] According to Miss Detzer's account, Senator Norris evaluated Nye in these words: "Nye's young, he has inexhaustible energy, and he has courage. Those are all important assets. He may be rash in his judgments at times, but it's the rashness of enthusiasm. I think he would do a first-class job with an investigation. Besides, Nye doesn't come up for election again for another four years; by that time the investigation would be over. If it reveals what I am certain it will, such an investigation would help him politically, not harm him. And that would not be the case with many senators. For you see, there isn't a major industry in North Dakota closely allied to the munitions business. Go and ask him again, Dorothy. If he refuses, then I'll have a talk with him. I think together we may be able to persuade him.[18]

Nye had already turned her down twice. But with the encouragement and support of the old senator, Miss Detzer arranged an appointment with Nye immediately after the Christmas recess. Late in the afternoon on January 2, 1934, she spent an hour explaining in detail the problem, the need, and the objectives. She concluded by saying that Norris considered Nye their man. Nye listened quietly, thought about it for a while without speaking, and then said: "I'm afraid my conscience won't let me refuse you again. I'll do it."[19]

When Nye began his crusade for a munitions investigation he was forty-one years old and had eight years of Senate experience behind him. He had already directed two previous Senate inquiries and was convinced of the importance of legislative investigations. In a radio address in May 1933, Senator Nye said: "Investigations serve a most healthy purpose in that they prevent many practices and serve as a caution against practices which might be considered proper and customary but for the development of a conscience by the existence of an investigating committee. . . . With economic and political influence coming into such concentrated control it is of greatest importance that legislative bodies be on closest guard against encroachment which further threatens a free government. Honest investigations, prosecuted by legislators determined to reach and develop the facts, and by legislators who in their work can and will abandon partisanship, are of greatest value to the government and its people. They afford necessary knowledge basic to helpful legislation. They educate people to practices unfriendly to their best interests. They throw fear into men and interests who would by any means at their command move governments to selfish purposes. They command respect for government and for law. They tend to make government cleaner and more responsive to public needs and interests. We should have not less, but more legislative investigations."[20] His views and background made Nye "a natural" for the munitions probe.

There were numerous conferences with pacifist leaders and others as the resolution calling for a munitions investigation was whipped into shape. Finally, at noon on February 8, 1934, with Dorothy Detzer eagerly watching from the gallery, Nye submitted his Senate Resolution 179 calling for an investigation of the munitions industry by the Senate Foreign Relations Committee. The handful present in the Senate at the time paid little attention to the move, and without objection the resolution was referred to the Foreign Relations Committee under Senator Key Pittman of Nevada. Pittman had no enthusiasm for the idea and did not want responsibility for the investigation. At his request the resolution was referred to the Military Affairs Committee.[21]

Lobbyists led by Miss Detzer then urged two steps to get it reported favorably out of committee. First, they recommended that the investigation be conducted by a special committee rather than by a standing committee, opening the door for selection of Nye to head the investigation. Second, they proposed that Nye's resolution be combined with one introduced earlier by Senator Arthur H. Vandenberg, Jr., of Michigan. Vandenberg's resolution, endorsed by the American Legion, advocated taking the profits out of war — an idea with which Nye wholly concurred. If the resolutions were combined, thus appealing for support from such dissimilar groups as the Legion and the pacifists, the chances for adoption would be improved. Nye and Vandenberg agreed to these moves, and on March 12, 1934, Nye introduced the new combined Senate Resolution 206. It was referred to the Military Affairs Committee which promptly reported it out favorably. Next the Committee to Audit and Control the Contingent Expenses of the Senate reported it out but recommended that the funds for the investigation be reduced from $50,000 to $15,000.[22]

At the same time organized pressure and popular enthusiasm for an investigation were reaching tremendous proportions. An article on

European munitions makers, "Arms and the Men," published in the March 1934 issue of *Fortune* magazine, was widely reprinted, distributed, and quoted. Senator William E. Borah delivered a powerful oration in the Senate on the subject. The book *Merchants of Death* by H. C. Englebrecht and F. C. Hanighen was widely read and discussed. Petitions, meetings, letters, telegrams, editorials, and personal appeals endorsed the resolution calling for a munitions investigation.[23]

The Women's International League polled senators and found that twenty favored the resolution, forty-five opposed it, and twenty-nine were not willing to commit themselves. Most of the uncommitted indicated they would give their support if it won administration approval. When the State Department announced its endorsement of an investigation the number of senators in favor of the resolution rose to forty. Fervent efforts were made to increase this number.[24]

The showdown in the Senate occurred on April 12, 1934. Senator Pat Harrison of Mississippi, chairman of the Finance Committee, was impatiently pushing for a vote on the pending revenue bill but was frustrated by lengthy debate on amendments to the bill. In introducing an amendment calling for a ninety-eight per cent tax on all incomes over $10,000 a year during wartime, Nye spoke for over an hour. Then Senator Vandenberg took the floor and began to speak on behalf of Nye's tax amendment. As Vandenberg talked on, Harrison's impatience grew. Finally, he consulted with Nye on the Senate floor and learned, to his horror, that eleven senators planned to speak for Nye's amendment and that this would probably consume five days. To head off this filibuster, Harrison proposed that the Nye-Vandenberg munitions investigation resolution be adopted immediately and that Nye's tax amendment be referred to the committee appointed to conduct the investigation. That was exactly what Nye and Vandenberg wanted. With Harrison's cooperation, Senate Resolution 206, as amended, was promptly adopted by the Senate on April 12, without a single dissenting vote.[25]

This resolution alleged that "the influence of the commercial motive is an inevitable factor in considerations involving the maintenance of the national defense" and is "one of the inevitable factors often believed to stimulate and sustain wars." It empowered the Vice President to appoint seven senators to a special committee to investigate all aspects of the manufacture, sale, and distribution of armaments and munitions. The resolution also directed the committee to study and report on the adequacy of existing legislation and treaties on the subject, instructed it to review the findings and recommendations of the earlier War Policies Commission concerned with taking the profits out of war, and empowered it to consider the desirability of a government monopoly in the manufacture of munitions.[26]

Vice President John Nance Garner of Texas met with Nye and Vandenberg, and the three men determined the composition of the committee.[27] It included four Democrats – James P. Pope of Idaho, Homer T. Bone of Washington, Bennett Champ Clark of Missouri, and Walter F. George of Georgia – and three Republicans – the two sponsors of the resolution, plus W. Warren Barbour of New Jersey. This committee overrepresented the agricultural sections of the country and underrepresented urban industry. Five of the seven were from south of the Ohio River and west of the Mississippi (four from west of the Mississippi). The Northeast and the South were internationalist strongholds, but only two of the seven came from these sections. The two members with the most substantial industrial constituencies, Barbour and Vandenberg, in 1934 both spoke the language of manufacturers who sold in protected domestic markets, although both New Jersey and Michigan had big industries that profited from munitions production and had important foreign markets. (When Vandenberg turned internationalist a decade later, he was following a road taken long before by the most powerful industry in his state – General Motors.) But Dearborn's Henry Ford was passionately isolationist, and Vandenberg's home was in Grand Rapids, famed for its protected furniture manufacturing industry. Michigan was also a leader in the processing of agricultural dairy and cereal products. Barbour himself was a manufacturer of light consumer goods and was a fervent protectionist. All seven members participated in committee affairs, but the most active and influential were two Republicans, Nye and Vandenberg, and two Democrats, Clark and Bone. Of these four, all but Vandenberg were distinctly liberal in their domestic views, and even he was no reactionary.[28]

Vice President Garner left the choice of a chairman up to the committee. Many assumed that a member of the majority Democratic party would be chosen even though the resolution had been introduced and sponsored by two Republicans. Senator Pope of Idaho, a New Deal Democrat, was a strong possibility. But at a brief organizing meeting on April 23, 1934, Democrat Clark proposed Nye for the chairmanship and another Democrat, Bone, seconded the nomination. Without dissent, Nye won the assignment.[29]

Secretary of State Cordell Hull was disappointed that a Republican isolationist was made chairman of the committee. He later wrote that he would have opposed the investigation if he had known this would happen. Nevertheless, Hull promptly assured Nye that the investigation would receive "the fullest and most cordial cooperation of the Department." Hull assigned Joseph C. Green, the department's expert on the munitions traffic, to serve as liaison between the department and the committee.[30]

On May 18, 1934, in a letter to the Senate drafted in the State Department, President Roosevelt endorsed the investigation and promised that the "executive departments of the Government will be charged to cooperate with the committee to the fullest extent." He contended that the "private and uncontrolled manufacture of arms and munitions and the traffic therein has become a serious source of international discord and strife." But his letter was also an appeal for an international approach to the problem – and a tacit warning against isolationism. He wrote that it was impossible "effectively to control such an evil by the isolated action of any one country. . . . this is a field in which international action is necessary." He urged Senate approval for the Convention for the Supervision of the International Trade in Arms and Ammunition and in Implements of War, signed at Geneva, June 17, 1925.[31]

Senator Nye appointed an Advisory Council of experts to consult with the committee. This council was composed of Manley O. Hudson of the Harvard Law School, Harold G. Moulton of the Brookings Insitution, and John T. Flynn, then a researcher and liberal writer with *New Republic* magazine.[32] Of the three, only Flynn played a major role in the course of the investigation.

Stephen Raushenbush became the committee's secretary and chief investigator. He was a tall, quiet, mustached, keen-minded, experienced investigator in his late thirties. Much of the work of directing the research, planning the hearings, and preparing the committee reports fell on his shoulders. The son of Walter Rauschenbusch, a prominent leader of the Social Gospel movement in America, Stephen had graduated from Amherst, had served in the ambulance corps in

UNITED PRESS INTERNATIONAL PHOTO

Young Senator Nye in 1928, with leading isolationist and western insurgent William E. Borah of Idaho

Two midwestern senators whose careers began at nearly the same time, Robert M. LaFollette, Jr., of Wisconsin and Nye

WIDE WORLD PHOTOS

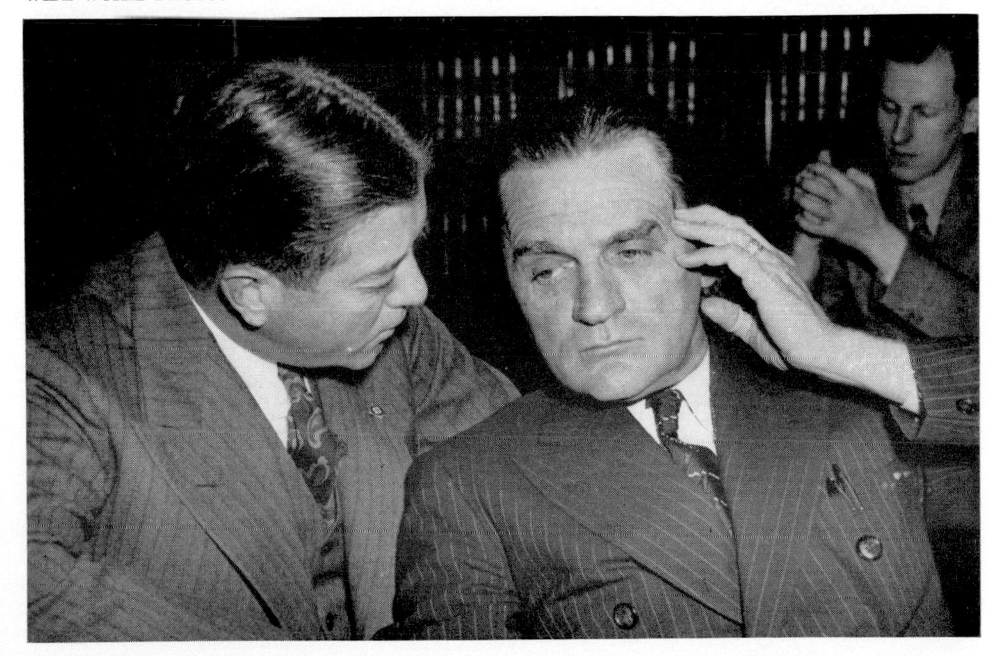

UNITED PRESS INTERNATIONAL PHOTO

Nye with two of the most prominent witnesses during the munitions hearings: above, Irénée du Pont; below, J. P. Morgan

COPYRIGHT BY HARRIS & EWING

UNITED PRESS INTERNATIONAL PHOTO

The Senate munitions committee in 1934: left to right, Senators Arthur H. Vandenberg, W. Warren Barbour, and Gerald P. Nye; Alger Hiss, committee counsel; Senator Bennett Champ Clark; Stephen Raushenbush, chief investigator for the committee; and Senator James P. Pope. (Two committee members are not pictured, Senators Homer T. Bone and Walter F. George.)

Nye with R. Walton Moore, assistant secretary of state, and Key Pittman, chairman of the Senate Foreign Relations Committee, during the 1936 campaign for neutrality legislation

WIDE WORLD PHOTOS

UNITED PRESS INTERNATIONAL PHOTO

Nye at America First rallies in 1941: above, addressing a Brooklyn meeting (Mrs. Nye is at the left); below, with Charles A. Lindbergh at Madison Square Garden in New York City

UNITED PRESS INTERNATIONAL PHOTO

France during World War I, and had investigated and written on the "power trust" in America. He gathered an able and dedicated staff of experienced workers for the committee. The legal assistant on this staff for a few months was a brilliant young Harvard Law graduate by the name of Alger Hiss who was borrowed temporarily from Jerome Frank's staff in the Agricultural Adjustment Administration.[33]

During the summer of 1934 Raushenbush and his staff, under the authority of Nye's committee, scoured the files of corporations and government agencies in their search for evidence and documents. By the end of the summer Raushenbush had arranged and planned the first series of committee hearings and had prepared material to be used by the senators in questioning witnesses.[34]

Public hearings before the Nye committee began on Tuesday, September 4, 1934, in the large caucus room of the Senate Office Building. This first series of hearings continued daily, except weekends, through September 21. During these three weeks the committee heard testimony from officials of the Electric Boat Company, a submarine manufacturer; the Driggs Ordnance and Engineering Company; the American Armament Corporation; the Curtiss-Wright Export Corporation; E. I. du Pont de Nemours and Company; Pratt and Whitney Aircraft Company; United Aircraft Exports, Incorporated; Federal Laboratories, Incorporated, makers of gas, airplane bombs, and machine guns; the Lake Erie Chemical Company; and U.S. Ordnance Engineers, a munitions export company. All the senators on the committee, along with Raushenbush and Hiss, shared in questioning witnesses, and the testimony and exhibits filled more than two thousand pages of fine print. The hearings did not attract so many spectators as were expected, but newspapermen from all over the United States and from other countries gave them detailed coverage, providing for readers throughout the world a daily round of headlines and sensations.[35]

The investigation brought out information about activities of shadowy, mysterious figures in the international munitions business. But the witnesses did not look like bloodthirsty "merchants of death." For the most part they were prosperous, respected businessmen telling of their corporate organizations, their business methods, and the profits and losses of their firms. The high point of the September hearings was the appearance of four du Ponts: the brothers Irénée, Pierre, and

Lammot and their cousin, Felix. These soft-spoken, unpretentious industrialists looked like "men who could pass the plate at any church service without anyone looking at them twice." A Congregational minister writing in *Christian Century* thus evaluated the testimony of the du Ponts and the other witnesses: "It will do no good to think of these men as fiends who rejoice in dealing in blood and death, for they are not. They are average men who are using the business ethics and techniques of the average business man around the world. . . . the only difference between these munitions men and many of the business men of the world is not in ethics or business technique, but simply in the commodity in which they deal. . . . let us put the blame where it belongs, on the business technique and ethics which go unchallenged among the leaders of our business life, and on our willingness to allow private business to conduct an international trade in armaments."[36] Not all observers or committee members shared this view—but it represented a widespread reaction to the investigation.

The Nye committee hearings had scarcely started before they provoked a storm of protests from home and abroad. Evidence and testimony introduced in the committee hearings alleged corruption, bribes, and "rake-offs" by officials of various governments in dealing with agents of American munitions firms. Some of this evidence was factually accurate; some of it was unsubstantiated rumor and hearsay. True or not, however, the allegations angered officials in countries with which the United States had friendly relations, Great Britain, China, and several Latin American governments among others.[37]

The State Department feared serious damage to American relations with these countries, particularly with Latin America. While Secretary of State Hull and his staff did not want to appear to be "blocking the inquiry," they did want to "protect our good name and friendship,"[38] and Hull spent more than two hours discussing the problem with the committee during the noon recess in the hearings on September 11, 1934. After this conference Hull issued a statement to the press saying that neither the committee nor any official of the United States government wanted to offend any foreign government or its officials. At the same time Hull made public a letter from Nye in which the senator emphasized that the insertion in the record of statements by foreign agents of American companies did not necessarily imply that the statements were true.[39]

American officials also warned the committee against releasing certain government documents. General Douglas MacArthur, army chief of staff, was seriously concerned lest the committee reveal records about secret War Department procurement plans relating to national defense.[40] In a different connection, Secretary Hull and Secretary of Commerce Daniel C. Roper again met with the committee for more than an hour on September 14, 1934. At that time they refused to permit the committee to put into the public record a confidential report by Douglas Miller, the American commercial attaché at Berlin, on German purchases of airplanes. Hull and Roper emphasized that if such reports were published essential sources of information for the United States government would dry up.[41]

The foreign diplomatic protests and Secretary Hull's closed sessions with the Nye committee provoked speculation that the committee was being asked to "soft-pedal" its findings. Nye denied this.[42] Although the committee and the State Department tried to cooperate with each other, problems of this sort continued to crop up throughout the entire investigation.

Businessmen also feared that the committee revelations would jeopardize their profits from foreign business. Governments in other parts of the world might not buy from them if they believed their dealings might be broadcast to the world as a result of the committee's probings. Furthermore, the investigation was pointing clearly toward either severe government regulation or government ownership of munitions industries. Businessmen, including the du Ponts, insisted that the government could not do the job adequately and that private munitions industries operating with the incentive of profits were essential to American national security. Irénée du Pont also hinted that attacks on munitions makers were partly Communist inspired.[43]

On Friday, September 21, 1934, the committee adjourned its hearings for two months. At the closing session Senator Nye said that the committee had "only scratched the surface in its work" and that it intended "to go as deeply into the entire subject as its means and its ability will permit."[44]

Between the adjournment and the beginning of the committee's next hearings on December 4, 1934, Nye divided his time between political campaigning in North Dakota and speaking engagements all over the country. From his early days in the Senate Nye had spoken with increasing frequency and effectiveness at public meetings and gatherings. By 1934 he was a powerful orator, not a "shouter," but with an earnest, intense, and moving style that repeatedly held large audiences in rapt attention for two hours and more. Even those who disagreed with him conceded that he was an unusually effective speaker. In the fall of 1934 he went on the first of his many nationwide speaking tours arranged through private lecture agencies. Nye enjoyed these speaking engagements and they brought him substantial financial returns, but in addition they provided an opportunity for him to take his foreign policy views to the people. From 1934 through December 7, 1941, many tens of thousands of Americans heard his addresses and millions more heard him on local and national radio broadcasts.[45]

In speech after speech, citing evidence from the findings of the munitions investigation, Nye pounded home his theme: "There may be doubt as to the degree but there is certainty that the profits of preparation for war and the profits of war itself constitute the most serious challenge to the peace of the world. . . . the removal of the element of profit from war would materially remove the danger of more war." To preserve peace the senator urged the United States to "be as severe with income and property as we are with lives in time of war." He was referring primarily to urban industrial and financial interests, not to farmers, so his theme was perfectly consistent with his agrarian frame of reference.[46]

At the same time Nye and his committee stressed the business "villain" in their analyses of foreign affairs, a second villain gradually began to loom larger in their findings and thinking: government, and particularly the executive branch of the government. Its role in promoting international friction and war was increasingly emphasized by Nye from 1934 onward. As his attitude toward government hardened he gradually began to move from liberalism to conservatism— without abandoning his agrarianism.

FIGHT FOR NEUTRALITY

6

The Nye Committee and Presidential Power

AFTER THE FALL RECESS the Munitions Investigating Committee under Senator Nye resumed public hearings on December 4, 1934, and continued them regularly for nearly five months. Late in April 1935 the committee adjourned and held no hearings for eight and one-half months until January 7, 1936. It heard its final witness on February 20, 1936, a year and one-half after the hearings first started. During those eighteen months the Nye committee questioned nearly two hundred witnesses and spent more than $130,000; the testimony and exhibits, when published, filled thirty-nine volumes, totaling 13,750 pages of fine print. The du Ponts, who testified in 1934–35, were the biggest of the industrial giants examined in the munitions inquiry, while the appearance of J. P. Morgan and his senior partners in January and February 1936 was the high point of the committee's exploration into financial aspects of the munitions traffic. Among the many other firms whose officers appeared before the committee in 1935–36 were the Winchester Repeating Arms Company, Colt's Patent Fire Arms Manufacturing Company, Remington Arms Company, New York Shipbuilding Corporation, Newport News Shipbuilding and Dry Dock Company, Carnegie Steel Company, and Bethlehem Steel Company. The Nye committee submitted a brief preliminary report and two major reports in the spring and summer of 1935, with five more major reports released before the end of June 1936. As a result of the inquiry the committee sponsored several legislative proposals. The investigation also helped set the tone for American attitudes toward foreign affairs during the remainder of the decade.[1]

Although Nye and his colleagues probed throughout the entire investigation the methods and profits of private businesses engaged in the manufacture, trade, and finance of munitions, from December 1934 onward the senator became increasingly alarmed by the role of the federal government itself in the munitions traffic. It is significant that the particular controversy that ended the investigation in 1936 involved President Woodrow Wilson's role in World War I – not the activities of munitions makers. From 1935 through 1938 Nye wanted to restrain *both* business and government in the name of peace. By 1939 he had relegated his criticisms of business to a distinctly secondary place in his public statements as his fears about the war-making potential of the executive branch of the government came to dominate his views.

Early in January 1935, four months after the hearings began, Senator Nye told a reporter: "I suppose nothing [in the munitions investigation] has astonished me so much as to discover the large amounts of evidence which indicate that, instead of munition-makers promoting the military activities of governments, governments – especially our own war and navy departments – have been actively promoting the munitions-makers, for years." He emphasized that the munitions business "would not be what it is without the support of government officials." On January 15, 1935, he told the Senate that "the most vicious feature of all the disclosures as a result of this investigation has been the revelation of a partnership . . . which our Government – your Government and mine – has in the business of selling American munitions of war."[2]

When the senator first expressed concern about the role of the government he singled out the War Department, the Navy Department, and the Department of Commerce. Though these were in the executive branch, Nye did not immediately denounce the presidency. Even as his fears about the direction and strength of presidential influence on foreign affairs steadily increased, Nye initially sympathized with the Chief Executive's difficulties in withstanding pressures from powerful economic interests. He said legislation limiting the President's role in foreign affairs would help him resist such pressures.[3]

Nye's growing opposition to presidential authority in foreign relations gradually brought him closer to economic conservatives who feared and opposed presidential power over domestic issues. From 1935 through 1938 he retained both his liberalism and his isolationism. By the end of 1938, however, his attitudes toward presidential power (and toward President Roosevelt in particular), as well as shifting political patterns in North Dakota and the nation, were drawing him irresistibly toward an alliance with conservative Republicans. This transition was not completed until later, but the trends were beginning to be visible from 1935 through 1938.

Nye's increasingly critical attitude toward the President was consistent with his agricultural frame of reference. As early as 1927 he said it was "the industrial east which is still making and unmaking presidents."[4] In the twentieth century urban groups have generally played a much larger role than farmers in selecting and influencing the President—in spite of the considerable political importance of the West in Roosevelt's early New Deal and of the South throughout his administration. Farmers for the most part have exerted their greatest political influence on the United States Congress and on state governments. From Nye's point of view the President in making decisions in foreign affairs was likely to use government authority to advance the privileged position of urban business and financial groups (labor unions were added later by Nye) at the expense of the farmer. If he had sought them, Nye could have found historical precedents for his agrarian-based fear of executive power that went back at least as far as Thomas Jefferson.

The causes of the senator's disenchantment with the presidency may be found partly in his own personal qualities and those of the President. Gerald P. Nye and Franklin D. Roosevelt were alike in some respects. Neither was scholarly or intellectual. Both were liberals who combined a compassion for the lower classes with a faith in political democracy. Both defended the private enterprise system. Both were skilled politicians who thrived on political battles. The differences between these two men, however, were much more striking than any similarities. Roosevelt was a wealthy easterner with an aristocratic social background; Nye was a relatively poor middle westerner who had never been east of Chicago before he went to the Senate. Roosevelt attended Groton, Harvard, and Columbia; Nye's formal education ended when he graduated from Wittenberg High School. Roosevelt had been to Europe many times; Nye never visited Europe and did not leave the United States until after he entered the Senate. Roosevelt loved the sea and the navy; Nye never saw the ocean until he was thirty-three and he rejected the view of those advocating a big navy. The President was urbane, charming, and informal, with a warm sense of humor; the senator was serious, earnest, direct, and intense. Roosevelt was pragmatic, Nye doctrinaire. In politics Roosevelt was the clever boxer, parrying blows, rolling with punches, and hitting sharply; Nye was a rugged, aggressive slugger. Roosevelt was positive in thought and action; Nye's crusades were generally against some evil. Roosevelt was a country gentleman whose values, personal ties, and political base were increasingly urban; Nye, while he never lived on a farm, had agrarian values and a predominantly rural constituency.[5]

Nye's policy differences with the President extended back to the early New Deal. His criticisms of the N.R.A. urged reforms to benefit small business, labor, and the consumer. But he also began to criticize the "oppression" and "usurped powers" of governmental administrators in the N.R.A., charging that "code authority administration in many cases has lost all semblance of a rule of law and has become a rule of men."[6] Conservatives endorsed this view even though they rejected Nye's liberalism.

President Roosevelt angered the Senate munitions investigators on December 12, 1934, when he announced appointment of a separate committee to consider the possibility of legislation to take the profit out of war, a group headed by Wall Street's Bernard Baruch who did not share Nye's more extreme views on the subject. The eleven others on Baruch's committee were General Hugh S. Johnson, Chief of Staff General Douglas MacArthur, Secretary of War George H. Dern, Secretary of Navy Claude A. Swanson, Assistant Secretary of Navy Henry L. Roosevelt, Secretary of State Cordell Hull, Secretary of the Treasury Henry Morgenthau, Jr., Secretary of Agriculture Henry A. Wallace, Secretary of Labor Frances Perkins, Federal Coordinator of Transportation Joseph B. Eastman, and Foreign Trade Adviser George N. Peek. No senator was included and many believed this was an administration move to sidetrack the Senate inquiry.[7]

Nye's reaction was prompt and vigorous: "The departments of our government are really codefendants with the munitions industry and the profiteers. . . . When I view, in part, the personnel of the conference, I cannot but think how unfortunate it is that [John] Dillinger is dead. He was the logical person to write the anti-crime laws." The

White House was flooded with letters protesting any effort to block the Senate munitions investigation. At Roosevelt's invitation Nye conferred with the President at the White House on December 26, 1934, and was assured that the Baruch committee would not undermine the Senate inquiry and that Nye's committee would have the President's continued support. The Baruch group in fact did not function, but the episode increased Nye's distrust of the administration.[8]

In the spring of 1935 the Senate committee differed with the administration over the examination of correspondence between New York banks and Allied governments during the period of American neutrality in World War I. The British and French objected, and the State Department did not want to irritate friendly governments on the issue. At Hull's request the committee delayed subpoenaing the records for a week. The secretary did not succeed, however, in his efforts to dissuade Nye from embarking on any study of the documents, for the senator insisted that the probe of private American loans to the Allied governments might be the most important phase of the investigation. At a White House conference on April 18, 1935, President Roosevelt and Secretary Hull tried to convince Senators Nye, Clark, and Pope that they should abandon or at least defer their examination of the files. But they failed. On March 20, Nye had promised that the committee would not publish any of these documents until the State Department had an opportunity to consult with the government involved. He repeated this assurance at the White House on April 18, but he firmly refused to yield further. Confronted with this stand, the administration (and the British, French, and Italian governments) had to accede.[9] Hull and the senators made a comparable agreement in August 1935, when the committee began its examination of financial accounts of the British and French governments in the files of J. P. Morgan and Company.[10]

On April 1, 1935, Nye submitted a brief preliminary committee report to the Senate,[11] and the first of its seven major reports was presented on June 24, 1935. It covered the committee's findings and recommendations on naval shipbuilding. In it the committee urged that naval defense should "be provided for without profiteering or collusion" and "that the national necessity for a purely defensive Navy shall not be confused with the private necessity of the shipbuilders for continuing profits." The committee insisted that private shipbuilders should either "be policed" effectively or "be cut off entirely from the building of ships for the Navy." It suspected some shipbuilders "of willingness to wave the flag or to circulate war scares in the plain and simple interest of their own pocketbooks, regardless of results." Complaining about lack of real competition among shipbuilders, the committee charged that there was collusion or "sympathetic understanding" among big companies bidding for naval contracts. The committee contended that there was "no effective profit-limitation law" and that the profits of shipbuilding firms were too high – 21.8 per cent to 36.9 per cent on the ships studied. It called private shipyards "expensive luxuries" and cited statistics to show that it cost more to build naval vessels in private yards than in government shipyards. The committee deplored the lobbying and influence of shipbuilders and warned against the dangers of allowing shipbuilders "to remain in a position where it is to their financial interest to confuse public opinion between the needs of the country for a purely defensive Navy and their own continued needs for profits." The report included more than 270 pages of evidence and testimony to support the findings and the recommendations made.[12]

In this first report the Nye committee did not reach a conclusion on the relative merits of government ownership and private ownership in naval shipbuilding. But pending a later decision on that issue, the committee recommended "an unusually strict reporting of the activities of all the representatives of the shipbuilders and allied interests." It also recommended approval of two bills "to prevent collusion in the making of contracts for the construction of naval vessels in private shipyards" and "to prevent profiteering in the construction of naval vessels in private shipyards." These bills (S. 3098 and S. 3099) were introduced by Senator Vandenberg on June 19, 1935, but they died in the Naval Affairs Committee.[13]

The committee's second report, issued in August 1935, dealt with methods of taking the profits out of war. The main responsibility for this phase of its inquiry had been assigned to John T. Flynn, who directed a detailed study of the subject. The central issue concerned the relative merits of price controls and taxation. In general, administration departments favored primary reliance on price controls. The Nye committee, on the other hand, believed controls would be insufficient and recommended extremely high wartime taxes in addition to price controls. The committee's proposals were similar to those introduced by Nye a year earlier when the Senate first authorized the munitions investigation.[14]

On March 19, 1935, all seven committee members met with President Roosevelt at the White House to discuss several phases of the inquiry. Before this meeting Hull had sent the President a detailed memorandum advising him on issues to be discussed with the committee, but Roosevelt failed to follow most of the secretary's suggestions. At the meeting Nye summarized Flynn's proposals for taking profits out of war—expecting the President to find them too drastic. To his surprise, Roosevelt endorsed the main ideas. The President also encouraged the committee to go into the matter of neutrality legislation. Nye was elated by the President's attitude. Hull was displeased, however, and later advised Roosevelt not to support any specific legislation on taking profits out of war.[15]

A week after the White House conference Bernard Baruch appeared before the committee in opposition to Flynn's proposals. Baruch said he wanted to prevent profiteering but opposed methods that might interfere with essential war production. He warned that "there is such a thing as taking the profits out of war at the cost of losing the war, by going too far." He favored high wartime taxes, but placed much more emphasis on rigid price ceilings. Administration departments, including the War Department, shared Baruch's general point of view, and the House of Representatives concurred when it adopted the McSwain bill (H. R. 5529) on April 9, 1935.[16]

In the Senate Nye arranged to have the McSwain bill referred to the Munitions Committee. There everything after the enactment clause was deleted and replaced with provisions conforming to the views of Flynn and the committee. As amended the lengthy document called for sharply increased wartime taxes, including what were in essence one hundred per cent tax rates on all corporate profits over six per cent and on all personal income of more than $10,000 a year during a war. The resolution also authorized the government to draft industrial managers in extreme cases when war needs plus lack of cooperation by executives made it necessary. Nye submitted the amended resolution to the Senate on May 3, with an accompanying report stating the committee's views on it. The resolution was then referred to the Military Affairs Committee and finally to the Finance Committee.

There it was eventually assigned to a subcommittee under Senator Tom Connally, a severe critic of Nye and his investigation.[17]

In the meantime the second of the major Nye committee reports was released. This 164-page document urged enactment of H. R. 5529 to cope with "the distressing inequalities, the shameless profiteering, and the staggering aftermath of the last war" and noted the need for adoption of three amendments to the Constitution, the first two authorizing the "power of commandeering [industries] and the power of taxing without uniformity – both without our customary elaborate court review," the third permitting Congress to tax the interest on tax-exempt securities during a national emergency. The report doubted, however, that even these drastic steps would eliminate war profiteering. And it emphasized that the first two amendments "contain dangers that may be far worse than the evil of profiteering" since they obviously would "increase enormously the power of the Federal Government." The report warned: "The opportunities for militaristic control in war-time are well known; the relaxing of constitutional restrictions will increase these opportunities. . . . If there is, therefore, the least danger that any group of industrialists, through the sheer size of their investment, or through their absolute necessity for war purposes, such as, for example, the steel and chemical industries, should be in a position of power in a war-time administration, the first two amendments would be dangerous weapons to place in their hands." The report did not express any fear that either farmers or laborers might gain the "position of power."[18]

Nye tried repeatedly to get a Senate vote on the committee's resolution. After months of delay Connally's subcommittee in the spring of 1936 revised it by increasing the war taxes to be levied on lower incomes and decreasing those on upper incomes, but even in this more moderate form it failed to be adopted by Congress. During the next five years Nye and his colleagues regularly re-introduced bills to tax the profits out of war – but they were never able to get them enacted.[19]

In the summer of 1935 Nye had also been absorbed in the battle to enact a neutrality law. And sandwiched between his activities on the committee and on the Senate floor was an almost continuous round of speeches on munitions makers and on neutrality. When Congress adjourned late in August only political fence-mending in North Dakota and a brief fishing vacation interrupted his speaking engagements all over the country. In October he joined a large congressional party for a long, leisurely ocean voyage to Hawaii, Japan, and the Philippines to attend the inauguration of Manuel Quezon as the first president of the Philippines. This two-month junket was Nye's first trip outside of the Western Hemisphere. He returned in the middle of December in time to help plan the final series of committee hearings.[20]

After years of attacking Wall Street, the youthful-appearing senator on January 7, 1936, came face to face with the biggest international banker of them all—J. P. Morgan and his senior partners. These hearings had been preceded by months of arduous work in Morgan company files by the committee's staff, during which period irritation had arisen all around: the committee believed the company was obstructing the search of its records; the House of Morgan partners objected to the probing; Britain and France disliked the examination of their accounts with the Morgan firm; and the State Department was caught in the crossfire.[21] In the dramatic hearings the committee investigated the House of Morgan's role in directing and financing the sale of American munitions to Allied governments in World War I from 1914 to 1917. These detailed and occasionally heated sessions with the Morgan witnesses, supplemented by the introduction of many documents, extended into early February and won daily headlines all over the nation and the world. After listening to all the testimony Senator Nye concluded: "It would not be fair to say that the House of Morgan took us to war to save their investment in the Allies, but the record of facts makes it altogether fair to say that these bankers were in the heart and center of a system that made our going to war inevitable. We started in 1914 with a neutrality policy which permitted the sale of arms and munitions to belligerents, but which forbad loans to belligerents. Then, in the name of our own business welfare, President Wilson permitted the policy to be stretched to the extent of permitting the house of Morgan to supply the credit needs of the Allies. After this error of neutrality, the road to war was paved and greased for us." He maintained that comparable conditions in more intensified form existed in the United States in 1936.[22]

While the Morgan hearings were in progress Nye was also busy working for extended neutrality legislation. At the same time he again was carrying an incredibly heavy load of speaking engagements. Because of his many responsibilities the senator urged the commercial speakers' bureau arranging for his addresses not to schedule any "except for weekends and then only in event the engagement is reasonably close at hand so I can get back." But the bureau accepted invitations from as far away as the Middle West and, as usual, Nye found it difficult to say No. As commitments of all sorts accumulated, the hard-pressed senator warned the bureau on January 14, 1936: "If I don't watch my step, I am going to be driven insane by reason of conflicting obligations created by the hearings which we have on the boards and by the engagements which I have consented to have scheduled."[23]

On the next day an incident occurred that promised to end the whole munitions investigation abruptly. The crisis did not involve munitions makers, shipbuilders, international bankers, or any other economic group directly. Rather, it concerned the political leader of the United States during World War I, President Woodrow Wilson. At the hearings on Wednesday morning, January 15, Senator Clark read documents and evidence into the record showing, among other things, that President Wilson, Secretary of State Robert Lansing, and Colonel Edward M. House had very early knowledge of Allied "secret agreements." Clark said: "the Committee has taken cognizance of information from official sources which has not yet been released for publication, which I am therefore unable to put into the record, which clearly indicates that [in the spring of 1917] before he departed from this country, [England's Foreign Secretary Arthur] Balfour left with Lansing, Secretary of State, a statement . . . [that] referred at length to the terms of peace to which Britain was committed and the secret treaties." The official source Clark alluded to was a memorandum from Balfour to Lansing in the State Department files. The Nye committee wanted to make it public, but the British had refused to grant the necessary permission. At the hearings Nye then said that "the Committee is informed by the highest possible sources that Secretary Lansing and President Wilson were fully apprised by Balfour of the secret treaties, to which Great Britain had been committed, and the record that has been made and is yet to be made will all clearly reveal that both the President and Secretary Lansing falsified concerning this matter, and declared upon occasion that they had no knowledge prior to their visit to the Peace Conference in Paris."[24]

Nye's statement that "the President and Secretary Lansing falsified" about their knowledge of the secret treaties was the match that set off the powder keg. Evening newspapers charged that Nye had said President Wilson "lied." After warning the senator what he planned to do and asking him to be present, Tom Connally, Democrat of Texas, rose from his seat the next day and proceeded to give Nye one of the most scathing tongue-lashings ever administered on the Senate floor. It was very difficult, Connally said, "within the compass of parliamentary propriety to find language adequate to express my contempt for efforts of this kind to besmirch the memory of the man Woodrow Wilson." But despite any theoretical inhibitions imposed by "parliamentary propriety," he managed to get his point across. "Some checker-playing, beer-drinking, back room of some low house," Connally roared, "is the only place fit for the kind of language which the Senator from North Dakota . . . puts into the Record about a dead man, a great man, a good man, and a man who when alive had the courage to meet his enemies face to face and eye to eye." Connally charged that the Nye committee did not have authority to meddle in such matters and he vehemently opposed making any more money available for the investigation. In the course of his tirade he struck his desk so hard that a knuckle of his left hand became enlarged and remained misshapened thereafter. Nye was presiding over the Morgan hearings at the time and did not hear Connally's assault. Only Senator Clark actively came to Nye's defense in the Senate.[25]

The altercation continued the following day when Nye took the floor to answer what he called Connally's "loud barking" and "gutter English." He refused to apologize or retract his statement about Wilson. Instead, he repeated it and cited evidence to demonstrate its truth. He said the committee had to study the Wilson administration to determine the effects of the arms traffic on the government's foreign policies. "If we find that one of the most idealistic Presidents this Nation ever had was unable to stem a flood of munitions orders, is it improper to report on that fact?" He reminded his listeners that as a newspaperman he had enthusiastically supported Wilson and his foreign policies. "When we go in search of pertinent truths we ought not dodge them when we encounter them — we ought not let partisan prejudices blind us to those truths, however embarrassing they may be to a mere political party." He promised: "Whatever the degree of threat or intimidation, however slimy may be the language used in criticism of the course pursued, I shall pursue that course and know that I have done that which is right." He was repeatedly interrupted and attacked by Connally.[26]

The heaviest blast on this second day came from Carter Glass, who had served as secretary of the treasury in President Wilson's cabinet. The old Virginia senator trembled with emotion as he told the packed galleries: "If it were permissible in the Senate to say that any man who would asperse the integrity and veracity of Woodrow Wilson is a coward, if it were permissible to say that his charge is not only malicious but positively mendacious, that I would be glad to say here and elsewhere to any man, whether he be a United States Senator or not, because the charge would be not only destitute of decency but it would be such a shocking exhibition as never has happened in the 35 years I have served in the Congress of the United States." He said the money spent on the investigation was "wasted" and, like Connally, he opposed giving the committee another dollar. During his talk Glass pounded his desk with such violence that his hand bled. Other senators joined in this verbal brawl and it continued a third day on the Senate floor with some echoes on still later occasions.[27]

The repercussions from Nye's criticism of Wilson were not limited to the Senate chamber. The State Department vigorously protested the references by Nye and Clark to the Balfour memorandum that had not been released for publication by the British government.[28] Allen W. Dulles, a New York lawyer who shared with his brother, John Foster Dulles, authority for granting access to the Lansing private papers, objected to the fact that Nye had shown certain senators – including Connally – extracts from the papers that were not to have been made public. (Actually, despite his allusions to them, for the public record Nye did not quote or indicate the specific contents of either the Balfour or the Lansing memorandum.)[29] In addition, two Democrats on the Munitions Investigating Committee, Pope and George, issued an angry statement criticizing Nye. They reaffirmed their support for the investigation and for remedial legislation, but they disassociated themselves from "head hunting or using an instrumentality of the United States Senate to promote the bias, prejudice, or animus of any member of the committee."[30] Even the sympathetic Senator George Norris feared that Nye's "unfortunate" and "unnecessary" remark might reduce the good results he hoped would come from the findings of the investigation.[31]

Nye's statement about Wilson was factually correct and none of his critics cited any evidence to disprove it. When the episode occurred the inquiry was nearly completed, and the committee was able to finish its hearings and issue its final reports. But the senator's statement was a political mistake and it was not essential to the investigation. It strengthened and unified the previously scattered opposition to Nye, his committee, and the foreign policies he advocated. Earlier, the munitions investigation got nearly as much support from Democrats as from Republicans. But seemingly gratuitous criticism of a Democratic President by the Republican head of the investigation helped drive Democrats into opposition to the foreign policies Nye favored.

On February 16, 1936, Nye was presented the Cardinal Newman Award "in recognition of his distinguished contribution to world peace."[32] Four days later the Special Committee Investigating the Munitions Industry held its last day of public hearings.[33] There remained, however, the work of preparing the committee's final reports and the even more difficult task of enacting laws to implement the committee's recommendations.

Even Nye's rugged constitution could not stand indefinitely the pace he was setting, and in March 1936 the overwrought senator was advised by his physician to take a rest and slow up considerably. Within three weeks he was feeling much better, but he resolved to put himself "under stricter regulation for the balance of the spring." He told the speakers' bureau that his health and legislative responsibilities would keep him close to Washington in April and May.[34]

On April 20, 1936, Nye submitted the committee's third major report to the Senate — a 282-page document on the activities and sales of munitions companies. The committee reported "that almost without exception, the American munitions companies investigated have at times resorted to such unusual approaches, questionable favors and commissions, and methods of 'doing the needful' as to constitute, in effect, a form of bribery of foreign governmental officials or of their close friends in order to secure business." The committee was convinced that these business methods carried "within themselves the seeds of disturbance to the peace and stability of those nations in which they take place." "While the evidence before this committee does not show that wars have been started solely because of the activities of munitions makers and their agents, it is also true that wars rarely have one single cause, and the committee finds it to be against the peace of the world for selfishly interested organizations to be left free to goad and frighten nations into military activity." The committee also charged that munitions companies had "secured the active support of the War, Navy, Commerce, and even State Departments in their sales abroad."[35]

All seven senators agreed on the seriousness of the problem, but they disagreed on the methods for dealing with it. The majority favored government ownership of munitions industries, while the minority favored reliance on strict government control of private munitions companies. The grouping of the senators on this issue is significant. Those who favored government ownership (Nye of North Dakota, Clark of Missouri, Bone of Washington, and Pope of Idaho) were all liberals from states west of the Mississippi River. Those who opposed government ownership (George of Georgia, Vandenberg of Michigan, and Barbour of New Jersey) were conservatives from east of the Mississippi. The senators with the largest farming constituencies outside of the South favored government ownership of munitions industries, while the senators with the most substantial industrial constituencies (Vandenberg and Barbour) opposed it. The economic and regional patterns were more clear-cut than the political patterns. Three of the four Democrats favored government ownership and two of the three Republicans opposed such ownership. Nye was the only Republican on the munitions committee who wanted government ownership – and the only Republican whose home state had little industry and much agriculture.

In urging government ownership the majority contended that private munitions companies could easily evade government regulation. Further, since the military services "already manufacture half of the naval vessels, their guns, their rifles, their ammunition, and, in the case of the Navy, their powder," the majority saw "no change in principle to extend the present practice in regard to this material to the same or other material." The minority feared "that if large Government plants are erected to provide these commodities, there will be inevitable local, political pressure to maintain these plants at full capacity production regardless of actual defense needs, and the result will be to encourage armament rather than disarmament." The minority believed government ownership would cost more than private ownership and concluded that "the public welfare, from the standpoint of peace, defense, and economy, can be better served by rigid and conclusive munitions control than by nationalization except in a few isolated instances."[36]

The fourth committee report, submitted by Senator Clark on June 2, 1936, dealt with seven bills on wartime industrial mobilization prepared by the War Department. The issues and the analysis in it were similar to those in the committee's earlier report on wartime taxation and control. The committee believed that much of the authority sought in these bills could be provided by enactment of H. R. 5529, still buried in committee. The Munitions Committee also had some serious objections to the War Department bills, particularly to one that called for a wartime military draft. The committee believed it would even permit drafting labor to operate industrial plants and feared this might lead to a military dictatorship and the destruction of American democracy. The War Department found little support in the Nye committee for its industrial mobilization proposals.[37]

On June 5, Senator Clark submitted the committee's fifth report covering findings and recommendations on neutrality legislation. In the interests of American neutrality, the committee recommended detailed restrictions on economic groups and on the administration in relations with belligerents in any war. Apropros of the crisis over Nye's statement about Wilson, this report included the following observation: "The Committee wishes to point out most definitely that its study of events resulting from the then existing neutrality legislation, or the lack of it, is in no way a criticism, direct or implied, of the sincere devotion of the then President, Woodrow Wilson, to the high causes of peace and democracy. Like other leaders in government, business and finance, he had watched the growth of militarism in the pre-war years. Militarism meant the alliance of the military with powerful economic groups to secure appropriations on the one hand for a constantly increasing military and naval establishment, and on the other hand, the constant threat of the use of that swollen military establishment in behalf of the economic interests at home and abroad of the industrialists supporting it. . . . President Wilson was personally impelled by the highest motives and the most profound convictions as to the justice of the cause of our country and was devoted to peace. He was caught up in a situation created largely by the profit-making interests in the United States, and such interests spread to nearly everybody in the country. It seemed necessary to the prosperity of our people that their markets in Europe remain unimpaired. President Wilson, himself, stated that he realized that the economic rivalries of European nations had played their part in bringing on the war in 1914."[38]

This fifth report also included a detailed study of the neutrality of the United States in 1914–17, prepared by Josephine Joan Burns, a member of the committee's staff who worked through the State Department's files. In her study she emphasized "the importance of determining a neutrality policy before war has begun and the desirability of mandatory rather than discretionary legislation."[39]

The sixth report, submitted by Senator Nye on June 6, 1936, was based largely on the committee's probe of the activities of J. P. Morgan and Company before the United States entered World War I. "Loans to belligerents militate against neutrality," it maintained, "for when only one group of belligerents can purchase and transport commodities the loans act in favor of that belligerent" and "profoundly affect the neutrality of mind and spirit of those holding them." "Loans extended to the Allies in 1915 and 1916, led to a very considerable war boom and inflation. This boom extended beyond munitions to auxiliary supplies and equipment as well as to agricultural products. . . . The nature of such a war-boom inflation is that, like all inflations, an administration is almost powerless to check it, once the movement is well started. Our foreign policy then is seriously affected by it, even to the extent of making impossible the alteration of our foreign policy in such a way as to protect our neutral rights." The committee, therefore, recommended the continuation and extension of neutrality laws restricting loans and exports to belligerents to help preserve American neutrality in future wars.[40]

It was on June 19, 1936, that Senator Nye presented the committee's final report to the Senate. It dealt, in 123 pages, with the question of government manufacture of munitions. It was largely a summary, drawing data and recommendations from the earlier reports on naval shipbuilding, on wartime taxation and price control, and on activities and sales of munitions companies. In its final recommendations the committee divided four to three in favor of government ownership of munitions industries – exactly as it had in its third report. Interestingly, though Vandenberg, George, and Barbour opposed government manufacture of munitions, in their minority report they did not base their opposition on the grounds of preserving private enterprise or opposing collectivization.[41]

Public opinion polls in 1936 indicated that the overwhelming majority of the American people in all sections of the country favored government ownership of the munitions industry.[42] In 1937 Nye introduced a bill that would have provided for government ownership of shipbuilding and munitions manufacturing facilities, but it was never adopted by Congress. As early as March 1935, Secretary of State Cordell Hull had advised President Roosevelt against a government monopoly of munitions manufacturing. He warned that "a Government monopoly would seriously dislocate our whole economic structure, would curtail or put an end to the business of several hundred private companies, and would put this Government in business to an extent unknown anywhere else in the world except in the U.S.S.R." Hull believed it "would probably result in an increase in the total quantity of arms manufactured and perhaps in an increased menace to peace." The War and Navy departments both shared his general point of view and opposed Nye's bill. It was the administration's position on the issue (not Nye's) that prevailed.[43]

The Senate authorized the printing of 44,000 copies of each of the seven reports and they were widely distributed throughout the country. Many who wrote or spoke about the munitions investigation, however, did so without ever reading the committee's reports. Neither Senator Nye nor his committee believed that munitions makers and international bankers were solely responsible for wars or for American entry into World War I. Nye and his colleagues did not believe that the causes for wars could be located exclusively in economic interests. Furthermore, Nye did not believe that the legislation recommended by the munitions committee would "eliminate all the dangers or causes of war." Among the many noneconomic forces for war that loomed increasingly large in Nye's thinking was political and military leadership—both in dictatorships and in democracies. At the close of the investigation he said he "had not been aware until recently that it was actually within the power of any President of the United States to provoke a war and whip the Nation into line behind him within a few days." But the Nye committee had not been authorized to study the noneconomic causes for war, and Nye and his committee did insist that among the more important forces for war were economic ones.

In a major Senate address in July 1939, Nye said: "No member of the Munitions Committee to my knowledge has ever contended that it was munitions makers who took us to war. But that committee and its members have said again and again, that it was war trade and the war boom, shared in by many more than munitions makers, that played the primary part in moving the United States into a war."[44] In this statement the senator described the committee's views (and his own) much more moderately than he had during the course of the investigation more than three years earlier. If his 1939 statement was not an accurate description of the committee's views, however, it was probably at least as accurate as the oversimplified descriptions of the committee's "thesis" in most history textbooks written since then.

In his farewell address to the Senate a decade after the investigation began Nye said he was "more proud of having been connected with the work of the Munitions Investigating Committee than of any other service in my 20-year career as a United States Senator." He said the investigation had clearly established four facts: "First, it showed that economic interests do lie at the bottom of modern war. . . . Second, our inquiry also discovered that economic interests which stand to make money out of war cannot be trusted not to work for war. I do not say, mark you, that they always do, but I do say that they cannot be trusted not to. . . . The third fact follows, namely, that the private armament industry stands at the top of the list of those which, because they stand to make money out of the arming of nations for war, cannot be trusted to work against the coming of war. . . . The fourth fact brought out by our inquiry is that any portion of the banking industry which is engaged in financing the armament industry is just about as dangerous to peace as the armament industry itself."[45]

Nye and his colleagues failed in their efforts to secure enactment of their recommendations for regulating the shipbuilding industry, taxing the profits out of war, and for government ownership of munitions industries. But the committee, its hearings and reports, and the speeches and legislative activities of its members undoubtedly strengthened isolationist or noninterventionist sentiment in the United States before World War II. The members of the Nye committee also played prominent roles in the controversies surrounding the neutrality legislation of the 1930's.

7

Legislating Neutrality

IN THE ENACTMENT of the neutrality laws of the 1930's Senator Nye was a key figure. These laws reflected the noninterventionist philosophy he believed in, of course. They also were in line with his agrarian economic and political views since they placed no direct restraints on farmers or on the export of agricultural products but did restrict urban business groups. They barred manufacturers from selling munitions to belligerents; they prohibited traders from carrying non-embargoed goods to belligerent ports in American ships; and they prevented financiers from making loans to belligerents. In urging these controls, Nye was not moved by a basic desire to destroy business profits. He was convinced that a misdirected drive for economic gain by many industrialists, traders, and financiers helped promote foreign policies that endangered American neutrality and peace. The neutrality laws imposed legislative restraints on executive power in foreign affairs as well as on urban groups. Nye knew that farmers could not control either the President or Congress. But since farmers had a greater influence on Congress than on the President, increasing legislative controls over foreign affairs and restricting presidential discretion would provide the greatest possibility for establishing foreign policies consistent with agrarian values.

The accident of transitory political and economic conditions in the 1930's made enactment of the neutrality laws possible. But the combination of Axis military aggression and dominance by urban groups in

America guaranteed eventual defeat for Nye's efforts to legislate neutrality.

Numerous congressmen, administration leaders, and private groups and individuals played roles in the controversy over the neutrality laws. The State Department studied the problem in 1934 and sent a memorandum on neutrality to the President late in August. Because the subject was "of such importance," Roosevelt asked Hull in September if he "should recommend legislation to the coming session of Congress."[1]

Although Nye's Munitions Investigating Committee was not explicitly authorized to deal with neutrality legislation, it was instructed to "investigate and report upon the adequacy or inadequacy of existing legislation, and of the treaties to which the United States is a party, for the regulation and control of the manufacture of and traffic in arms, munitions, or other implements of war within the United States, and of the traffic therein between the United States and other countries." Nye had mixed feelings on the relative merits of international agreements and national legislation on the subject. On January 15, 1935, he told the Senate: "We should hope for, we should anticipate, ultimate international agreement. It will simplify matters very, very much indeed. Surely, however, we can proceed in a domestic way in very large measure to straighten out and bring into the line of fair play and decency our own munitions makers."[2]

In February 1935 the senator asked Joseph C. Green of the State Department to prepare a memorandum for the committee on legislation that might precede or supplement a treaty to control munitions manufacture and traffic. Hull wanted to defer action on neutrality legislation, but he gave Green permission to draft the memorandum and legislation Nye had requested.[3]

Paradoxically, it was a suggestion by President Roosevelt that triggered the Nye committee's decision to plunge headlong into the whole matter of neutrality legislation. Hull advised Roosevelt to encourage the committee to approve Green's proposals for registration and licensing of munitions makers and traders. But at the White House conference with the Nye committee on March 19, 1935, the President strayed far from the paths Hull had recommended. The discussions centered for the most part on methods for taking profits out of war and on American neutrality legislation. Senators Nye and Pope told Green the next day that Roosevelt discussed American neutrality policy at length and said "he had come around entirely to the ideas of Mr. Bryan, in regard to that matter, and that he was preparing to propose legislation which would prohibit American ships or American citizens from visiting belligerent countries in time of war." While encouraging the committee to study neutrality policies and to formulate appropriate legislation, the President asked the committee to consult him before introducing bills on the subject. A few days later Stephen Raushenbush told Green "that the President had pushed the Committee into the study of this subject of neutrality which, up to the time of their conference with him, they had not considered in connection with their program of proposed legislation." As a result, the committee was "hot on the trail" of the neutrality matter. Green advised delay in consideration of the subject until it had been "threshed out more thoroughly" with the President. But Raushenbush doubted that the committee would be willing to wait.[4]

In a major address in Lexington, Kentucky, on March 30, 1935, Nye warned that German rearmament made it necessary for the United States "at once to consider and write law such as would largely guarantee our neutrality in the event of European hostilities." He emphasized that President Roosevelt had urged his committee to study the neutrality question. The senator recommended: "America's neutrality program should prohibit the flotation of any public or private loans in the United States on behalf of any foreign government or national of any foreign government engaged in armed conflict. There should be strictness in withholding the issuance of passports to citizens of the United States when nations at war are jeopardizing safety upon the high seas. There must be provided a clear defining of the term 'arms and munitions of war,' and utter prohibition of sale or exportation of such from any place in the United States to countries engaged in armed conflict."[5]

The Nye Munitions Committee planned that its preliminary report on April 1, 1935, "would contain a general statement to the effect that the Committee, having studied the question of neutrality at the request of the President, was approaching agreement upon legislation to withdraw the protection of the American Government from American ships and American citizens entering a war zone or visiting belligerent countries." After Key Pittman and William E. Borah complained that this subject was under the jurisdiction of the Senate Foreign Relations Committee, the reference to neutrality legislation in the preliminary report was toned down. The report, which endorsed "more rigorous international control of the arms traffic," announced in Article IV that the committee was in "substantial agreement on a principle to govern the export of munitions and contraband in case of a major war and expects to make certain recommendations to the Senate on this subject in the immediate future and for action in the present session of Congress. This," the report promised, "is the only phase of the neutrality problem which the committee considers to be within its jurisdiction."[6]

Pittman, a tall, lean, and hard-drinking Democrat from Nevada, was chairman of the Senate Foreign Relations Committee from 1933 until his death in November 1940. He was a shrewd but pessimistic politician who was inclined to emphasize the strength of the opposition and the weakness of his own forces. Except for his crusades for the silver interests of Nevada, he preferred maneuver and manipulation in politics rather than frontal assaults.[7]

His Foreign Relations Committee included some able spokesmen for internationalism – particularly from the South and East. Among these were Joseph T. Robinson of Arkansas, Tom Connally of Texas, and Robert F. Wagner of New York. But the opposition in the committee – particularly from the West and Middle West – was even more powerful: William E. Borah of Idaho, Hiram Johnson of California, Arthur H. Vandenberg of Michigan, Arthur Capper of Kansas, Robert M. LaFollette, Jr., of Wisconsin, and Henrik Shipstead of Minnesota, among others. Pittman officially cooperated with and provided leadership for the internationalists in support of the administration's foreign policies. But he shared some of the attitudes of the opponents and, in any event, was reluctant to risk pitched battles against them. He was jealous of his prerogatives as chairman of the committee, and he guarded against incursions from either the administration or other legislative committees.[8]

Because the Foreign Relations Committee under Pittman firmly claimed jurisdiction, the Munitions Investigating Committee eventually decided not to sponsor any neutrality legislation of its own. The joint resolutions on neutrality policies of which Nye was co-sponsor were technically introduced by the individual senators – not on behalf of the Munitions Investigating Committee – and they were referred to the Foreign Relations Committee for consideration. Pittman did not object to this procedure.[9] But the vital role of Nye's committee in the enactment of neutrality laws should not be obscured by the parliamentary tactics. The munitions hearings helped arouse public interest in the general subject. The committee's staff did much of the work and planning behind the scenes. Nye and his colleagues on the Munitions Committee helped force legislative action on neutrality policies. Given the prevailing public attitudes and political patterns, Secretary of State Hull would have preferred no neutrality legislation, except for registration and licensing of munitions makers and shippers.[10] Without the Nye committee the neutrality laws probably would not have been adopted by Congress. And if they had been, they almost certainly would have been significantly different from what they were.

Teamed with Nye in the sponsorship of neutrality legislation in 1935 (and during the entire neutrality and noninterventionist crusade before Pearl Harbor) was Bennett Champ Clark, Democratic senator from Missouri, the son of Champ Clark, long-time speaker of the House. Over six feet tall and weighing more than two hundred pounds, he had been an army colonel in World War I and was a charter member and national commander of the American Legion. After developing a successful law practice in St. Louis, he went to the Senate in 1933. He was a liberal on domestic issues and a noninterventionist on foreign affairs. Round-faced and amiable, Clark enjoyed eating, drinking, and talking with people. He lacked Nye's intensity and capacity for hard work, but he had a keen mind and plenty of political courage.[11]

In 1935 Nye and Clark were co-sponsors of four resolutions on American neutrality policies. Nye introduced two of these for himself and Clark on April 9. The first (S. J. Res. 99) would have required the President to withhold passports from American citizens traveling in war zones or on belligerent ships. It was designed expressly to avoid the loss of American lives that resulted from incidents like the sinking of the British *Lusitania* in World War I. The second resolution (S. J. Res. 100) would have prohibited private American loans and credits to all belligerents at the outbreak of war. On May 7, 1935, Senator Clark, for himself and Nye, introduced S. J. Res. 120, which would have automatically prohibited American export of arms and ammunition to all belligerents at the outbreak of war. It also would have required exporters of non-embargoed contraband to ship the goods at their own risk or at the risk of the belligerent to which they were sent. These resolutions were mandatory and their application was not to be left to the President's discretion. They would have applied to all belligerents—not just to aggressors.[12] The fourth resolution (S. 2998) had been drafted by Green and was introduced on June 5, 1935, by Senator Pope, for himself, Nye, Clark, Bone, and George. It provided for the establishment of a National Munitions Control Board under the secretary of state to register and license munitions makers and shippers. It won approval from President Roosevelt and from the Departments of State, War, Navy, Commerce, and Treasury. The Foreign Relations Committee promptly reported it out favorably on June 20.[13] The other three resolutions, however, had rougher sledding.

The President's advisers did not agree on specific neutrality proposals—or even on the desirability of any neutrality legislation at that time. If legislation were enacted, however, Roosevelt and Hull wanted considerable presidential discretion in the application of the law and preferred authority to apply embargo and loan provisions only against aggressors, not necessarily against all belligerents. Since the three resolutions introduced by Nye and Clark were mandatory and did not permit discrimination against aggressor states, Hull opposed them. But the Foreign Relations Committee reported out favorably S. J. Res. 99 (passports) and 100 (loans and credits) on June 26, and planned to consider S. J. Res. 120 (arms embargo) on July 10.[14]

Pleased with this initial success, Nye directed his committee staff under Raushenbush to prepare a memorandum on the resolutions. This thirteen-page document, mimeographed and sent over the names of Nye and Clark to Pittman and the other members of the Foreign Relations Committee a week before S. J. Res. 120 was scheduled for consideration, said that the three resolutions formed "a unified program designed to avoid the entangling economic alliances created by the growth of a vast trade in munitions, by the granting of huge loans and credits which link our financial and economic interests with one group of warring nations and by the activities of private citizens who involve the nation in their pursuit of war profits." It emphasized the importance of mandatory provisions to help the President resist the "tremendous pressure" that would accompany the drive for "profitable trade in war materials after war has broken out." While the bans on munitions and loans to belligerents were mandatory and absolute, warring countries could purchase "cotton or wheat or machinery" and "make their own arrangements about securing their safe shipment."[15]

At the same time, the administration brought heavy (and decisive) pressure upon Pittman and his committee to block the Nye-Clark neutrality resolutions. Norman Davis, acting for the State Department, spent several hours with Pittman on June 27, to persuade him to "stifle" the resolutions. President Roosevelt met with Pittman on June 29, and Hull also talked to the senator to ensure his cooperation.[16]

At the Foreign Relations Committee meeting on July 10, at which Hull appeared, the Nye-Clark forces — as Raushenbush phrased it — suffered a "complete rout." The committee not only failed to vote out S. J. Res. 120, but also recalled S. J. Res. 99 and 100 for further consideration and agreed to appoint a subcommittee under Pittman to study neutrality proposals.[17]

Though discouraged, Nye and his colleagues immediately regrouped for "a real scrap" on the issue. In the weeks that followed both the Nye group and the State Department worked feverishly planning their respective maneuvers. The State Department hurriedly drafted a neutrality bill as an alternative to the Nye-Clark resolutions and submitted it to the subcommittee on July 31. In it discretion was "vested in the President to decide whether in time of war shipments of arms shall be prohibited and if they are prohibited whether they shall be prohibited to all parties to a conflict, or, in his discretion, to one party and not to another." This was directly opposite to the mandatory Nye-Clark resolutions. On August 7, the subcommittee rejected the State Department draft, and there was a mad scramble to prepare a compromise measure that could win committee approval. Senator Nye arranged to delay Senate action on the munitions control resolution (S. 2998) so that neutrality amendments might be attached to it if the Foreign Relations Committee failed to report out a neutrality bill before Congress adjourned. During these frenzied activities in July and August 1935, Nye was frequently out of Washington for speaking engagements, but he kept in close touch with developments and was on hand in the capital city when he was needed.[18]

The neutrality controversy was given special urgency by the probability of war in Africa and the serious possibility of a general war in Europe. Adolf Hitler was consolidating his Nazi dictatorship and was rearming Germany rapidly in violation of the Versailles Treaty. Even more ominous in 1935 was the determination of Italy, under the Fascist dictatorship of Benito Mussolini, to seize the independent African state of Ethiopia. Whether the United States would cooperate with European countries opposing Fascist aggression or avoid ties that might involve America in foreign wars depended partly on the kind of neutrality legislation Congress adopted.

The whole controversy in 1935 culminated in the week beginning on Monday, August 19. In a letter to Pittman, released to the press on that day, Nye insisted that if "Congress imposes no restrictions on munitions sales and shipments before a war breaks out in Europe, it will be impossible for Congress to form a policy later without incurring representations that such a new policy involves the taking of sides against one particular belligerent." This letter also included copies of documents released by the State Department on neutrality policies before American entry into World War I.[19]

On the same day Secretary Hull handed President Roosevelt a letter urging him to "make a vigorous effort" to secure legislation that would give the President discretionary authority to embargo shipment of arms and munitions to Italy and Ethiopia. The White House immediately consulted Senator Pittman by telephone about this proposal and found the senator vehemently opposed. He agreed to introduce the resolution as an administration measure if Roosevelt were determined to proceed, but insisted that it would "not receive the approval of the Committee on Foreign Relations, or a majority of the votes of the United States Senate." He also warned the President that "an adverse report by the Foreign Relations Committee and the defeat of the resolution upon the floor of the Senate would do great harm to our foreign policy." In a personal note to the President's secretary, Stephen Early, Pittman vividly expressed his feelings on the issue. "I have been trying to harmonize things and get away from that fool Munitions Committee," he wrote. "I do not want the Administration put in the position that it is opposed to Neutrality, and I do not want the Committee put in that position. . . . I tell you, Steve, the President is riding for a fall if he insists . . . on designating the aggressor in accordance with the wishes of the League of Nations. He had better have nothing than to get licked, and I assure you that is what he is facing." Confronted with this ominous evaluation from the chairman of the Senate Foreign Relations Committee, the President and Hull yielded.[20]

Instead, after lengthy and heated discussion at its meeting on August

19, the Foreign Relations Committee agreed to report out a compromise neutrality resolution (S. J. Res. 173). Pittman submitted it to the Senate the next day. The resolution was intended partly to appease public opinion on the issue but probably both Pittman and the administration hoped Congress would adjourn without adopting it.[21]

Nye and his colleagues, however, had absolutely no intention of permitting Congress to adjourn without voting on neutrality legislation—and they had the voices to back up their determination. At three o'clock on Tuesday afternoon Nye and Bone, with other senators in reserve, began a filibuster to force consideration of the neutrality resolution, "We hold the whiphand," Nye warned, "and we intend using it to the limit." Until it voted on the neutrality resolution Nye promised "nothing will happen in the Senate." And he was not bluffing.[22]

Confronted with this obstacle to the quick adjournment senators had hoped for, the Senate on Wednesday, August 21, gave unanimous consent to a motion by Senator Pittman to lay aside the Guffey coal bill then under discussion until the neutrality resolution was considered. Without objection, the Senate promptly approved S. J. Res. 173 and sent it to the House of Representatives. Equally eager for adjournment, the House passed it without delay but added an administration-sponsored amendment providing that the arms embargo provisions would expire in six months, on February 29, 1936. Nye agreed to the House amendment, but he did not like it and promised to battle for more comprehensive and permanent legislation when Congress reconvened in January. By a vote of 79 to 2 the Senate concurred in the House amendment to the neutrality resolution on August 24, 1935. Nye called it "the most important bit of legislation with which this session of Congress has dealt."[23]

S. J. Res. 173 was a scissors-and-paste combination of the Nye-Clark resolutions, the State Department's proposal, Green's munitions control resolution, and innovations of Pittman's. It was more mandatory than the administration desired, but it was less sweeping and more discretionary than Nye wanted. It included the main parts of the munitions control provisions of S. 2998, the mandatory arms embargo specified in S. J. Res. 120, and restrictions on American travel on belligerent ships comparable to those sought in S. J. Res. 99. Unlike S. J. Res. 120, it did not deal with the export of non-munitions contraband. Moreover, it did not include the ban on loans and credits that would have been provided by S. J. Res. 100. The omission of these financial restrictions was partly covered, however, by the Johnson Act of 1934 that prohibited private loans to governments that had defaulted on their war debts. Although the Neutrality Act of 1935 did not permit the President to discriminate against aggressors in the application of the arms embargo, it did give him authority to determine when key provisions of the act should become operative. For example, he was to invoke the arms embargo when a foreign war began "or during the progress of war." He could also determine what specific munitions would be embargoed, whether and when the embargo should be extended to states that later became involved, and if and when the restrictions on travel on belligerent ships should be invoked.[24]

Senator Tom Connally and others hoped the President would veto the resolution. Secretary Hull did not like it—particularly the mandatory arms embargo—but he told Roosevelt that he could not advise against its approval. Hull welcomed the National Munitions Control Board it authorized, and he believed the mandatory arms embargo would hurt Italy more than Ethiopia in the pending African war. He feared that a veto would provoke a battle with Congress in which the administration could lose. In any event, the embargo would expire in six months when Hull hoped more acceptable legislation might be adopted.[25]

President Roosevelt approved the resolution on August 31, 1935, and a pen used in signing it was given to Senator Nye. At the same time the President issued a statement, largely drafted in the State Department, calling the objective of the law "wholly excellent" but warning that its inflexible provisions might have unfortunate effects and insisting that the United States not only must try to stay out of wars but must also cooperate with like-minded states to maintain peace. "It is the policy of this Government to avoid being drawn into wars between other Nations, but it is a fact that no Congress and no Executive can foresee all possible future situations. History is filled with unforeseeable situations that call for some flexibility of action. It is conceivable that situations may arise in which the wholly inflexible provisions of Section I of this Act [arms embargo] might have exactly the opposite effect from that which was intended. In other words, the inflexible provisions might drag us into war instead of keeping us out. The policy of the Government is definitely committed to the maintenance of peace and the avoidance of any entanglements which would lead us into conflict. At the same time it is the policy of the Government by every peaceful means and without entanglement to cooperate with other similarly minded Governments to promote peace." [26]

When the undeclared Italian-Ethiopian War began in October 1935, Nye commended Hull for the spirit with which the neutrality policies were invoked, while denouncing the New York shipping interests that wanted government economic restrictions rescinded. "Where commerce and business conflict with neutrality," Nye said, "commerce must be tossed overboard, if the United States is to remain neutral." It should be noted that the Neutrality Act did not bar the sale to Italy of mineral or agricultural products such as oil, cotton, or wheat. Nye emphatically opposed American cooperation with League of Nations sanctions against Italy, fearing such cooperation would involve the United States in war.[27]

In the early winter of 1935, while the temporary neutrality law was being tested by Italian aggression in Africa, both administration and congressional leaders laid plans for renewed struggles on the issue when Congress reconvened. The State Department prepared a revised draft for legislation, and even before their return from the Philippines in December, Nye and Clark authorized Raushenbush to draw up a revised neutrality resolution. The schedule of the Munitions Committee hearings was altered so that the Morgan testimony would be presented before Congress acted on neutrality proposals.[28]

Key Pittman introduced the administration resolution in the Senate on January 3, 1936, the same day that Samuel D. McReynolds introduced it in the House of Representatives. Three days later Nye and Clark introduced their revised neutrality resolution and Maury Maverick, a Texas Democrat, presented an identical measure in the House. Pittman thought prolonged hearings would not be essential, but his Foreign Relations Committee held closed hearings at which Hull and his aids testified at length. Nye and Clark also appeared before the committee.[29]

By 1936 the administration was convinced that it was politically impossible to win discretionary authority to apply the arms embargo only against aggressors, so that provision was omitted from the Pittman-McReynolds bill. Like the Nye-Clark resolution, the administration measure called for an embargo on the shipment of arms to all belligerents and a ban on loans and credits. The most obvious administration innovation in 1936 was a provision giving the President discretionary power to limit to normal peacetime levels the export to belligerents of non-embargoed war materials (not including food, medical supplies, and clothing). It could have limited the export of such non-munition commodities as oil, cotton, iron, steel, and copper that were as essential to war as munitions. Hull had attempted to restrict the flow of these goods to Italy through a "moral embargo," but he felt statutory authority was needed to make it fully effective. The Nye-Clark resolution contained a comparable provision – though it would have extended to all non-munition materials (including food, medical supplies, and clothing) and was mandatory (not discretionary). In fact, despite administration concessions, the issue of mandatory versus discretionary provisions remained central in the controversy in 1936. In nearly every part of the proposed legislation, the Pittman-McReynolds bill would have given the President greater discretion than the Nye-Clark resolution. For example, the Pittman-McReynolds bill would have continued to give the President the option of applying the law when a foreign war began "or during the progress of war."[30]

Both the Pittman and Nye resolutions encountered heavy going in committee. The fact that it was an election year made congressmen and the administration exceptionally cautious. While the arms embargo and loan ban would directly restrict only certain urban segments of the economy, the provision limiting export of non-munition war materials could affect diverse economic groups in every section of the country – industrialists, miners, oil producers, cotton planters, traders, and laborers. One of the more vigorous opponents of the provision was Senator Hiram Johnson from the oil-rich, cotton-producing state of California. In contrast, the provision probably would not have had serious effects on North Dakota wheat and cattle producers, even if Nye's resolution which did not exclude food had been enacted. Many Italian-Americans opposed severe restrictions on trade with their mother country. But the congressmen directly affected by these constituents were from eastern and urban districts. Nye of North Dakota did not have to concern himself very seriously about the attitudes of Italian-American voters. Early in February 1936, Senator Pittman summarized the situation concisely when he wrote that "the necessity for foreign commerce is so great and political pressure at this particular time is so strong that possibly it is advisable to avoid weeks of acrimonious debate with probably no accomplishment, and simply extend the existing law for one year."[31]

That was essentially the course of action followed. The Senate Foreign Relations Committee did not report out either the Pittman-McReynolds bill or the Nye-Clark resolution. Instead, on February 12, 1936, it unanimously reported a measure that extended the main provisions of the 1935 Neutrality Act, with certain modifications and amendments, until May 1, 1937.[32]

The following day Senator Nye summoned a dozen senators to plan a last-ditch battle for more sweeping neutrality legislation. They decided to seek a sixty- to ninety-day extension of the 1935 act to give Congress time to adopt a permanent neutrality measure before it adjourned. If this effort failed, they proposed amendments to make the committee measure more acceptable to the "peace bloc." Nye's group decided not to filibuster because that might cause the existing law to expire without anything to take its place. Though Nye and his cohorts wanted the law strengthened, they considered the committee measure an improvement over the 1935 act and preferred it to no neutrality legislation at all. But they did want to put senators on record for or against more drastic proposals. Included in the group that met with Nye were eight Democrats, two Republicans in addition to Nye, one Progressive, and one Farmer-Laborite. Though they did not attend the meeting, Nye also claimed the support of Norris and Vandenberg, making a total of fifteen senators. All but four of them represented states located west of the Mississippi River. Only one (Rush Holt, a young West Virginia Democrat) was not from the West or Middle West.[33]

On February 14, the House Foreign Affairs Committee unanimously approved a stop-gap bill similar to the one reported in the Senate. Its sponsors arranged to push it through the House under a suspension of the rules that would severely limit debate and bar amendments. Representative Maverick protested to the President that this was "the cruelest type of gag rule." He said the steamrolling tactic "may help in a few districts like New York City, Boston, and San Francisco but it will definitely hurt politically in all agricultural districts." But Roosevelt answered that it would be "improper" for him to "take part in legislative procedure," and the House adopted the measure by a vote of 353 to 27 on Monday, February 17, 1936.[34]

To speed action in the Senate, Pittman immediately substituted the House measure for the slightly different resolution reported by his committee and pushed for an immediate vote. All amendments proposed by

Nye's colleagues were easily beaten down, and Senator Clark only marshaled sixteen votes for his amendment to extend the 1935 act until June 1, 1936. After only four hours of consideration in the chamber, the Senate on Tuesday afternoon, February 18, 1936, adopted the House bill without a record vote.[35]

Ironically, the speed with which the Senate moved caught Nye in the Middle West on a speaking tour arranged for him in spite of his warnings to the speakers' bureau that he must keep close to Washington. He fulfilled his engagement in Minneapolis on Monday evening before hurriedly taking a chartered plane to Cleveland. There he hoped to catch a commercial flight that would get him to Washington on Tuesday morning in time for the Senate debate. Bad weather caused him to miss his connection in Cleveland, however, and he did not arrive in the Capitol until the middle of the afternoon — just in time for the final Senate action on the neutrality resolution.[36]

On February 29, President Roosevelt signed the Neutrality Act of 1936. Like its predecessor, it was a temporary measure. In extending the main provisions of the 1935 law until May 1, 1937, the 1936 act included a number of changes in phrasing and certain substantive amendments. The new act gave the President some discretion in putting its key provisions into effect by stating that they would become operative "Whenever the President shall find that there exists a state of war." It exempted American republics from the application of the law when they were involved in war with a non-American state. It was made mandatory for the President to extend the arms embargo to states that became involved in a foreign war after it started. And the act also banned loans to belligerents.[37]

The Neutrality Act of 1936 did not restrict abnormal export of nonmunition war materials to belligerents. Roosevelt and Nye had had different objectives in urging such restriction. Roosevelt and Hull expected it to hurt aggressor Italy more than Ethiopia; Nye saw it as another step to prevent American economic entanglement in a foreign war. Furthermore, Nye opposed the discretionary features of this provision in the Pittman bill, while the administration objected to the mandatory character of the provision in the Nye resolution. Neither the internationalists nor the isolationists were wholly justified in blaming the other for the defeat of the proposal. Roosevelt and Nye both failed to win enactment of the general proposal partly because of the political power of particular economic and ethnic groups that feared the effects of the restriction.

With the adjournment of Congress in 1936 Nye undertook a speaking campaign in thirty-eight states between July and December on behalf of a five-point neutrality program. It included nationalizing the munitions industry, expansion of the arms embargo to cover petroleum products, a ban on public and private loans to belligerents, a "cash-and-carry" arrangement for the sale of non-embargoed goods to belligerents, and rigid restrictions on Americans traveling in war zones. Nye also endorsed a constitutional amendment requiring a national referendum on American participation in war and urged unifying the War and Navy departments into a single department of national defense.[38]

By the middle of 1936 the Italian conquest of Ethiopia was completed, but the Spanish Civil War was posing new challenges to American neutrality policies. From July 1936 to 1939 rebel troops under General Francisco Franco battled to crush the Loyalists supporting the republican government of Spain. Great Britain and France organized twenty-seven countries in a Nonintervention Committee hoping to prevent the war from spreading to the rest of Europe. The Fascist governments of Germany and Italy, however, supplied men and material to Franco. At the same time Communist Russia, then an advocate of collective security against Fascist aggression, gave limited aid to the Loyalists. To that degree, it was already a European war and a prelude to World War II.

In twentieth-century civil wars the United States generally permitted exports to established governments and barred sales to revolutionary forces. Such a course from 1936 to 1939 would have helped the Loyalists against the Nationalists under Franco. The American ambassador to Spain, Claude Bowers, favored this policy as did many American liberals and spokesmen for collective security. Sale of arms to Loyalist Spain, however, would have conflicted with the noninterventionist policies of Britain and France. And Roman Catholics were opposed to aid for the Spanish government because of its anti-clericalism and because of the role being played by the Communists in the Loyalist cause.[39]

The issues in the Spanish Civil War aroused passionate emotions both in Europe and in America, leading to unusual political alignments and patterns. Desire for Anglo-American cooperation, plus sensitivity to the predominantly urban Catholic vote in America, drove the Roosevelt administration in a noninterventionist direction.[40] At the same time, Nye's liberal ties, his opposition to the administration, his anti-British views, and other factors moved him, paradoxically, into a position similar to that of anti-Franco spokesmen who advocated collective security. In August 1936, shortly after the Spanish Civil War began, Nye joined with other congressmen in urging the President to "prevent shipment of war supplies to Spain."[41] But he soon modified this view.

With administration encouragement and support, Senator Pittman on January 6, 1937, introduced a joint resolution to prohibit the shipment of arms from the United States to both sides in the civil war. This was not an amendment or extension of the existing neutrality law. It was an emergency measure concerned with the specific crisis in Spain. In urging enactment of the Spanish arms embargo, spokesmen for the administration used essentially the same arguments that noninterventionists had used earlier and would use later in different situations. Nye voted with the eighty-one senators who immediately approved the resolution. But first he made it clear to the Senate that he had serious reservations about the wisdom of the embargo. It was not, he protested, consistent with American neutrality. He also feared that the cooperation with Britain and France, represented by the resolution, might lead America in interventionist directions later. Nye insisted that he was not moved by sympathies for one side or the other in the Spanish Civil War, but his statements and recommendations from 1937 to 1939 revealed his anti-Franco biases. Not a single senator voted against the Spanish embargo on January 6, and it was adopted in the House of Representatives with only one dissenting vote. A legal technicality kept the President from signing it until January 8, 1937 – too late to prevent one shipload of airplanes and engines from leaving New York en route to Spain.[42]

Noninterventionist policies blocked the flow of munitions to Spain from Britain, France, and the United States. But it became increasingly apparent that Franco was obtaining active assistance from Germany and Italy. Consequently, in March 1937, Nye introduced a resolution asking the secretary of state whether the existing neutrality laws were sufficient "to provide an embargo against nations whose armed forces are engaged in active warfare in a nation where a state of civil war exists." The senator also introduced a resolution that, in effect, would have provided for an embargo on exports of munitions to Germany and Italy. Such a trade ban would have coincided with the desires of collective security advocates and friends of the Loyalist government. Nye's resolution, however, would not have limited its effects to the Spanish controversy—or even to foreign wars. It proposed to prohibit the exporting of munitions from the United States at any time to any country in the world "except to nations on the American continents engaged in war against a non-American state or states." This broadly phrased resolution was not aimed simply against Franco and his friends. It was a sweeping extension of Nye's consistent drive for national legislation to stop the international munitions traffic.[43]

Both Pittman and Hull, of course, opposed Nye's resolution. Hull did not believe it would "promote the cause of world peace" and he feared that it "might indeed have the contrary effect." He also worried about its effects on American exports and predicted "disastrous" results for the American aircraft industry because "nearly one-third of its production is now exported." On May 19, 1937, on a motion by Senator Connally, the Foreign Relations Committee voted to postpone "indefinitely" consideration of Nye's arms embargo resolution.[44] In June 1937, after returning from a European trip, Socialist Norman Thomas urged President Roosevelt to take essentially the action Nye proposed. In a letter and again at a White House meeting Thomas strongly recommended extending the arms embargo to Germany and Italy. If that were not done, Thomas insisted, the United States should lift the embargo on shipment of arms to the Loyalist government. He called the administration's policy toward Spain "a kind of left-handed aid to Franco, the Fascists, and the dictators who are supporting him." Ambassador Bowers expressed essentially the same point of view. In a "private and confidential" memo to Cordell Hull on June 29, 1937, Roosevelt suggested that if Germany or Italy made "any official admissions or statements that their Government armed forces are actually taking part in the fighting in Spain on the side of Franco" the United States would "have to act under the Neutrality Act"—i.e., extend the arms embargo to Germany and Italy.[45] The administration never actually took this action, however, and Nye's resolution died in committee.

The senator, therefore, introduced on May 2, 1938, a joint resolution that would have lifted the embargo on shipment of arms to the Spanish government and placed such exports on a cash-and-carry basis. Nye said he was not motivated "by the interest of either side involved in Spain." But he insisted that the efforts to make "an effective embargo against all exportation of arms to both sides in Spain" had not only failed but had resulted in "aid for one side as against another, and neither neutrality nor non-intervention is accomplished." He wanted to end what he called "the policy of coming to heel like a well trained dog every time England whistles." Both Pittman and Hull vigorously opposed Nye's resolution, and Roosevelt concurred with them. As a result, the Foreign Relations Committee on May 13, 1938, voted seventeen to one to postpone action on the resolution "indefinitely." Only Pope of Idaho kept the vote from being unanimous.[46]

Nye's recommendations on Spanish policies were unpopular with the large Catholic population of North Dakota. Some suggested that his proposals were "an evidence of sympathy for Communism and a thrust . . . at Catholicism." But in his campaign for re-election in the fall of 1938 he denied these charges and said he was only moved by a desire for "fair play and consistency of principle."[47]

When Congress convened in January 1939, Nye repeated his appeal for lifting the embargo in the interests of "a consistent position and a position of greater neutrality in the Spanish situation than is that prevailing with the embargo in force." He again denied that he was moved "by any sympathy for communism . . . or by any feeling against any church or religious cause."[48] At the same time, according to Harold Ickes' diary, Roosevelt told his Cabinet that the Spanish embargo had been "a grave mistake." The President said the United States should have prohibited the transportation of munitions to Spain in American ships thus enabling the Loyalist government "to come to us for what she needed to fight for her life against Franco."[49] This was essentially the policy Nye had been urging for months. But not until April 1939, after Franco completed his triumph over the republican government, did the administration finally lift the Spanish embargo.

Throughout the entire Spanish controversy the Roosevelt administration took a noninterventionist position and used arguments almost identical to those used by isolationists in other situations. At the same time, the effects of Nye's proposals would have been consistent with the idea of collective security against the spread of Fascist power in Europe. Doctrines, politics, and diplomacy sometimes lead men in unexpected directions!

But in the debate over "permanent" neutrality legislation in 1937 Nye continued along the path he had followed when the Neutrality acts of 1935 and 1936 were being considered. Both the Munitions Investigating Committee and its chairman made concrete recommendations for neutrality legislation before Congress convened in January 1937. The Nye committee's fifth report, submitted in June 1936, had included detailed proposals for extending, clarifying, and tightening existing neutrality legislation. Its sixth report had made comparable recommendations for financial, export, and shipping controls – including "limiting exportations of commodities other than medicines and hospital supplies to belligerents to the normal amount exported to such nations during a typical peacetime period." In the fall of 1936 Nye promised to urge enactment of a comprehensive neutrality program at the next session of Congress.[50]

The senator summarized his general views on neutrality legislation in a nationwide radio broadcast on January 18, 1937: "Any proposal of genuine neutrality must first of all recognize the necessity of American resignation from any appetite for profit from the wars of other nations. . . . Some, including myself, are in favor of an embargo against the exportation of anything to a nation at war, but recognize the futility of trying to accomplish so much in one bite. Embargoing only munitions leaves a very large field of commerce open to challenge our neutrality and peace. . . . In any policy adopted some discretion must be given the President but not to the extent of choosing sides through the power to determine who is the aggressor in a conflict. The discretionary kind of policy had its trial back in 1914 and 1915 when we were trying to be neutral. . . . But our neutrality crumbled because of the chance given selfish interests to bring to bear such pressure as no man could possibly stand up under. . . . We ought never again leave a President up against such odds as Woodrow Wilson found in his path in those days. . . . the time has come when America will not permit the interests of a few profit-bent men to drag an entire population into a life-and-death struggle thousands of miles away from native shores. . . . all the foreign trade possible isn't worth a repetition of our experience of 20 years ago. . . . we cannot be in other people's wars in an economic way and stay out of them politically. Then we should be ready, if we would really avoid war, to deny ourselves any taste of the profits available in the blood of other nations at war."[51]

By 1937 there was no practical possibility that Congress would pass neutrality legislation in tune with the internationalist views of Hull and the President. The Department of State deliberately stayed in the background, refrained from recommending specific legislation, and generally left the initiative to congressional leaders. As Hull explained later: "I felt that Congress was determined on neutrality legislation of an inflexible nature, and our arguments in favor of flexible neutrality legislation that would leave the widest possible discretion to the Executive would have little effect. Where we could, we obtained slight modifications more in conformity with our ideas."[52]

Senator Pittman introduced his proposals (S. J. Res. 51) on January 22, 1937. Ten days later Senator Clark introduced S. J. Res. 60 for himself, Nye, Vandenberg, and Bone. Both of these resolutions were in the form of amendments to the existing Neutrality Act. Senators Elbert D. Thomas of Utah and J. Hamilton Lewis of Illinois introduced separate bills to replace the existing law. Comparable measures were introduced in the House of Representatives.[53]

The Senate Foreign Relations Committee met in executive session on Saturday, February 13, 1937, to consider the four measures. R. Walton Moore and Green H. Hackworth represented the State Department at the meeting. Moore told the committee that the Pittman and Clark-Nye resolutions were "not very different." He said that neutrality legislation "should be permissive to a very large extent," insisting that "the more legislation you put on the statute books which tends to tie the hands of the government, the more definitely you advertise to war-minded nations what they can count upon when a war occurs." He also warned against "legislation which will induce all the other nations of the world to channel their trade to other markets than the American markets." In spite of his preference for permissive legislation, however, Moore recognized that "in all human probability the Congress is going to retain the mandatory provisions" and under the circumstances considered the Pittman resolution reasonably satisfactory.[54]

Late in February the Foreign Relations Committee reported out the Pittman resolution, modified as a result of detailed committee consideration. Nye, Clark, Vandenberg, Bone, Borah, and Johnson considered it too discretionary. "It seems to to me," Nye told the Senate, "that experience definitely dictates that whenever we leave a discretion in providing a neutrality policy, we at once issue an invitation to selfish corporations and selfish individuals to hammer away and to exert pressure on the one holding such discretionary power. . . . we ought to wish to prevent ever placing a President 'on the spot,' as it were."[55] But on March 3, 1937, the Senate adopted the Pittman resolution by a vote of 63 to 6. In a letter to the President, Assistant Secretary of State Moore called the resolution "a fairly liberal measure and the best that anyone knowing the situation could expect the Senate to pass."[56]

The measure introduced by Samuel D. McReynolds, and passed by the House 376 to 12, allowed slightly greater presidential discretion than the Pittman resolution, particularly in the application of cash-and-carry restrictions. A conference committee wrestled for weeks with the task of reconciling the two measures. President Roosevelt urged Senator Joseph T. Robinson of Arkansas to try to persuade Pittman to yield as far as possible to the House bill and authorized Robinson to use the President's name if he thought it advisable in talking with Pittman. The conference report on April 28 generally compromised in favor of the more discretionary House resolution.[57]

A "mandatory bloc" led by Senator Nye, and including five of the seven members of the old Munitions Investigating Committee (Clark, Bone, Pope, and Vandenberg in addition to Nye), vigorously opposed the conference report. Nye told the Senate on April 29, 1937: "I am not one of those who are undertaking to pretend that it is possible to draft and enact a neutrality policy which will be a genuine cure-all and assure our nonparticipation in more foreign wars. . . . I am sure experience rather clearly dictates that if we would really undertake to stay out of other people's wars in the future, we must deny ourselves any taste of the profit from other people's wars before we get into them. . . . If we are really going to enlarge upon our chance of staying out of other people's wars, we shall have to do more than we have done in our pending neutrality program. . . . I, for one, cannot understand why a President should want some of the discretionary powers which are being granted him; for what we are doing, in fact, is to put a President, whoever he may be at the time an emergency may arise, on an utterly impossible spot. . . . There must be and always will be a large discretion left with the President, but in some fields experience has taught us that we should lessen that discretion so far as we can." In this address, as he did repeatedly from 1935 through 1938, Nye warned against the war-making potential of *both* economic interests and executive authority. But he portrayed the economic interests (particularly those tied to urban industry and finance) as the moving forces, and the executive as a political instrument used by these interests.[58] After 1938 he emphasized the presidency as a moving force in its own right.

In spite of the opposition from Nye and his colleagues, the Senate and House both adopted the conference report promptly and Roosevelt signed it into law on May 1, 1937. In this "permanent" Neutrality Act of 1937 were many of the provisions in the earlier laws – including a mandatory arms embargo, a ban on loans and credits to belligerents, continuation of the National Munitions Control Board, and a ban on travel by Americans on belligerent vessels. It also prohibited the arming of American merchant ships trading with belligerents and the use of American ships for transporting munitions to belligerents. In addition it gave the President discretionary authority to put the sale of non-embargoed goods to belligerents on a cash-and-carry basis – that is, title to the goods had to be transferred to non-American hands and the goods had to be carried to the belligerent in non-American ships. The President also was given discretionary authority to prohibit use of American ports by armed belligerent ships. Like the 1936 act, it did not apply to a war between an American republic and a non-American state. But it did apply to civil wars in addition to international conflicts. Most of its provisions were "permanent," but the cash-and-carry restriction would expire on May 1, 1939.[59]

Clark, Nye, Bone, and Vandenberg sponsored an amendment on May 10, 1937, in a futile effort to make cash-and-carry mandatory. But the State Department opposed the amendment and it was not adopted.[60]

Two years later, in a letter to columnist Walter Lippmann, Senator Nye protested against associating his name with the Neutrality Act of 1937. He pointed out that he voted against the conference report. "Could I have my way about it," he wrote, "the neutrality law would forbid all trade with nations at war as well as financing through loans or credits. In the absence of chance for this complete accomplishment, I should have to be content with a strict forbiddance of loans, credits and munitions sales to belligerents with a provision that All other commodities be placed on a strict cash and carry basis, with no right or power left with the President to determine what commodities should be included in the cash and carry category, and all of the provisions to be invoked when once a state of war existed, not at the discretion in whole or in part of the President. . . . I believe the existing law, while not all that it should be or could be, good law nevertheless. It is far better than having no law in its field whatever and leave an executive to occupy the hot and impossible spot President Wilson was on starting in 1914. The fact that President Roosevelt wants to occupy the same spot makes no difference."[61]

Less than two and one-half months after the Neutrality Act of 1937 became law, Japan began her undeclared war against China—essentially the beginning of World War II in Asia. Americans generally sympathized with China, but were unwilling to risk war for her. The Neutrality Act of 1937 required the President to invoke its mandatory provisions whenever he found "that there exists a state of war between, or among, two or more foreign states." It did not have to be a "declared" war. During Italy's undeclared war against Ethiopia the administration invoked the Neutrality Act of 1935 in the belief that it would work against aggressor Italy. But the administration was convinced the 1937 law would benefit Japan against China. In his *Memoirs* Secretary Hull explained that "invocation of the Act would have shut off supplies of arms to both Japan and China. Japan did not need them, but China did. . . . If 'cash-and-carry' went into effect, Japan had the ships to transport our goods to herself, and the means with which to pay for them; China had not." For this reason, the Roosevelt administration never invoked the neutrality law in the Sino-Japanese "incident."[62]

Nye promptly and repeatedly criticized the administration on this issue. He viewed the refusal to invoke the law as concrete evidence of the need for more mandatory legislation. He urged evacuation of Shanghai and the withdrawal of all American troops and vessels. In a joint statement with Senators Clark and Bone, Nye doubted "that any action—short of economic, which could finally become military, war on the part of the United States—would hold Japan back."[63]

At the same time Nye denounced the shipment of scrap iron and steel by American firms to Japan. In a short speech in the Senate on August 10, 1937, he predicted that "the only return we may expect from a continuation of this exportation [of scrap iron and steel to Japan], aside from the munificent return in dollars to the several exporting companies, is the probability that one day we may receive this scrap back home here in the form of shrapnel in the flesh and in the bodies of our sons." He warned that it was "quite conceivable that our exports may one day be used for war against our own country." Long after he was voted out of office, many North Dakotans remembered and commended this prediction made more than four years before the Japanese attacked Pearl Harbor.[64]

On October 5, 1937, President Roosevelt delivered his famous Quarantine Address in Chicago. With Japan clearly in mind, the President told Americans that "the epidemic of world lawlessness is spreading. When an epidemic of physical disease starts to spread, the community approves and joins in a quarantine of the patients in order to protect the health of the community against the spread of the disease." But this parable on behalf of collective security did not appeal to Senator Nye. In an interview he said: "There can be no objection to any hand our Government may take which strives to bring peace to the world so long as that hand does not tie 130,000,000 people into another world death march. I very much fear that we are once again being caused to feel that the call is upon America to police a world that chooses to follow insane leaders. Once again we are baited to thrill to a call to save the world. We reach now a condition on all fours with that prevailing just before our plunge into the European war in 1917. Will we blindly repeat that futile venture? Can we easily forget that we won nothing we fought for then — that we lost every cause declared to be responsible for our entry then?"[65]

When Japanese airplanes bombed and sank the United States gunboat *Panay* on the Yangtze River in China on December 12, 1937, Nye suggested that the incident would not have occurred if Roosevelt had invoked the Neutrality Act. In April 1938, the senator even urged immediate independence for the Philippine Islands "to eliminate the possibility of conflict between the United States and Japan."[66]

Among Nye's legislative proposals designed to guard American neutrality were Senate versions of the so-called Ludlow amendment. This proposed constitutional amendment would have required that any declaration of war be approved by a direct vote of the American people, except in case of armed attack on the United States, its territories, or the Western Hemisphere. It was not a new idea. Pacifist groups as well as William Jennings Bryan and other agrarian radicals had suggested it many years earlier. In a 1924 editorial the young Nye himself had written: "At the polls is the proper place to fight war."[67]

The Ludlow amendment was in tune with Nye's faith in political democracy and with his belief that wars are prompted by the few in the interests of economic gain. It also was an answer to his growing alarm about the dangers of presidential power in foreign affairs. If "the people" had control over final decisions for war or peace, Nye was convinced they would block the war-making influences of international bankers, munitions makers, and the executive branch of the government.

The proposed amendment won its greatest political support in the House of Representatives. The high point came when Representative Louis Ludlow, a Democrat from Indiana, forced a House vote on a motion to discharge the amendment from committee. The administration actively opposed the amendment and before the vote on January 10, 1938, Speaker William Bankhead dramatically read to the House an appeal from Roosevelt to defeat it. In his letter to Bankhead the President said he considered the amendment "impracticable in its application and incompatible with our representative form of government." He feared it "would cripple any President in his conduct of our foreign relations; and it would encourage other nations to believe that they could violate American rights with impunity." In answer to those who thought it would help keep America out of war, Roosevelt said he was "convinced it would have the opposite effect." The House rejected the motion to discharge it from committtee, 209 to 188, and the amendment itself was never voted on in the House of Representatives.[68]

In the Senate the proposal won even less support. But Nye repeatedly sponsored resolutions calling for such an amendment. He introduced one in 1937. In February 1938, he along with eleven colleagues sponsored S. J. Res. 270, which called for an amendment requiring that "Except in case of attack by armed forces, actual or immediately threatened, upon the United States or its territorial possessions, or by any non-American nation against any country in the Western Hemisphere, the people shall have the sole power by a national referendum to declare war or to engage in warfare overseas." All but one of the sponsoring senators were from the Middle West and West. Most of them were liberals with substantial farming constituencies. A statement issued by these senators said: "We believe there is no sound basis for a contention that this new bill in any way weakens our national defense. . . . The measure we propose is not intended to replace representative government by 'pure democracy,' but to place a democratic check on a completely unlimited executive power. . . . The people have demonstrated their capacity for self-government and we feel that they should have the right to pass upon a question which might involve the life of the Republic." The senators insisted that the referendum was "not an isolationist measure, except in the sense of President Roosevelt's phrase, 'Isolation against war,' which he approved in 1936. It puts a check only on a cooperationist program of which war is an essential part. It does not, however, prevent such a program. What it does prevent is the unrestricted power of one individual to commit the Nation to war."[69] In testifying on behalf of a similar resolution in 1939 Nye said a "constitutional amendment to afford a war referendum would be the greatest victory for democracy since American independence."[70]

The whole idea, however, was opposed by the President, Secretary Hull, Senator Pittman, the War Department, the American Legion, the Veterans of Foreign Wars, Communists, and most internationalists. It was never adopted in the Senate.[71]

Throughout his fight for neutrality Nye continually pointed to the "lessons of history," especially of World War I—its origins, American neutrality and involvement, the peace settlement, and the postwar dislocations. His emphasis on the "lessons" of World War I was partly a product of his Senate investigation of American financial and trade policies from 1914 to 1917. But it also resulted from his own experience and personal disillusionment with the results of the war. The world peace and democracy he had hoped for were not achieved. And the ill effects of the war on American farmers had been serious. The brief wartime prosperity had been followed by deflation, tight credit, falling prices, high taxes, and foreclosures for farmers. At the same time urban industry and finance strengthened their hold on America. In every speech Nye made on neutrality policies from 1935 through 1938 he insisted that the history of America's role in World War I demonstrated the need for the neutrality program he advocated.

Most of Nye's neutrality proposals in the 1930's were enthusiastically backed by pacifist organizations such as the National Council for the Prevention of War, the Women's International League for Peace and Freedom, and the Fellowship of Reconciliation. The leaders of peace organizations, including Dorothy Detzer, Frederick J. Libby, and Florence B. Boeckel, played important roles in the lobbying and maneuvering behind the scenes. Their organizations were responsible for countless letters, petitions, and resolutions on neutrality received by the administration and congressmen. Pacifist leaders frequently consulted and advised Nye on particular issues.[72] Although not a pacifist, he shared some of their attitudes on armaments and he played a prominent role in Senate debates on military policies and appropriations.

8

Armaments and Disarmament

GERALD P. NYE was a member of the Senate Military Affairs Committee from 1936 to 1940. He spoke repeatedly and forcefully in the Senate against large military and naval appropriations, and delivered many public addresses all over the country on the subject. His attitudes on American defense policies, like those on neutrality, were consistent with his noninterventionist convictions and also with his agrarian values. He repeated his views on armaments hundreds of times with many variations in his speeches, but five main ideas stand out. First, Nye was not a pacifist and he advocated American military preparedness sufficient to defend the Western Hemisphere. Second, he was convinced that much agitation for large military appropriations was not inspired by actual defense needs, but rather by the lust for profits by munitions makers and shipbuilders. Third, it pained Nye to see hundreds of millions of dollars channeled to "selfish interests" in the name of national defense, when there were farmers, workers, small businessmen, and consumers in need. Fourth, the senator believed that military forces in excess of those essential for continental defense led to armaments races, international friction, and war. And finally, he became more and more convinced that the large military appropriations sought by the Roosevelt administration were not essential for hemispheric defense, but were designed to prepare for war in Europe or Asia. Each of these themes deserves elaboration in an analysis of Senator Nye's role in American foreign relations.

Nye's sympathy with American pacifists was evident early. In a 1921 editorial commending Mennonite immigrants he said he believed Christ hated war.[1] Nominally a Presbyterian, he was not active in the church and it did not directly influence his actions in public life,[2] but in 1932 he told the Senate: "We, the people of the United States, hold as our proudest boast that we are followers of the Prince of Peace. We are Christians – except in practical things. We read and outwardly accept the teachings of that faith. . . . Then we close the book with its perfect theory, and, untouched by the essence of Christianity, we come here as Christian men and women, to vote unstinted millions for a haughty and merciless work of slaughter, and having denied the faith before the world, leave this Chamber justified."[3] In 1938 he introduced a bill that said an alien should not be denied American citizenship because he was "conscientiously opposed to war as a method of settling international controversies or has expressed an unwillingness to serve in the armed forces of the United States in time of war with a foreign country."[4]

At the same time, the senator repeatedly and consistently stressed the need for adequate military defense. In 1929 he approved "such acts as will afford complete and adequate means of defensive warfare," and urged that "every reasonable precaution [be] taken against any possible attack upon us."[5] Again, in April 1938, he asserted: "I want my country adequately prepared at any hour successfully to defend itself against any attack, singly or jointly, by a foreign foe or foes." Further, he wanted to "destroy any chance" for the establishment of bases by non-American states in South America. But for him the zone of operations for American military defense was restricted to the Western Hemisphere, including Latin America, Hawaii, and Alaska. He advocated "only that degree of armaments which are required to amply protect us against possible invasion from abroad. Beyond that point . . . we certainly have no right to go." By the middle of the decade he was convinced the United States had sufficient military forces for national defense. He completely rejected the idea that America might have to fight in Europe or in Asia to protect its national security.[6]

His conception of "adequate" defense forces minimized the role of the navy and stressed the importance of the army and particularly the air force. By the middle of the 1930's he believed the existing navy was "more than adequate, to repulse any nation that is going to be so foolish as to attack us." In 1938 he was convinced that "if Germany,

Japan, and Russia were to consolidate all of their forces and move cooperatively against us, still, in the matter of naval tonnage, we would have adequate preparation for any attack they might make upon us." The United States, in his view, had "over-emphasized the part the navy can possibly play in our defense program."[7] In 1942 in a proposal reminiscent of Thomas Jefferson's "gunboat policy," Nye urged construction of "a tremendous fleet of mosquito boats and others of that type" if the Axis operated out of Dakar, Africa.[8]

While he attacked the "big navy" emphasis of the administration, Nye, in 1938, urged construction of a more adequate air defense "as a unit of the Army, providing our own soil as the base for the ships that we will depend upon to take off and provide defense against attack if and when it ever comes."[9] In January 1939, he said: "We have the advantage of air bases, and, with an adequate air defense, need not worry much about the power of anyone's fleet."[10] In May 1940, he favored "putting the brakes on spending for battleship construction" and urged that America "shoot our money into airplane building." "If we had spent our money for aircraft and anti-aircraft guns and other materials for use in the event we were attacked instead of for these floating fortresses costing from fifty to a hundred million dollars apiece, we would find ourselves much better prepared for what might be our future emergency than is now the case."[11]

Nye's second major premise concerning armaments — that profit-seeking industrialists and shipbuilders were responsible for much of the agitation for large military appropriations — emerged in his thinking even before his munitions investigation. He was not convinced that their patriotic appeals for enlarged defense forces were inspired solely by disinterested concern for national security. He felt the 1929 naval building program was "wholly uncalled for" and was "engineered in the main by our Admiral Plunketts, aided by the private shipbuilders."[12] He labeled the naval construction bill of 1934 "a bill for the relief of the munitions makers of the United States." He was moved and inspired by an Army Day parade in Washington in April 1934, but he reminded himself (and the Senate) that "those glistening steel helmets . . . were the profit-returning products of American manufacturers, a product intended to protect those fine heads under the helmets against the shrapnel and shells which the same manufacturers had sold to the military departments of other nations which might some day be our foe in war." He called this "rotten commercialism," an "inhuman trade," and an "insane racket."[13] With urban business interests clearly in mind, he charged in 1932 that "our greatest dangers are from within, not from without our borders."[14] His crusades for arms embargoes, strict controls over private construction of naval vessels, nationalization of the munitions industry, and taxing the profits out of war were products of his desire to restrict or eliminate the militaristic effects of the profit motive in urban industry.

In this connection, the senator contrasted the obsessive demands of business for government economy in expenditures for human welfare with its silence on the need for economy in military appropriations. "If the chamber-of-commerce spokesmen were really sincere in their economy urge," he said in 1932, "they would broadcast to the people the story of what a terrific part armaments play in our present-day budgets." Three years later he pointed out that "the 'economy' leagues and the 'liberty' leagues . . . have not yet seen fit to protest the increased appropriations for the Army and the Navy."[15]

To a lesser (but growing) extent, he also blamed military officers for seeking armaments in excess of actual defense needs. As Nye saw it, "the man who makes the Navy his career would be destroying his own career if he by any chance argued against building more ships." This general attitude provided the incentive for a resolution he and Clark introduced in July 1935, designed to prohibit military officers from making public statements or publishing articles on international affairs without express authority. It also was responsible in 1935 for the Nye-Kvale bill that would have made R.O.T.C. elective rather than compulsory in nonmilitary schools and colleges. Like most of the measures he introduced in the Senate, both of these died in committee.[16]

Just as he blamed business interests and military leaders for unnecessarily large armed forces, he denounced them for undermining disarmament conferences. During the Washington Conference of 1921–22 he predicted that "a band of militarists, war material manufacturers, and ship builders" would probably "be sufficiently influential at the conference tables to build a disarmament program that looks good but is so completely meaningless that they will not have lost much, if any, of their grand old power."[17] In March 1934, he charged that disarmament conferences fail because they "are manipulated, are played with, are influenced, by lobbyists for the munition makers." In December 1934, he said he had "become more and more convinced that until we can have a disarmament conference . . . divorced . . . from those who have selfish purposes to serve, we are not going to make much headway in international agreements." He said if the United States really wanted to contribute to disarmament "she would set the example and show the way by eliminating the influence of the private manufacturer of munitions of war."[18] In 1938 he suggested that disarmament conferences failed partly because delegates "invariably leaned most heavily upon the naval authorities who are dispatched as delegates or who go as experts with the delegation."[19] Here, as in other contexts, Nye implied that not even "experts" escaped from the principle that "ideas reflect interests."

As the third key to Nye's thinking on disarmament it should be recognized that his attacks on munitions makers and shipbuilders were indirectly attacks on the government's distribution of its largess. In the senator's opinion, armament appropriations subsidized urban industrial profits—with limited amounts trickling down to a small part of urban labor. He preferred an allocation that would have channeled a larger proportion of federal funds to farmers, wage earners, small businessmen, and consumers. He also objected to the fact that the taxes paid by the lower income groups were greater because of these thinly veiled subsidies to big business. In opposing a naval appropriation in 1932 he urged the Senate to "show more solicitude of the needs of the many and vote against this pending bill."[20] In 1934 he charged: "When we resort to programs looking to the relief of those who are in great distress, those who are without employment, we find ourselves at moments ready to abandon, in many instances, efforts which have been undertaken to provide for the immediate needs of men and women throughout the country. . . . Yet the same . . . Congress . . . when confronted with a program, a request to build a larger, stronger Navy, does not bat an eye."[21] Speaking in 1935 he contrasted the great effort required that year to persuade Congress to appropriate $403,380 for the Children's Bureau with the almost casual appropriation of more than seven times that amount the previous year for "the care and maintenance of the horses owned by the National Guard of the United States." He also contrasted the meager appropriations for the State Department with the much larger expenditures for increasing enlisted army personnel.[22] In opposing the large naval appropriation in January 1938, he said: "Before we decide that there must be slashing of the budgets for farm help, for relief, and for the other essential purposes of the government, before we determine that instead of meeting these needs at home we should pour the billion and a half dollars into the Atlantic and Pacific, we have a right to ask what in the world the administration thinks it is up to in asking for these mad increases for the Navy."[23] Clearly, Nye did not believe they were essential for continental defense. He preferred that the government make expenditures directly for individual needs rather than stimulate prosperity indirectly through military appropriations.

The fourth theme in Nye's views on military defense was based on a psychological, rather than an economic, analysis of international affairs. He repeatedly insisted that armaments aroused fears and insecurity in other countries, thereby promoting armaments races, friction between countries, and war. "Peace suggests compassion, trustfulness, good will, good faith, and at least reasonable forbearance," he said in 1929. "War and the instruments of hostility are supported by hate, greed, brutality, and the right of might." He denied that there was "any foundation in fact or historical experience for the claim that preparation for war maintains peace."[24] In 1934 he called this idea "a myth, sponsored and nursed by those whose unclean profits would vanish if ever they permitted the world to know that preparation for war is marvelously profitable for a few."[25] In the middle of the decade he charged: "No nation on earth spends more to maintain military machines than does the United States of America today."[26] In 1938 came this comment: "We operate on fear; we operate on suspicion. How long will it be before we start operating on hate? Not very long at the rate at which we have been moving." To illustrate his point he told of the imaginary experience of a friend who wrote: "'I have a neighbor with whom I wish to be a friend. He also wants to be a friend of mine, and we both agree that we must get along peacefully together, doing everything possible to further mutual understanding and friendship. In order to show him my good intentions I built a high barbed-wire fence with steel pickets on top between his house and mine. He, in turn, to convince me of his friendship, put a ferocious dog in his back yard. I then put bullet-proof glass in the window on his side and started wearing large pistols in my belt. The other day I saw him moving supplies of poison gas and hand grenades into his house. Now I have a machine gun mounted in the front yard, and for the life of me I can't understand why we don't get along better.'"[27]

In this same vein, the senator contended that "the military dominance in Japan would have died of its own weight long ago except for the fact that at least once a year the United States gives the Japanese military some ground or other upon which to stand when they say, 'We have to be better prepared for the trouble that the United States is getting ready to make for us.'"[28] "Japan would not be prepared with the armaments she has today" – he was speaking in 1938 – "if it had not been for the year after year challenge which the United States has laid down to Japan in the form of increased armament programs, in the form of speeches made here and elsewhere whose theme has been 'Look out for Japan! War with Japan!' and if it had not been for editorials in American newspapers depicting the danger of war with Japan."[29] He thought that the United States could not defend the Philippine Islands successfully even if the American navy were five times as large as it was in 1936. But he thought that even if the Japanese navy were twenty times larger than it was, it "could not get within hundreds of miles of our shores."[30]

Finally, Senator Nye repeatedly emphasized the intimate relation between military policies and foreign policies. If the foreign policies of the United States were dedicated to continental security and to neutrality and nonintervention in the wars of Europe and Asia, Nye believed that a huge navy was not necessary. If, on the other hand, American foreign policies were aimed at internationalism, collective security, and "policing the world," he feared that there was "no limit to what we require" in military forces. He advanced this general point of view many times during the 1930's. But he stressed it more and more late in the decade as his distrust and dislike of the Roosevelt administration grew more intense.

In 1936, for example, the senator insisted that armament appropriations were based on plans "not for national defense, but . . . for a national offensive."[31] A year later he said that every day he became more convinced "that the things we do in the name of national defense do not really, honestly, sincerely have national defense as their purpose." American military leaders, he warned, were "not thinking in terms of territorial defense but almost exclusively in terms of another major war abroad."[32] In April 1938 he charged that the administration's naval appropriation request was "most emphatically a preparation, not to defend ourselves, but to carry on aggressive warfare thousands of miles away from the shores and the homes for which national defense should be provided." He told the Senate: "Our naval program must of necessity be linked directly with our foreign policy. If our foreign policy . . . is one which dictates the need for an increase of one and a quarter billion dollars in our Naval Establishment, I say that foreign policy is one which directly jeopardizes the future of America. In that event the policy is one which contemplates fully and completely America's participation in other peoples' wars."[33]

Year after year Senator Nye crusaded against increased naval appropriations that he believed were not essential to national security and promoted foreign policies and economic groups he opposed. He orated, he maneuvered, and he organized the opposition — but he was always beaten. Congress never failed to appropriate the funds requested by the Roosevelt administration for the army and navy. Generally the legislature provided more than the administration asked. Both the army and navy were strengthened during the decade, though not so rapidly as Nazi Germany expanded its land and air forces. Nye realized that he could not win his legislative battles against increased naval appropriations, but he tried, and his efforts were popular with voters in North Dakota.

His battles against increased military appropriations were an integral part of his broad crusade against big business and international bankers in eastern cities. A more immediate practical influence was the unfavorable position of his home state in defense spending: the federal government channeled only a relatively small amount of its defense funds into North Dakota. For example, from June 1940 to March 1941, North Dakota ranked last among all states in the value of defense contracts its businesses received from the government, whether the calculation is based on the total value of the contracts or on the value per capita. In those months North Dakota firms secured $534,-359 in defense contracts. The top states (New Jersey and New York) were each awarded contracts totaling roughly 2,500 times that amount. North Dakota's contracts averaged eighty-three cents per person. New Jersey's per capita average (top for the nation) was nearly four hundred times greater. The three states of New Jersey, New York, and

Pennsylvania won contracts totaling more than those awarded to businesses in the bottom forty states plus the District of Columbia.[34] North Dakota had not yet discovered mineral resources that might have attracted defense funds indirectly. In 1938 North Dakota's senators, Nye and Lynn Frazier, sponsored an appropriation of $403,000 for new buildings at Fort Lincoln at Bismarck.[35] The North Dakota climate was not, however, well suited for new army or air bases, and the state obviously was not available for the navy. Americans living on the coasts, in industrial cities, in mineral producing areas, and in warm climates benefited directly from increased military appropriations. Prosperity was restored for agriculture during World War II, but North Dakota farmers and townspeople did not experience significant direct economic gains from defense expenditures.

9

Political Struggles and Transition

NYE'S CAREER reached its zenith between 1935 and 1938. His munitions investigation and crusade for neutrality established him as a leading spokesman for the Senate "peace bloc." His investigation, legislative activities, and public speeches helped arouse sentiment favoring American neutrality. He still had status as an agrarian liberal. By 1936 the forty-three-year-old senator was even mentioned as a possible presidential nominee – either as a Republican or on a progressive third-party ticket. Like all aggressive politicians, he made enemies, but from 1935 to 1938 he was praised much more than he was criticized.

At the same time, he was moving toward more conservative political alignments. The senator retained his faith in democracy and his compassion for the lower classes – the hallmarks of his liberalism. But his growing opposition to President Roosevelt led to differences with liberals (particularly from urban areas) who followed the president's leadership. These differences, plus the senator's increasing fear of executive authority in principle, pointed to the path that he followed to conservatism later.

Developments in North Dakota moved him in the same direction. His break with William Langer in 1934 was complete and irreparable. During the next decade North Dakota politics revolved around the emotion-packed question of whether one was pro-Langer or anti-Langer. Nye led the latter group. Since Langer dominated the left wing of the Nonpartisan League and Republican party in North Dakota, Nye gradually was forced into political harness with state Democrats and conservative Republicans.

In 1935 his peace crusade absorbed most of his time, but Nye continued to battle on the progressive side of domestic issues. As he had for many years, he blamed the depression partly on "the private control of money and credit." He denounced the Federal Reserve system for placing control of American money and credit in the hands of the private "banking crowd" that "had not the interests of the people at heart." The Nye-Sweeney bill he sponsored would have preserved private banking "but with a central bank, owned by the Government, over it all." The proposed Bank of the United States would have been the sole agency of Congress to issue money. Nye's monetary, credit, and banking proposals were rooted in the agrarian radicalism of North Dakota's Nonpartisan League. But they also paralleled the views vociferously expounded by the Reverend Charles E. Coughlin. Nye warmly endorsed the Roman Catholic priest and his monetary views in 1935.[1]

In other areas of domestic policy Senator Nye supported the Social Security Act and the Wagner Labor Relations Act—key measures in Roosevelt's liberal "Second New Deal." In June 1935, he joined with twenty-one other progressive senators to force action on the administration's tax measure that called for increased income, corporation, gift, and inheritance taxes. He warned that the President's performance on the tax question would "decide whether he can hope to have the Progressive Republicans with him" in the 1936 campaign.[2]

The progressive Republicans (including Senator Nye) faced a difficult dilemma in the presidential race of 1936. Most of them (including Nye) wanted to wrest control of the Republican party from old-guard conservatives. Failing this, several alternatives were available, none of them particularly satisfactory. They might support a conservative Republican party in spite of their progressive views; they might support a progressive third-party movement; they might cross party lines and support Roosevelt in the name of progressivism; or they could remain "neutral" in the presidential race. To support a conservative Republican candidate would be ideologically distasteful and might be politically risky, given the acute dissatisfaction in drought-ridden farming regions. Supporting a Democratic national ticket, however, might hurt congressmen whose political fortunes depended on Republican support at the state level. A third party posed the same problem—and there was in addition the probability of defeat for a third-party national ticket. (In February 1935, President Roosevelt believed "Progressive Republicans like LaFollette, Cutting, Nye, etc." were "flirting with the idea of a third ticket . . . that . . . would defeat us, elect a conservative Republican and cause a complete swing far to the left before 1940."[3]) Senator Nye carefully considered the several alternatives and did what he could to bring about the ideal situation: a Republican party dedicated to and working for progressive principles.

For example, in March 1935, he urged the party "to separate itself from big business and take an aggressive attitude in support of the small business man who has been ruined by the NRA." More than a year later he insisted that unless the Republicans developed "a more complete liberalism it would hardly be progressive than to do other than hope for the reelection of President Roosevelt." Nye's name occasionally was proposed for the Republican presidential nomination in 1936, but he repeatedly urged the nomination of Senator William E. Borah of Idaho. Before the Republican national convention met in Cleveland Nye warned: "Unless the Republican party ignores the Old Guard crowd and writes a safe and sound agricultural plank, it will take a worse trimming than it did in 1932." He urged party approval of a cooperative marketing program for agricultural products.[4]

After the convention Nye labeled the Republican platform "a keen disappointment to progressives." "Farmers and wage earners," he believed, would "find little in the platform to aid in the practical solution of their problems." He was disappointed that it ignored proposals for supporting neutrality and taking the profits out of war. He also denounced its failure to endorse the St. Lawrence Seaway. Senator Nye finally refused to support either the platform or the candidates of the Republican party in the national campaign of 1936.[5]

In July 1935 a meeting in Chicago called by the American Commonwealth Political Federation considered the creation of a third party. Presiding over the sessions, at which there were delegates from more than thirty states who represented varied shades of American radical opinion, was Paul H. Douglas of the University of Chicago. Senator Nye, as a guest speaker, voiced hope that the meeting would lead to the creation of a third party, but he urged the delegates to "look ahead five, ten or twenty years," not to "next year." He said that "without

President Roosevelt the Democratic party would be the same old stand-pat institution it always has been." He warned the delegates to divorce themselves "from communism or anything that smacks of communism."[6] In August 1935, Nye predicted that there would be a third party in the next presidential race. But he feared that it "would draw the extreme Liberals away from Mr. Roosevelt. So, if the Democrats were to remain Liberal and Progressive, a third party would tend to hinder the execution of its own principles." At that time, fifteen months before the election, Nye said that "unless the Republicans nominate a real Liberal I imagine I'll support Roosevelt in 1936 provided he remains Liberal. Otherwise I'll support a third party candidate always with the proviso that it isn't a demagogue."[7] Early in 1936 Nye himself was suggested as a progressive third-party presidential candidate.[8] In practice, however, he rejected the third-party approach in 1936. He even refused to support the Union party whose presidential nominee, William Lemke, was a fellow North Dakotan. He charged that the Union party was launched with poor methods and did not have the support of liberals. He predicted a new progressive political alignment by 1940 but felt the time was not ripe in 1936.[9]

Despite their differences on specific issues during Roosevelt's first term and despite their later hostility, there was a possibility as Nye himself had indicated that the senator would support Roosevelt for reelection in 1936. The President had listened to Nye's demands for reforms in N.R.A. The administration officially had cooperated with the munitions investigation. The President had signed the Neutrality acts. And Nye and Roosevelt consulted about emergency relief for drought-ridden North Dakota in the summer of 1936.[10] The two men were never close; but their differences did not appear irreconcilable in 1935–36.

After the national conventions, Secretary of the Interior Harold L. Ickes (a progressive Republican himself) was particularly eager to win Nye to the Roosevelt colors. He wanted the President to persuade Nye to organize progressive Republican support for Roosevelt's reelection. Ickes believed the President could win over the senator if he made a public and unequivocal "statement to the effect that so long as he is President he will leave nothing undone to keep us from becoming embroiled in another European war." Nye's support, in Ickes' view, "would have a profound effect on the country."[11]

President Roosevelt made the statement Ickes wanted in his foreign policy address at Chautauqua, New York, on August 14, 1936. Parts of this major address pleased Nye and his followers. The President said: "We are not isolationists except in so far as we seek to isolate ourselves completely from war. . . . I have seen war. I have seen war on land and sea. I have seen blood running from the wounded. I have seen men coughing out their gassed lungs. I have seen the dead in the mud. I have seen cities destroyed. . . . I have seen children starving. I have seen the agony of mothers and wives. I hate war. I have passed unnumbered hours, I shall pass unnumbered hours, thinking and planning how war may be kept from this Nation." Critics of Roosevelt's foreign policies repeatedly quoted these passages in the years that followed. In his speech the President also referred to adverse consequences of war on agriculture. "It was the prospect of war profits that made our farmers in the West plow up prairie land that should never have been plowed, but should have been left for grazing cattle. Today we are reaping the harvest of those war profits in the dust storms which have devastated those war-plowed areas."

The address, however, was not an appeal for isolationism. Subtly but clearly Roosevelt emphasized that developments abroad affected American peace and security. He said he had "sought steadfastly to assist international movements to prevent war." He warned that "so long as war exists on earth there will be some danger that even the Nation which most ardently desires peace may be drawn into war" and emphasized that "any Nation which provokes war forfeits the sympathy of the people of the United States." The President commended the neutrality legislation and believed it would "reduce war profits." But: "No matter how well we are supported by neutrality legislation, we must remember that no laws can be provided to cover every contingency, for it is impossible to imagine how every future event may shape itself." Members of the "peace bloc" lauded the Chautauqua speech; but so did internationalists—and with greater justification.[12]

A few days after the address, at Ickes' urging, the President invited Senator Nye to visit him at Hyde Park. Ickes hoped the meeting would cause Nye to "give out a statement endorsing the President for reelection on the basis of his peace record and his peace talk" and showing "very clearly that those elements in this country who would profit from a war, namely the international bankers and the munitions makers, are all on the side of Landon." In response to the President's invitation Nye traveled from Yellowstone Park where he was vacationing and met with Roosevelt in his Hyde Park home on Friday, August 21, 1936. Exactly what transpired at the meeting is not known, but the results fell short of Ickes' hopes. A few days after the meeting Nye announced that he would keep "hands off" the presidential race and would not endorse either Roosevelt or Landon.[13]

A month before the election Nye was inadvertently brought into the national campaign. The publication *Aero Digest* revealed that the President's son Elliott had in 1934 made an agreement with Anthony Fokker to sell military airplanes to the Soviet Union. This episode had been uncovered long before by the Nye committee, but the contract had been canceled and no planes had been sold, so the committee decided not to make it public. When the publisher of *Aero Digest* intimated that the Nye committee had concealed the incident, the senator reluctantly decided to release a deposition on the subject. He emphasized that the President's son had done nothing illegal and that as far as his committee was concerned the episode was closed. Although Elliott Roosevelt did not criticize Nye for releasing the deposition under the circumstances, Senator Bennett Champ Clark called Nye's action "as cheap a political trick as has been seen in years."[14]

This brief episode aside, Nye did not participate directly in the national political campaign. As late as October 30, Ickes sent the senator a telegram urging him to endorse Roosevelt, but he got no reply before the election. Many progressives, including LaFollette, Norris, and Shipstead, backed Roosevelt in 1936. But Nye did not. Part of his reticence may have resulted from his belief that Alfred M. Landon had the political edge in North Dakota. On one occasion Nye said he abstained as "a matter of courtesy to the Presidential candidate from my own State"—William Lemke. It is at least possible that Nye feared endorsing the Democratic presidential candidate would jeopardize his chances for winning the Republican presidential nomination in 1940. Part of the explanation probably may be found in the complicated political situation in North Dakota, where the senator faced election again in 1938. Whatever his reasons, Nye limited his political campaigning in 1936 to the state level—largely in North Dakota.[15]

Like the rest of the Great Plains, North Dakota in 1936 was staggered by the worst drought, dust storms, and clouds of grasshoppers in its history. In July one correspondent from southwest North Dakota wrote Nye: "Seventy five per cent on farms and ten percent in towns now in need, ultimately ninety percent on farms and twenty percent in towns will need help. . . . Morale bad and everyone extremely discouraged; A few cattle in Southwest corner dying on range but look for greater numbers in the very near future unless aid is given; Grasshoppers have destroyed whatever forage remained; Late rains of no benefit . . . Wells running dry, farmers hauling water long distances and clamoring for help to dig wells."[16] The rest of the state was not hit so severely, but the situation was extremely serious. All this came on top of a decade and a half of economic depression and followed another severe drought of two years before. Many people literally were saved from starvation and bankruptcy by federal aid. The Roosevelt administration had poured an average of $309 in gifts, loans, and grants for every man, woman, and child into the state during its three and one-half years in office. New Deal relief won many plaudits, but there were complaints about the administration of aid. And the New Deal clearly had not ended the farmers' difficulties in that state. Furthermore, the reciprocal trade agreement with Canada was anathema to Dakota farmers who did not relish competition from Canadian agricultural products.[17]

At the same time "Wild Bill" Langer, who had been acquitted in his third trial in federal court of the charges that had removed him from the office of governor two years earlier, was now on the comeback trail and had his eyes on Nye's Senate seat. In 1936, however, he was content to regain the governorship. He won endorsement from the regular Nonpartisan League convention and was pitted against the incumbent, Walter Welford, in the Republican primary in June 1936. Nye rushed back from Washington to help Welford defeat Langer for the Republican gubernatorial nomination by the narrow margin of 695 votes.[18] But Langer, as always, was a hard man to down. With the support of the left wing of the League, he ran for governor as an independent in the general election. Nye again campaigned against him and said the "real issue" was "clean government." Fearing that anti-Langer votes would be divided between the Republican Welford and the Democrat John Moses, Nye warned that Moses could not win and that a vote for him would increase the possibility of a Langer victory.[19]

The election results were discouraging for the senator, even though the "reactionaries" he despised were repulsed nearly everywhere. In spite of Nye's efforts, Langer managed to squeak through to victory in the general election on November 3, 1936. Thus, as governor of North Dakota, Nye's main political adversary was in a strong position from which to seek his Senate seat in 1938. Furthermore, in spite of Nye's neutrality and opposition from both Langer and Welford, Roosevelt won North Dakota's electoral votes again. He got nearly fifty per cent more popular votes in the state than Landon and Lemke combined, while carrying all but two of the rest of the states.[20] Nye's refusal to commit himself in the presidential race did not enhance his stature with either national party.

The urban strength in Roosevelt's national sweep was of fundamental significance. The President carried both rural and urban America, but in the North he won his most overwhelming support among lower income voters in the cities. Both major parties gradually were becoming more urbanized, but this urban orientation was particularly striking in the Democratic party of the North.[21] With his overwhelming victory in 1936 and with his impressive urban strength, Roosevelt was less obliged to cater to the wishes of western agrarian progressives than he had been during his first term. Nye's farmers were declining in political power, and this augured ill for the senator's national political fortunes and for the foreign policies he advocated. During the two years before he faced election his bad relations with the new chief executive of his state did not improve, while his relations with the chief executive of the nation got worse.

The court-packing controversy in 1937 highlighted and accelerated Nye's differences with Roosevelt, his growing fear of executive power, and his drift toward accord with conservatives. The senator initially declined comment on the President's proposal on February 5, 1937, to increase the size of the Supreme Court. Like Roosevelt, Nye was unhappy when the Court struck down liberal legislation – including the Agricultural Adjustment Act. (Nye had felt no remorse, however, when the Court had killed N.R.A. in 1935.) But it was a fellow progressive, Democratic Burton K. Wheeler of Montana, who led the Senate fight against the President's proposal, and in a meeting with Wheeler and four other senators Nye was persuaded to deliver a nationwide radio address against the court-packing bill. Before he faced the microphone, he was summoned to the White House where the President tried to dissuade him from making the address. William Thatcher of the Farmers' Union also tried to call off Nye, fearing it would hurt North Dakota farmers who needed federal farm legislation.[22]

Nye persisted, however, and delivered his address on Sunday evening, February 21, 1937. He made it clear that he was "completely out of sympathy with those processes by which the Supreme Court majorities have thwarted the will of the people when they have sought to build for better opportunity for themselves and to win a larger share of reward for their labors." But he insisted that "to preserve our form of government it was and is essential to limit strictly the power of the Executive." He said: "However foreign to the President the thought of dictatorship may be, in connection with his present request, it is good warning to look out, not for him necessarily, but for those who would in other days have opportunity to use the power which he would have us now extend." Nye, instead, endorsed the constitutional amendment proposed by Senator Wheeler that would have enabled Congress, by two-thirds votes in both houses, to pass laws over the Court's opposition.[23]

Mail reaction to Nye's address was largely favorable. Most liberals, however, were loyal to their presidential benefactor and were fearful lest the Court wipe out the social gains made under the New Deal. They brought pressure on the North Dakota senator to persuade him to reverse his position. In addition to the appeals of spokesmen for the liberal Farmers' Union, Nye heard from A. F. Whitney of the Brotherhood of Railroad Trainmen, Daniel J. Tobin of the Teamsters Union, and others. As a result, Nye wavered on the issue, and in May 1937 Thomas Corcoran assured Ickes that the senator would vote for the court-packing bill.[24]

Then the Court (or two of its members) suddenly reversed itself and began to sustain New Deal measures — thus making court packing seem less essential. The resignation of Justice Willis Van Devanter in May assured Roosevelt of an opportunity to appoint a man more sympathetic to New Deal philosophies. Finally, the death of Joseph T. Robinson, who was leading the administration's fight in the Senate, assured defeat for the President's proposal. When Nye voted with sixty-nine other senators on July 22, 1937, to return it to the Judiciary

Committee, the measure was already dead.[25] His opposition to court packing (like that of Senators Wheeler, Borah, Bone, Johnson, and Clark) did not represent an abandonment of liberalism. It is significant that Nye voted to confirm the appointment of the liberal Hugo Black to the Supreme Court in August 1937.[26] Nevertheless, liberalism was increasingly associated with strong executive leadership in general and with President Roosevelt in particular. Conservatism, on the other hand, in the twentieth century commonly has been associated with congressional and judicial restraints on executive authority. Thus the episode aligned Nye and Wheeler with the President's conservative opponents, and the gradually intensified emotional antagonisms on both sides made reconciliation on subsequent issues increasingly difficult.

In 1937–38, Senator Nye also voiced views on labor and farm policies that, without repudiating his progressivism, moved him within shouting distance of conservatives. In July 1937 this spokesman for North Dakota farmers criticized the National Labor Relations Board for being "a partisan body rather than a judicial institution." He reaffirmed his "support of the cause of labor" but did not want "the governmental umpire batting for either side." He called the N.L.R.B. "a kangaroo court" with "such a pronounced pro-C.I.O. bias that the average man regards it as an adjunct." In Nye's opinion it "would be equally bad or worse if it had a pro-capital bias." In a Senate speech he said he "would not take away from American labor, organized or unorganized, one iota of any advantage which may accrue to it today." But he believed the Wagner Act should be changed to restrict the powers of the N.L.R.B. in promoting what he called "compulsory labor organizations." He cast his vote against the Black-Connery wage and hour bill.[27]

Nye's position could simply be written off as conservatism. A more thorough analysis, however, reveals more subtle, meaningful, and consistent explanations. First, he had always opposed "special privileges" extended by the government to particular economic groups. When the recipients of government favors were business and financial groups—as they were in the 1920's—his position was consistent with the attitudes of liberals, progressives, and radicals everywhere. When the privileged group was labor, Nye's hostility to government "favoritism" put him in company with conservatives. Even when agriculture was concerned, the senator preferred to limit positive government aid largely to temporary emergency situations. What he sought ideally was not special privileges for farmer or labor, but the elimination of government favoritism to business and finance, a *laissez-faire* arrangement with special favors for none. Second, though he broadened the base for his liberalism in the early 1930's, his outlook was fundamentally agrarian. He did not want political and economic dominance by urban business, but neither did he want dominance by urban labor. Like Jefferson, Nye's feeling of kinship with urban labor was tenuous and transient. Third, the senator's concern over the powers of the National Labor Relations Board went along with his growing fear of executive authority in principle and in practice. In all these respects Nye's attitudes were within the philosophical and value systems spelled out so brilliantly a century and a half earlier by Thomas Jefferson. The views of both these men were made meaningful partly by the agricultural society they revered. In addition, Nye's growing opposition to the Roosevelt administration was probably already making him a little more receptive to the views and attitudes of conservatives who opposed the New Deal. In 1937, however, he was not yet operating from a conservative frame of reference.

Nye's attitudes on farm legislation in 1937–38 came out of the same mold. The Supreme Court had invalidated the first Agricultural Adjustment Act in January 1936, and the Soil Conservation and Domestic Allotment Act of 1936 did not fill the gap. Nye, of course, wanted to improve conditions for American farmers, but he believed the most essential remedies lay in credit and monetary policies. Though he welcomed the emergency aid it provided, he had never been enthusiastic about the New Deal's first Agricultural Adjustment Act. He recognized the need for new farm legislation in 1937–38, but he had serious reservations about the administration's proposals.

The senator realized that limiting production helped urban industry sustain prices for its products, and he conceded that acreage controls were probably necessary to support farm prices. Nevertheless, he opposed reliance upon scarcity as a long-range solution to the farm problem. He believed that farmers would rebel in normal times "against anything resembling controlled production." He was convinced that "farm price difficulties were at least as much a problem of underconsumption as they are problems of over-production." He objected to "the inconsistency of programs that would create scarcity in the present scene of great want on the part of millions of our people." He did not, however, have specific proposals for making need, rather than markets, the basis for a farm program.

He believed world markets would not contribute significantly to the solution of the American farm problem. Ultimately, he said, "the American farmer is going to have to learn to make the domestic market quite his entire market." Hence he distrusted and opposed the reciprocal trade agreements. "When I see how the agricultural products of other countries are pouring in under these agreements, to interfere with our own market, it increases my belief that the reciprocal trade program is adverse to our own agricultural interests."

Nye thought that the parity levels were set too low and that real parity for farmers would not be obtained under the provisions of the bill. He stressed the need for including a crop-insurance feature. As he had for many years, Nye emphasized the farmers' credit difficulties. He objected to the vigorous collection methods used by government credit agencies and introduced a bill that would have authorized the secretary of agriculture to be extremely lenient in dealing with farmers in debt to the federal government. He consistently supported the Frazier-Lemke bill to protect farmers against mortgage foreclosures.[28]

Senator Nye clearly believed the administration farm bill was "not going to loom overlarge in the stocking of the American wheat producer on Christmas morning." Nevertheless, he voted for it in December 1937. He voted against the conference report that reconciled differences between the House and Senate measures, hoping it would be sent back for improvements. He based his opposition to the conference report on three grounds: First, he thought the parity level was too low and would not restore the farmer to real parity with the rest of the economy. Second, he objected to the "inconsistency" of cutting acreage and production while the reciprocal trade program "lets the bars down and admits into this country products from other lands which enter into direct competition with the American farmer's production." He said "if the American farmer is entitled to anything, he is entitled to his own home market." These attitudes were completely in harmony with his foreign policy views. Third, he believed the bill discriminated against North Dakota producers of spring wheat. There had never been "any surplus or any overproduction of hard spring wheat"; the surpluses were in winter wheat. If there were separate acreage allotment programs for winter and spring wheat, North Dakota farmers, he said, would not be obliged to cut production significantly. Nevertheless, when the conference report became the second Agricultural Adjustment Act in February 1938, over Nye's objections, he insisted that Congress appropriate funds to implement it fully.[29]

Nye circulated his speeches on farm policies widely in North Dakota, for he faced his most formidable state political adversary in his efforts to win re-election for a third full Senate term in 1938. Governor William Langer was determined to win Nye's seat and there was a strong possibility he might succeed. For one thing, the governor dominated most of what remained of the Nonpartisan League that had previously helped elect Nye. The governor won enthusiastic support among hard-pressed prairie farmers. Despite Nye's progressive record, he was to the right of Langer. The governor charged that Nye spent too much time dashing around the country on speaking tours and insisted that Nye's search for headlines through the munitions investigation and the campaign for neutrality legislation caused the senator to neglect the interests of North Dakotans. According to Langer, Nye was so busy acting like a "big shot" out East that he did not have time for the common people who had sent him to Washington. There is little doubt that Nye had not kept his political fences adequately mended. Furthermore, the senator's sympathy for the Spanish Loyalists and his efforts to repeal the Spanish arms embargo antagonized the large Roman Catholic voting population in North Dakota. He clearly had a battle on his hands in the race for re-election.

Langer, nevertheless, had a powerful adversary. Nye was one of the most successful vote-getters in the state's history. To counter Langer's control of the League, the senator was endorsed by the convention of anti-Langer Republicans in March 1938. In answer to the governor's bid for support from the farmers, Nye could point to his own continuing efforts in the Senate on behalf of progressive legislation. Some criticized him for spending so much time on his national peace drive, but his foreign policy views were approved by most of the people in his state. Even Langer shared these views. If Nye sometimes failed to pay enough attention to the home folks, he gave North Dakotans a feeling of pride as one of theirs made a splash on the national political scene. Furthermore, his crusade for honest government and against "Langerism" got a warm reception among many.[30]

The senator also won impressive support from liberals and radicals outside the state. Under the chairmanship of the historian Charles A. Beard, a National Nonpartisan Committee for the Reelection of Senator Nye was formed in May 1938, with headquarters in Washington, D.C. Among those on the committee were Harry Elmer Barnes, historian; Alfred M. Bingham, editor of *Common Sense*; Bruce Bliven, editor of the *New Republic*; Dorothy Dunbar Bromley, columnist with the *New York Post*; John Chamberlain of *Fortune*; Dorothy Detzer of the Women's International League for Peace and Freedom; author Sherwood Eddy; H. C. Engelbrecht; John T. Flynn; Hubert C. Herring; Paul Hutchinson, managing editor of *Christian Century*; Frank Kingdon, president of the University of Newark; Daniel L. Marsh, president of Boston University; Charles Clayton Morrison, editor of *Christian Century*; Methodist Bishop G. Bromley Oxnam; Jeannette Rankin of the National Council for the Prevention of War; Stephen Raushenbush; the Reverend Ralph W. Sockman of Christ Church in New York; Oswald Garrison Villard, contributing editor of the *Nation*. This National Nonpartisan Committee distributed an elaborate folder supporting Nye's primary campaign. It included endorsements by numerous prominent Americans, including William Allen White, the Kansas newspaper editor who led the opponents of Nye's foreign policy views two years later. In a letter printed in the folder William Green, president of the American Federation of Labor, called Nye "one of the most consistent supporters of labor legislation" in the Senate, and urged "all labor organizations in North Dakota to appoint committees for the purpose of aiding him in his renomination and reelection." The senator also was lauded in the folder by the Washington representative of the National Grange. Other endorsements came from progressive senators of both parties including William E. Borah, George Norris, Burton K. Wheeler, Homer T. Bone, Arthur Capper, Henrik Shipstead, and Lynn Frazier.[31]

Paradoxically, at the same time Nye also won support from conservative Republicans in eastern North Dakota who previously had been his dedicated opponents and from the *Fargo Forum*. Most of these conservatives, however, were more interested in beating Langer than in re-electing Nye. For many of them, it was "a choice between evils."[32]

Most of the Nonpartisan candidates won nomination in the Republican primary late in June 1938. Nye, however, defeated Langer by a little more than five thousand votes out of more than 177,000 votes cast. Nye lost most of the counties in the central part of North Dakota and did less well than Langer in the west. But he carried nearly all of the eastern third of the state. Fargo's Cass County, which generally had been a center of opposition to Nye, gave its votes to him by more than a two-to-one margin in its determination to beat Langer.[33]

The campaign before the general election in the fall was virtually a re-run of the primary race. Though beaten in the Republican primary, Langer announced late in September that he would run for the Senate as an independent with Nonpartisan League endorsement, a tactic he had used successfully in the gubernatorial race two years earlier. The Nonpartisan newspaper controlled by Langer charged that Nye's "interest centers upon the vote harvest rather than upon crop conditions." The governor accused Nye of getting interested in the problems of North Dakota farmers only when he was up for re-election every six years; he criticized the senator for neglecting state problems while "lecturing on some abstract European and Asiatic cause." The governor pitched his appeal particularly to small farmers and endorsed a $40-a month state pension plan for the aged.[34]

J. J. Nygaard, the Democratic candidate, campaigned aggressively on a program endorsing President Roosevelt and the New Deal. He called Nye a "reactionary" who "'yesses' the progressive people of North Dakota and then goes down to Washington and 'noes' them at every chance." He pointed to the senator's criticisms of N.R.A. and A.A.A. – but neglected to mention that generally Nye had attacked the New Deal from a progressive (not a conservative) frame of reference. Nygaard's slim chances for election virtually disappeared after Langer entered the race in September. He was up against two of the most successful politicians in the state's history. Moreover, thousands of Democrats were convinced that Nygaard could not win and that the only possible way to stop Langer was to vote for Nye.[35]

Senator Nye campaigned energetically all over the state. He emphasized his efforts in Washington on behalf of farmers and progressive legislation. He spoke pridefully of his munitions investigation and his crusade for neutrality and peace. He repeatedly denounced Langer and his alleged corruption and political irresponsibility. Though he had rejected the Townsend old age program earlier, in 1938 he endorsed it in opposition to Langer's pension proposal. The following excerpts from his campaign literature illustrate his tack in the campaign: "Nye has fought the most powerful forces in the world (the Morgans, International bankers, the Du Ponts, billion dollar oil interests) and has stood his ground without flinching under such attacks as were brought against him. Nye's recognition as the most influential and appealing speaker on the platform in the United States today, casts an enormous credit upon the State of North Dakota. . . . Senator Nye has particularly been instrumental in bringing a larger share of WPA, PWA, Farm Security and other federal help to North Dakota than accorded any other state. In this respect North Dakota has received far more per capita than any other state in the union. Nye has sponsored legislation to liquidate debt owing by farmers to the various governmental agencies. . . . Nye made the last ditch fight in support of Scandinavian and German immigration quotas. . . . Nye's record has been one of the most progressive known in Congress. . . . Nye's greatest contribution to his state has been his leadership in that effort which would avoid a recurrence of the distressing economic situation visited upon all people since the world war. HIS FIGHT AGAINST OUR COUNTRY BEING DRAWN INTO MORE WARS HAS RECEIVED NATION-WIDE RESPONSE. . . . North Dakota should be exceedingly proud of him."[36]

Among the many liberals and progressives inside and outside of the state who endorsed him were the North Dakota Brotherhood of Railway Trainmen, Representative William Lemke, Senators Hiram Johnson, Ernest Lundeen, George Norris, Burton K. Wheeler, Arthur Capper, and William E. Borah, the national headquarters of the Townsend Recovery Plan, the Women's International League for Peace and Freedom, and some of the old Nonpartisan Leaguers. He won the support of many Democrats – including John Moses, the Democratic candidate for governor who was opposed by a pro-Langer Republican, John N. Hagen. Nye-Moses clubs were organized with bipartisan support throughout the state late in the campaign.[37]

In addition, as before the primary, Nye won support from conservatives – including the most conservative Republicans in North Dakota. In 1938 Nye was still a progressive, but conservatives backed him as the man most likely to beat Langer.[38]

Passionate determination to defeat Langer thus brought together extremely dissimilar factions in support of Nye's candidacy: conservative Republicans, New Deal Democrats, former Nonpartisans who opposed Langer's tactics, and almost everyone else who disliked the governor. In all probability Nye could not have beaten Langer in 1938 if he had not joined forces with these diverse groups in opposition to the governor. But the coalition accomplished its goal.

On November 8, 1938, Senator Nye was re-elected for a third full term by a margin of nearly 20,000 votes over Langer out of more than 263,000 votes cast in the Senate race. Nygaard got less than 20,000 votes. Nearly twice that many people had voted for Senate contenders in the June Democratic primary, but undoubtedly thousands of those Democrats voted for Nye against Langer in November. Nye lost one western county he had carried in June, but he won five counties he had lost at that time. Nye still had thousands of friends among western farmers, but he could not have won without substantial support from conservative voters in the cities and richer farming areas of eastern and east-central North Dakota.[39]

The changing political bases from which Senator Nye operated presaged changes in his political principles. The new political bases along with his growing fear of executive authority served as hinges for his swing to conservatism during his last term in office. These changes did not, however, represent an abandonment of the agricultural point of reference for his domestic and foreign policy views. Indeed, the senator's agrarian-based fear of executive authority was comparable to Thomas Jefferson's attitude a century and a half earlier. These changes did not lessen in the slightest the determination and vigor of Nye's crusade for neutrality and noninterventionist foreign policies. They did, however, encourage the senator to focus his crusade more against presidential power and policies in foreign affairs. Munitions makers and international bankers gradually faded into the background of his foreign policy analyses after 1938.

BATTLE AGAINST INTERVENTION

10

The Advent of Foreign War

EARLY IN 1939, before war began in Europe, the already strained relations between Senator Nye and President Roosevelt were severed completely. Previously the President and the senator had tempered their differences with official courtesy and restraint. At least on the surface, each had credited the other with honorable, though sometimes misguided, motives. This civility, however, ended in 1939, when the lines of battle were drawn between the two men—and between the foreign policy views each represented. Roosevelt cautiously stepped up his efforts to lead America away from isolationism and toward collective security in international affairs. At the same time, Nye became more vehement in his attacks on the President and his policies.

The crises in the early months of 1939 involved most of the issues on which Nye and Roosevelt (and the so-called isolationists and internationalists) differed. The immediate problem centered on military defense policies—what military forces and what areas and countries were essential for American security. These differences over military policy quickly expanded to a broader disagreement concerning foreign policy and the proper roles for the President and Congress in foreign affairs. In Nye's opinion, administrative secrecy and the implications of such secrecy for American democracy were also at issue. And finally, the two men differed in their analyses of economic aspects of defense and foreign affairs.

In his message to Congress on January 4, 1939, and in a special message eight days later, President Roosevelt emphasized the seriousness of the international situation and urged the appropriation of additional funds for military defense. "Events abroad," he urged, "have made it increasingly clear to the American people that dangers within are less to be feared than dangers from without."[1]

As it usually did before Pearl Harbor, Congress appropriated more than the President requested—but it did so over the objections of Senator Nye. He thought it "highly improbable that anyone would seek to invade our shores or the shores of South America." With "an adequate air defense," the North Dakota senator believed, the United States "need not worry much about the power of anyone's fleet. Of course, if we are going to be foolish enough again to fight on foreign soil, to cross the ocean looking for a fight, then there is no limit to what we require." He opposed fortification of Guam in the Pacific. "If this is but to afford larger preparation to defend the Philippines, then let me ask: How soon must we fortify still more islands to defend Guam?" He elaborated his view in a radio address on January 24: "I should count myself derelict in my duty if I found myself ready to jeopardize American security against attack by refusing the machines, equipment, supplies, and men necessary to repulse any possible attack upon us. But I am equally derelict in my duty if I become party to a rearmament cause that entertains large prospect of inviting war and that is sponsored by man-made hysteria which can but lead my country under a greater load of debt and into greater economic difficulty." The senator emphasized that "we've a sizable war to win right here at home, the war against suffering and need that exists in a land of plenty." In his opinion the United States had "rather miserably failed to win that war."[2]

Then on January 23, 1939, near Los Angeles, California, a Douglas bomber on a test flight crashed. Among the dead was a French Air Ministry representative secretly arranging for the purchase of American military airplanes. Senators Nye, Bennett Champ Clark, Ernest Lundeen, and Robert R. Reynolds—all members of the Military Affairs Committee—were aroused by the revelation and threatened a probe of the administration's military and foreign policies.[3]

President Roosevelt invited the committee to meet with him in the White House on January 31, where he spoke earnestly and forthrightly about American policies in the face of the serious Axis menace. He explicitly rejected the "school of thought that says we can draw a line of defense around this country and live completely and solely to ourselves." The President contended that Germany, Italy, and Japan were dedicated to "world domination." America's "first line of defense" on the Atlantic, he said, was "the continued, independent existence" of forty or fifty countries in Europe and Latin America – including England and France. In explaining the sale of military planes to France he said: "We want France to continue as an independent nation. We don't want France to have to yield to this, that and the other thing because if France yields and England yields, there won't be any independent nation in Europe or Africa or anywhere else. Therefore, it is to our interest, quite frankly, to do what we can, absolutely as a matter of peace, peace of the world, to help the French and British maintain their independence. Literally, their independence is threatened today." To the charge that sale of planes to France would be "unneutral," he responded that it was essential for "self-protection." He promised to do everything he could "to maintain the independence of these other nations by sending them all they can pay for on the barrelhead, to these about forty or fifty now independent nations of the world." He contended that planes for France "may mean the saving of our civilization." Roosevelt assured the senators, however, that "about the last thing that this country should do is ever to send an army to Europe again."[4]

Roosevelt urged the senators to keep his statements "as confidential as you can." Several of those present, including Nye, Clark, Lundeen, and Reynolds, were greatly disturbed by Roosevelt's views and by his emphasis on secrecy. The next day Nye told the Senate that he would withdraw from executive sessions of the Military Affairs Committee "in its present consideration of national defense measures . . . until such time as a reasonable part of the record, devoid of any military secrets of those meetings, shall be available to the people." He considered the secrecy "intolerable and completely out of step with what ought to be practice under a democratic representative form of government."[5]

One danger in the failure to make the record of meetings public is that "leaks" occur, and they are often inaccurate or misleading. After the White House conference of January 31, when reporters eagerly sought out those who had attended, one of the senators charged that Roosevelt had said America's frontier was on the Rhine. The White

House transcript of the meeting does not include this wording or any direct variant of it. The alleged statement angered both the President and his critics, for different reasons. Isolationists were irate at the thought of placing America's defense frontier in Europe. Roosevelt resented both the leak and its inaccuracy. At his press conference on February 3, he called the leak a "deliberate lie" and said that "some boob got that off." The President also denied that "The American frontier is on the Rhine" summed up his views. Two weeks later, in off the record comments, he further explained to newsmen what he had told the Military Affairs Committee. He restated his view that the "continued independence" of "thirty or forty countries" was "of tremendous importance to the safety of the United States." He again denied "that the frontiers of the United States are on the Rhine or in France," charging that the phrase was coined to "make political capital." In the course of his comments on this subject he referred to Nye as "an unscrupulous person."[6]

The senator's understanding of what transpired at the President's press conferences was somewhat different. Nye understood Roosevelt had said that he did not know who had leaked the phrase to the press, but that this person was a "boob" and a "liar" and "spelled his name N-y-e." Nye later insisted that he had not leaked the statement—that Senator Lundeen had done so. If this was so, Nye's anger over what he understood to be Roosevelt's direct reference to him in the press conference was natural. When Marvin McIntyre, the President's secretary, called the senator soon after and said Roosevelt would like him to come to the White House to talk over matters, Nye refused the invitation. He believed that if Roosevelt considered him a "boob" and a "liar" nothing would be accomplished by further discussion. After this refusal, Nye was never again invited to the White House for consultation with Roosevelt. The episode marked the final break in personal relations between the President and Nye.[7]

The clash between them assumed somewhat different proportions in the minds and emotions of each of the two men. In Roosevelt's view, Nye was one among several troublesome, blind, and irresponsible isolationist senators whose baneful influence had to be countered if peace and security were to be preserved or restored. In Nye's view, Roosevelt personally was the formidable barrier to accomplishment of the senator's goals for America and for himself.

Their mutual hostility was based partly on differences in principle—between Nye's isolationism and Roosevelt's internationalism. Each was moved by sincere dedication to his own conception of the proper course for the United States in world affairs and by the conviction that the other's approach would have tragic consequences for the nation.

Aside from these very real ideological differences, the feud was partly a product of politics. Party loyalty played a role, though Nye was not noted for his party regularity. Personal ambitions for position, power, and status were involved. Further, Nye and Roosevelt represented a struggle for power between different political alliances. Roosevelt inspired support from remarkably diverse interests. As he shifted his emphasis from the New Deal to foreign affairs after 1938, he carried most liberals (including urban labor) with him. But he also won new support from many conservatives who had vigorously opposed his New Deal. Many of these conservatives were southern Democrats, both rural and urban. Many others, however, were from urban business, industrial, and financial circles, particularly in the Northeast. Executives of the House of Morgan, General Electric, United States Steel, and many other corporations, big and small, became part of the coalition behind Roosevelt's foreign policies. The enthusiasm with which the conservative *New York Herald Tribune* and the Henry Luce publications rallied to the President's foreign policies before Pearl Harbor was part of this pattern.[8] In this context, Nye's battle against Roosevelt was partly a continuation, in new garb, of his long-term agrarian crusade against urban dominance.

If the clash had resulted only from rational ideological and political differences, however, it would have been less heated than it was. Nye had conducted many aggressive battles, but his emotions were never more aroused than when he fought Roosevelt after 1938. Roosevelt was angered and contemptuous of Nye and his foreign policy views, but the President's emotional stability, sense of humor, self-confidence, and power helped keep his reactions to Nye somewhat within bounds. For the senator, the situation was different. His feelings of inferiority were probably aggravated by Roosevelt's sophisticated, confident personality. While Nye was riding the crest of the isolationist tide in the mid-1930's, these feelings were kept in check. Roosevelt's official courtesy and consideration for the senator and his views helped. By 1939, when the isolationist tide was beginning to recede, probably both Roosevelt and Nye were beginning to suspect that the President was moving with the political currents in foreign affairs, and the senator may have begun to fear the powerful undertow that eventually carried him to his political death in the waters of World War II. Nye's belief that the President had called him a "boob" and a "liar" in front of newsmen was a blow to his pride. His feelings of inferiority and the frustration of his political and foreign policy goals caused him to strike out aggressively and passionately at "that man" in the White House. As he suffered repeated defeats in his skirmishes with the administration from 1939 onward, and as his position was subjected to growing criticism and scorn, the senator's hostility toward the President intensified. Indicative of his emotional stress was the fact that on the advice of his physician Nye took a two-week rest in the middle of March 1939 "to recover from a strained nervous condition" and to regain "a vitality which has been pretty largely spent this winter." His marital difficulties in 1939–40 may have been partly a cause and partly a result of his emotional state. Whatever the explanation, Senator Nye became an increasingly vehement critic of the President and his policies.[9]

On February 18, 1939, the day after Roosevelt's second press conference reference to the "frontier" episode, Nye addressed the National Republican Club in New York City. This speech was a classic statement of his views and clearly suggested trends in his attitudes. Characteristically, in an address on "America's Place in the World," Nye devoted much of his time to domestic affairs, particularly to agriculture. He maintained that "America's place in the world is in a very definite and large way dependent upon her own strength of mind and body." Consequently, he advised "correcting our own ills . . . saving our own democracy rather than soliciting the trouble to come from any move to police and doctor the world." As he had hundreds of times before, the senator insisted that "a healthy agricultural industry was basic to an economic state that would serve well the interests of business, capital, and labor." His incipient conservatism was apparent when he criticized government spending and "tinkering," and charged that the farmer was "exceedingly weary of the New Deal agricultural program, sick to death of the control program." America's "greatest contribution to the welfare of mankind and to future generations is to preserve intact our way of life and our democracy."

Nye denied that Hull's reciprocal trade program would serve "as an instrument of promoting peace"; in fact, he said, it had hurt the farmer and, therefore, the nation: "While the farmer is asked by his own Government to reduce his production to the requirements of American consumers, he has had to watch the same Government bringing him new competition. Imports coming from Canada for instance, imports in competition with the American farmer, are permitted in the name of helping Canadian farmers to buy Michigan automobiles, thus aiding business and labor. But what of the American farmer who by reason of the Canadian competition loses his own market and ability to buy the same product of the automobile manufacturer? Preservation of an expanded American market for the American farmer is the greatest contribution which this or any other administration can make toward stabilizing our economic life. No longer is the foreign market the hope of the American farmer. His hope is an enlarged domestic market protected against the low-cost producers abroad. Instead of worrying about increasing the standard of living abroad we should set ourselves to work to increase the standard of living in America through increased consumption and new industrial uses for American farm products. The very least to which the American farmer is entitled is the American market. Let him have that, and we shall have started down the road to economic recovery – because increased purchasing power on the farm means employment for workers in the cities – and once we achieve economic recovery we need not worry about the future of our civilization or institutions, irrespective of what happens in other parts of the world." When he denounced the New Deal farm programs, controls, and spending, while endorsing protectionist policies, Nye was speaking a language that most conservatives understood.

After his comments on economic bases for America's role in world affairs, the senator turned in his address to the administration's foreign policy. He claimed that it was based on the "fallacious and erroneous" belief that "if there is another general war in Europe the involvement of this country in that conflict is inevitable." Nye called this "a counsel of despair, generated by emotion and hysteria, without a basis of either fact or realistic appreciation of world affairs." He rejected "the contention that America must give aid and support to the democracies of Europe." Nye denied "emphatically that religious freedom in this country will be imperiled by whatever happens abroad." In his view "the greatest threat to American democracy is to be found in policies which ultimately will have the effect of making us participants in the quarrels of Europe and in any war which should break out." Reverting once more to his concern with economic bases for foreign affairs, Nye said that Roosevelt was "seeking to draw a red herring across the trail of his failures in domestic policies." And finally, he lamented that critics of the administration's foreign policy "are cast aside as 'boobs' or 'liars' and are being referred to as profascists, prompted by partisan prejudices." This major address before the Republican gathering included an agrarian-oriented analysis of the domestic economy as well as an anti-executive noninterventionist foreign policy. It contained seedlings of Nye's emerging conservatism, and it put the senator openly in the vanguard of Roosevelt's more vigorous critics.[10]

Ten days later Nye said that the dictatorships did not want war any more than the democracies did. "There will be no war in Europe," he told the Senate, "unless the United States shows a definite will to help out when war comes, and an inclination to finance it. There will surely be a war in Europe when the United States gives the word 'go' and gives Europe reason to anticipate that the United States will be standing by and ready to go on when the hour comes." This statement set off a spirited donnybrook in which Senator Scott Lucas, Democrat of Illinois, asked who in the United States Nye believed would give the "go" sign for war. In reply the North Dakota senator mentioned "selfish commercial interests" and those "whose foreign favors and prejudices are so strong as to blind them to truly American interests." But he contended that "the greatest force or influence of all that may dictate war is composed of those who shape and direct the foreign policy of our great Nation." He emphasized the inability of Congress to prevent war if those conducting foreign affairs took the nation step by step "to the gates where there is no alternative to a declaration of war."[11]

The foreign policy differences between Nye and Roosevelt were further highlighted by the controversy over revision of the Neutrality Act in 1939 – both before and after war began in Europe. In his message to Congress on January 4, the President warned that the neutrality laws "may actually give aid to an aggressor and deny it to the victim." He insisted that the "instinct of self-preservation should warn us that we ought not to let that happen any more." In the same message he recommended "methods short of war, but stronger and more effective than mere words" to oppose aggressor states.[12]

Ideally, the President and Secretary Hull would have preferred complete repeal of the Neutrality Act or at least discretionary executive authority to apply the arms embargo only against aggressor states. Key Pittman warned the administration that such legislation simply could not be obtained in Congress at that time; the most that could be hoped for was repeal of the arms embargo and the application of cash-and-carry to all exports (including munitions) from the United States to belligerents. Administration leaders reluctantly accepted Pittman's political analysis as correct and cooperated with his strategy. Since the British and French presumably would control the seas, such a law would operate to their advantage against the Axis in any European war, although the reverse would be true in the Pacific, where such a law would, in effect, open American ports and production to Japan but close them to China.[13]

Pittman contended that the chances for revision of neutrality legislation would be greater if the administration remained in the background and left the initiative to congressional leaders. In general, the President and Secretary Hull acceded to this plan. On March 20, 1939, Pittman introduced his bill with apparent confidence and hearings began in April. Several other bills were also introduced, ranging all the way from proposals to repeal the Neutrality Act completely, through proposals for giving the President discretionary authority to impose discriminatory arms embargo against aggressors, to the rigidly mandatory proposal introduced by Senators Nye, Bone, and Clark.[14]

Pittman failed even to obtain repeal of the embargo. Early in May he informed Hull that he would be unable to secure Senate passage of his bill because of the strength of the opposition. On May 27, Hull made a special appeal in identical letters to Pittman and Sol Bloom, chairman of the House Committee on Foreign Affairs, and administration leaders worked diligently behind the scenes to get the the bill through the House. When it passed a measure that provided for continuance of the arms embargo, the administration was forced to turn again to the Senate. On July 11, however, the Foreign Relations Committee, on a motion by Senator Clark, voted 12 to 11 to postpone further consideration of neutrality legislation until January 1940. Even a dramatic White House conference between the President, Hull, and congressional leaders failed to break the jam. When the war in Europe began in September 1939, the Neutrality Act of 1937 (including the arms embargo) was still binding, except that the cash-and-carry provisions had expired four months before. As Cordell Hull correctly wrote later, this was "the last effective stand of the powerful isolation movement in the United States. The movement continued its fight by every means at hand . . . but after war came in Europe it was never again able to thwart an Administration proposal."[15]

Most of the activity on the neutrality issue in the spring and summer occurred in the White House, the Department of State, the Foreign Relations and Foreign Affairs committees, and the House of Representatives. Since the Foreign Relations Committee never reported out any neutrality proposal, and the issue was not brought to a vote on the Senate floor, Nye, not then a member of the Foreign Relations Committee, did not play a central role in the maneuvers at this time. Nevertheless, he spoke repeatedly and forcefully in and out of the Senate on the issue. And he played an active role in the group that promised to oppose the administration's bill if it reached the Senate floor. He charged that Pittman's proposal for repeal of the arms embargo was designed to help England and France. The only purpose of the neutrality law, he said, was "to help the United States keep out of other people's wars"; until America entered a foreign war in spite of the law, no one could justly call it a failure. In private letters he wrote that if he could have had his way "there would be no exportation of war materials to any land in peace time or in war time," and "the neutrality law would forbid all trade with nations at war as well as financing through loans or credits." In the absence of such extreme restrictions, he wanted a complete ban on loans, credits, and munitions sales to all belligerents, and only cash-and-carry sale of non-embargoed goods to belligerents. He wanted the existing law tightened to limit further the President's discretion. He insisted that the United States could stay out of war "if we have a will to do it."[16]

In July 1939, a few days before the Foreign Relations Committee voted to postpone consideration of neutrality legislation, Nye joined with Hiram Johnson and other senators in a statement "unalterably" opposing "repeal or modification of the present neutrality law." Fourteen senators (including Nye) attended the meeting that drafted the statement, but they boasted support from a total of thirty-four senators. They threatened a filibuster if necessary to block the administration's drive for repeal of the embargo. The group of fourteen provided seven of the twelve votes for postponing consideration of neutrality that were cast in the Foreign Relations Committee on July 11.[17]

With the battle temporarily won, Nye told the Senate late in July that "the time and events inviting our participation in Europe's squabbles should be determined by Congress, never by the President and his Cabinet alone." In a single sentence in this speech he concisely summed up his views: "We can stay out of war if we will break the possibility of selfish profiteering by Americans from other people's wars, if we will curb Executive power to secretly move toward war." In answer to the complaint that the economic restrictions in neutrality legislation would undermine prosperity, he commented that America had "been prosperous heretofore without yielding our independence from Europe, and we can and will be so again." America should never wish "to copy the Hitler program of prosperity through armament production and sale." He urged greater coordination between the President and Congress in foreign affairs "by including Congress in policy matters rather than by giving all powers and responsibility to the President."[18]

In August, Nye charged that Roosevelt was "preaching a determination to keep this country of ours out of war, but pursuing a course of activity that can only be inviting ourselves to another war." He contended that the administration "drifted from a strict 'keep out of war' policy . . . at precisely the time when that administration saw itself failing miserably in its domestic policy." He advocated looking out for "America first!"[19]

Throughout 1938–39, alarming events signalized the rapidly deteriorating prospects for peace. Japanese forces made impressive gains in China. Hitler added Austria to his domain in the *Anschluss* of March 1938. In the fall of 1938, after appeasement at Munich, Hitler seized the Sudetenland, and in March 1939, the rest of Czechoslovakia was dismembered. The Russo-German Non-Aggression Pact of August 23, 1939, opened the door for Hitler to pursue his ambitions in Poland. Fears grew that general war would soon erupt.

Up to the moment it began in Europe in September 1939, however, Senator Nye minimized the likelihood of war, portrayed the European struggles in terms of imperialism rather than democracy, and charged the administration with encouraging war. Early in the summer he said his sympathies were "with Britain and France as against Italy and

Germany" and he conceded that Americans could "entertain little or no sympathy for such internal and external exploits, such racial prejudices, as the dictator countries have demonstrated." He believed, however, that the European struggles did not involve democracy "in any serious degree." He contended that Britain's "love for democracy" was "utterly lacking of sincerity" and was designed "only to win allies to the saving of her imperialism." In Nye's opinion, "Saving British imperialism isn't going to save the world." He urged Britain and France to "adjust the injustices" of the Versailles Treaty and to recognize that "they are going to have to give up something which is theirs, not only that which belongs to others."[20]

In July, before the Russo-German Pact, the senator said that "a combination of the great naval powers plus Russia and the non-German states of eastern Europe" could "successfully withstand attack from the Central European Powers." He believed the United States should not "carry the military burden which would otherwise fall to Russia." "What good reason," he asked, "can there be for substituting American soldiers for Russian soldiers on the European front?"[21]

On August 18, 1939, Nye asserted that "there isn't going to be any war in Europe." He believed no government wanted war. On August 24, he said that Roosevelt was responsible for causing Britain and France to take a stiffer stand in Europe. Three days before Hitler unleashed his blitzkrieg on Poland, Nye insisted that Germany was not ready for war and did not want "a war of the kind the English and French would give him." To think that Hitler wanted war was, Nye believed, to assume that the Nazi dictator was "the kind of sportsman who fishes with a barbless hook to give the fish a better break or hunts with a bow and arrow to even the odds between man and his prey." In less than a month Hitler's "bow and arrow" had destroyed Poland.[22]

The German forces invaded Poland on September 1, 1939, and England and France, resolved to appease no more, declared war on Germany on September 3. Poland's antiquated military forces were no match for Germany and Russia, and England and France were unable to render effective assistance. After the collapse of Poland, Nye suggested that Roosevelt mediate among the European belligerents. In the summer of 1940, during the Battle of Britain, Nye publicly charged that the Roosevelt administration had given "England and France reason to believe that if they would declare war on Germany, help would be forthcoming." He predicted that "some day history will show, as one of the blackest marks of our time, that we sold out, by deliberate falsification, the two European nations with which we had the closest ties. We sent France to her death and have brought England perilously close to it. Had they stalled Hitler for a while, while they prepared to meet him, the story might have been different."[23]

With the beginning of the European war, President Roosevelt called a special session of Congress. In his message to it on September 21, 1939, the President urged repeal of the arms embargo and re-enactment of cash-and-carry. Fearful of isolationist strength, however, neither the President nor Secretary Hull publicly based these recommendations on the grounds of protecting American security by helping Britain and France. In his message he said: "I give you my deep and unalterable conviction . . . that by the repeal of the embargo the United States will more probably remain at peace than if the law remains as it stands today. I say this because with the repeal of the embargo, this Government clearly and definitely will insist that American citizens and American ships keep away from the immediate perils of the actual zones of conflict." In this key passage the President was citing the merits of cash-and-carry as an argument for repealing the arms embargo—even though the two were not causally related except in a political sense.[24]

This essentially noninterventionist emphasis in official administration statements on the issue coincided with the approach recommended by Senator Pittman, who again urged the administration to leave legislative initiative and responsibility to congressional leaders. The bill he sponsored provided for the repeal of the arms embargo and the re-enactment of cash-and-carry that the President wanted. In an effort to appease noninterventionist fears, however, the measure also contained more severe restrictions on American shipping than the administration desired. Pittman resisted administration objections to his measure, though later amendments modified the final act somewhat. In presenting the bill to the Senate on October 2, Pittman argued that the revised bill was more likely to keep the United States out of war than was the existing law. He did not make use of the idea that American security would be protected by extending aid to the victims of Axis aggression. He did, however, bolster his case by an appeal to economic considerations, asserting that the "condition with regard to industry and labor in this country today is so deplorable that further obstructions to our exports would bankrupt large sections of our country."[25]

Senator Nye played a leading role in the battle against repeal of the arms embargo. Ten days before the special session, he announced formation of a "senatorial peace bloc" to oppose repeal and promised a "last ditch fight" on the issue. More than a dozen senators, including Hiram Johnson, William E. Borah, Arthur H. Vandenberg, Bennett Champ Clark, Robert M. LaFollette, Jr., Henrik Shipstead, Ernest Lundeen, Arthur Capper, Lynn Frazier, Rush Holt, and D. Worth Clark, held meetings with Nye to plan their strategy. Most of these senators, like Nye, represented predominantly agricultural constituencies and held progressive views on domestic issues. A private source provided $3,000 for a research bureau to aid senators with data against repeal. Nye restricted his speaking engagements late in September and canceled some previously scheduled for early October to clear his calendar. The North Dakota senator made radio broadcasts as well as speeches in the Senate to rally support for the embargo.[26]

Like the administration, Nye and his colleagues urged re-enactment of cash-and-carry, so the only real issue in the debate was the arms embargo. Nye emphasized over and over again that repeal of the embargo would be "the first, most important step toward our eventual participation in the war in Europe." He charged that the President had not stated the issue "frankly," and that "the purpose of the administration in this arms-embargo repeal effort is to help the Allies, on the theory that they are 'our first line of defense.'" Nye denied that the United States could "make the world safe from Hitlerism by becoming the silent partner of the British Empire," and asked: "If our supplies alone are not enough to help England win, what will happen then?" If the United States "determined to fight this war with materials," it would "inevitably end up by fighting it with men."[27]

The senator conceded that the arms embargo did not cover all commodities important in war trade, but argued that this problem could (and should) be handled by expanding the embargo to include these additional products, not by repealing the embargo entirely. To contend, as some did, that the arms embargo endangered American economic recovery was, he said, like acknowledging that "it is trade and profits, not security about which we are most solicitous." If the arms embargo were repealed, Nye predicted that it would be only a matter of time before the administration wanted the "cash" part of the Neutrality Act repealed, and then the "carry" part. The last step would be a declaration of war. The arms embargo, he warned, had become "a kind of traffic light. If it is repealed, the light will turn green— 'Go ahead'—along the road to war." He repeatedly emphasized that the United States could not "take steps 'short of war' against Germany and not end up in military war against her."[28]

In September the White House, Department of State, and congressmen received huge quantities of mail opposing repeal of the arms embargo—mail inspired partly by the efforts of Nye, Borah, Clark, Vandenberg, and others. Nye's mail from North Dakota on the subject was two to one against repeal.[29]

But those who opposed the embargo also conducted an all-out effort to obtain its repeal,[30] and the "aid-short-of-war" formula (implied or expressed) was unbeatable during the twenty-seven months of European war before Pearl Harbor. The various amendments to Pittman's bill introduced by Nye's colleagues were overwhelmingly rejected by the Senate. Nye was subjected to growing criticism on and off the Senate floor. In the final Senate vote on October 27, 1939, there were only thirty votes against repeal, while sixty-three were cast for the Pittman measure. Those voting with Nye against repeal included most of the western agrarian liberals, including Borah, Capper, Clark, Frazier, Johnson, LaFollette, McNary, Shipstead, Lundeen, and Wheeler, plus a few from industrial areas such as Vandenberg and Henry Cabot Lodge. Nye warned that the revised Neutrality Act gave the United States "an economic interest in the war." It had no immediate effects on farmers, but it did open British and French markets for munitions produced by management, labor, and capital in American cities. When Britain restricted certain agricultural imports in 1940 to preserve her dollars for industrial war goods, Nye charged that trade with belligerents inevitably turned toward munitions. The combination of repeal of the arms embargo and re-enactment of cash-and-carry, in his view, expanded industrial munitions exports, reduced agricultural and other non-munition exports, and increased pressure for removing restrictions on loans and credits to belligerents.[31]

By the time the embargo was repealed, Hitler's forces had crushed Poland and there was a temporary lull in the fighting. During the winter of 1939–40 headlines went not to Hitler but to the war between the

Soviet Union and Finland. The Russo-Finnish war encouraged Nye's belief that war between the Soviet Union and Nazi Germany was inevitable. He lauded the Finns and emphasized his hatred for the Russian cause. But he opposed an American loan to Finland on the ground that "to aid any belligerent" would be "a step toward war."[32]

Though no senator was more active and vocal on foreign affairs in the 1930's than Gerald P. Nye, he was not a member of the Senate Foreign Relations Committee. Not until January 1940 did he finally win a seat on that powerful committee, filling the vacancy left by the death of William E. Borah. (At the same time, Nye lost his place on the Military Affairs Committee.) As chairman of the Republican Committee on Committees in the Senate since 1934, Nye had helped arrange the assignment of other isolationists to the Foreign Relations Committee. In 1940 on the isolationist side it included Johnson, Vandenberg, Capper, LaFollette, Shipstead, Clark, Reynolds, and Nye. When Key Pittman died in November 1940, his successor as chairman was Walter George, who earlier had been a member of Nye's Munitions Investigating Committee. He gave all sides their day in court. Tom Connally of Texas, however, took over chairmanship of the committee on July 31, 1941, when George became chairman of the Finance Committee. Connally vehemently opposed the isolationists in general and Nye in particular. Under his leadership the isolationists were held in check in the committee, but although Nye had relatively little influence there,[33] this did not inhibit his interest or activity on foreign policy issues.

By 1940, "isolationist" was being used as a derogatory and smear term, but Nye wrote an article for the *New York Times Magazine* urging a return to isolation. He pointed out that he and other isolationists did not want "to cut off commercial intercourse with other nations or to be entirely indifferent to the political, moral and social problems of other nations." They rejected "the theory of the Chinese Wall." He contended that isolationists were "first of all realists" who wanted to base American actions "on an honest estimate of our national physical strength, on an honest weighing of the gains and losses to us and to other peoples of each practical measure suggested." He emphasized that isolationists were looking out for American national interests: the United States did not have sufficient power "to make itself the guardian of international virtue" — American power was "not evenly distributed over the earth but localized sharply in this hemisphere, where there is a job big enough for us to do." Americans could "be self-sufficient and live within ourselves without regard to what happens in the outside world," and this "would result in a better distribution, a better sharing, of that which we have than the present economy affords us."[34]

In the spring and summer of 1940, the Nazi German military forces made important parts of "the outside world" extremely unpleasant places to be. In April, Adolf Hitler's forces overwhelmed Denmark and Norway. On May 10, 1940, the German armies drove into the Netherlands, Belgium, and Luxemburg, and within a few days they were rolling into northern France. Less than a month after the attack began, the British army in Europe was driven into the sea at Dunkerque. As France reeled from the German blows, made more crippling by her own internal weakness, Italy chose to attack the unhappy nation in the south. Finally, with the Germans in control of their capital city and considerably over half of their area, the French under Marshal Pétain signed an armistice with Hitler on June 22, 1940. Even before the fall of France the German *Luftwaffe* had begun its assault on the British Isles. By August and September the Battle of Britain was raging. At the same time German submarines were taking a heavy toll of British shipping. The outlook for the Western democracies in Europe was indeed dismal in 1940.

Nye's determined noninterventionist views were not shaken by the terrifying Axis successes, however, and they got him into difficulty with the large Norwegian-American population in North Dakota and elsewhere. Scandinavians, like German-Americans, generally had approved Nye's foreign policy views, but with the Nazi conquest of Norway many Norwegian-Americans had second thoughts on the subject. On April 15, 1940, Senator Nye told a college audience in Pennsylvania that "not one single cause" in the European war was "worthy of the sacrifice of one American mule, much less one American son." Norwegian-Americans, understandably, were somewhat less than enthusiastic about the idea of attaching greater value to "one American mule" than to their mother country just overrun by the Nazis. As protests poured in, Nye tried to explain — but he did not retreat. He assured critics that Hitler's invasion of Norway had stirred within him "a bitter hatred toward the invaders who would thus violate the neutrality of a peaceful nation of people." But he said he would not permit his hatred of "the ruthlessness and lawlessness of Hitler and his kind" to blind him to the things he loved most—"my country, its institutions and its ideals which I fear cannot possibly survive involvement in another war if that war assumes proportions on a par with those suffered in the last war." He contended that only "Russia, Stalin and communist ideology" would win in the European war. Nye's response may have satisfied a few critics, but later he was convinced that the Norwegian-American vote contributed to his defeat at the polls in North Dakota in 1944.[35]

President Roosevelt, in June 1940, named Henry L. Stimson to be secretary of war and Frank Knox as secretary of the navy. Nye unsuccessfully opposed Senate approval of both these appointments. The fact that Stimson and Knox were Republicans did not impress the senator at all. The important thing, in his view, was that they were avid interventionists. Both of them were "ready to stick out the American 'neck' farther . . . in involvement in the European conflict." The positions should be filled instead, he said, "by men who are avowedly determined that this country is not going to be drawn into other people's wars; certainly not by men of the caliber of Mr. Stimson, who has found so many fine reasons why we ought to go to war."[36]

Nye also opposed adoption of compulsory military conscription in 1940. He called the proposal "totalitarianism" and "a direct thrust at the very heart of true democracy." He considered it "a serious departure from the American way," and said it "ought to be possible to resist foreign dictators without building a dictatorship out of this great democracy of ours." In the course of his attack on conscription in the Senate on August 23, 1940, Nye provided a moving glimpse of the loneliness and self-doubts that must surely, at some time, assail all who find themselves repeatedly in minority and unpopular positions: "Sometimes as I watch and listen to others, intelligent, conscientious, and forceful, as they work themselves into fevers over what they allege to be the grave emergency confronting this country of ours, I come up wondering if I am 'all there,' if I have lost my reason, if I ever had the power of reasoning well. I will swear to a genuine concern when I find myself failing to respond, and feeling the fears which others do feel and show." If the international emergency were sufficiently serious to justify drafting young men, however, he wondered why it was not sufficiently serious to justify drafting profits as well, through adoption of the war-profits tax bill he had introduced repeatedly. In spite of his efforts, Nye (as usual after 1938) was beaten. Peacetime military conscription became law with the President's signature on September 16, 1940.[37]

Logically, Senator Nye also opposed the "destroyer deal" in which the President exchanged fifty over-age American destroyers for bases on British possessions in the Western Hemisphere. He charged that the exchange would "plant" the United States "in the middle of war as an actual belligerent" and would "seriously weaken our own defense."[38]

Despite his Republican political affiliations, Senator Nye had actively supported his party's presidential nominee only once before 1940. If Franklin D. Roosevelt sought a third term, however, Nye's passionate hatred for the President virtually assured his support for almost anyone the Republicans might nominate. At least as early as 1936 the North Dakota senator had begun to hope that some bolt of political lightning might elevate him to the presidency in the election of 1940. Roosevelt was unbeatable in 1936, but the "no-third-term" tradition might give the Republican party its chance four years later. In 1936, Nye's foreign policy views were widely acclaimed and were considered (by the senator and by others) as a political asset. Conceivably Nye's unwillingness to support either Lemke or Roosevelt in 1936 was rooted partly in his desire not to endanger his chances, however remote, for winning the Republican nomination in 1940. Republican gains (and Nye's own re-election) in 1938 may have encouraged his hope. In August 1939, he said that "if the Republican party is going to get anywhere in 1940, it has got to make up its mind that its candidate and platform are going to have to be forward-looking and progressive." He, of course, emphasized that the party and its candidate must oppose vigorously American involvement in "other people's wars."[39]

Scattered support for Nye's nomination for President on the Republican ticket did develop in 1939. But contrary to his hopes the political currents in 1939–40 did not benefit him. The relatively conservative atmosphere that was gaining ascendancy in the nation was not receptive to Nye's progressive reputation. Even among many liberals, his agrarian orientation was not in vogue. Furthermore, the beginning of the war in Europe hurt Nye's chances for a first term as President, just as surely as it enhanced Roosevelt's for a third term. Despite the President's fear of isolationist strength, the war in Europe and the urban dominance in America helped make Nye's foreign policy views increasingly a political liability rather than an asset. Many had considered Nye statesmanlike in the middle of the 1930's, and some remained his enthusiastic followers, but he came under growing attack and criticism. The senator had had an unusually good press in the middle of the decade, and he still got headlines in 1939–40. But now he received increasingly rough treatment at the hands of editors – particularly from large-circulation dailies in the Northeast. When Drew Pearson and Robert S. Allen charged, in October 1939, that the senator's secretary, Gerald W. Movius, was directing a Nye-for-President drive, the senator and his secretary felt obliged to deny it and urge one of his more enthusiastic "tub thumpers" to cease his efforts. Nye contended that no one from a state with only four electoral votes was likely to be considered seriously as a major party's presidential candidate.[40] He might have said, with equal accuracy, that no one from a predominantly agricultural state was likely to win nomination in the urban America of 1940.

With political realities blocking his own way to the presidency, Nye in January 1940 threw his support to Senator Arthur H. Vandenberg of Michigan. Vandenberg had been an active member of the Munitions Investigating Committee and shared Nye's foreign policy views. Nye said that he could not "see the industrialists fighting him and his agricultural record ought to bring him a grand response from the farming sections." It is significant that he did not mention labor. On domestic issues Vandenberg was a conservative – the first conservative Nye had ever backed in any of his pre-convention efforts through the years. The North Dakota senator actively campaigned for Vandenberg in both the Wisconsin and Nebraska presidential primaries. In Wisconsin he particularly urged progressives to vote for Vandenberg. When Governor Thomas E. Dewey of New York beat Vandenberg in both states, the Michigan senator's chances for the nomination dwindled, and it was Wendell Willkie of Indiana and New York who, with vital support from eastern financial, business, and newspaper sources, won the Republican presidential nomination in Philadelphia on June 28, 1940. To appease western agrarians, the Republicans chose Senator Charles L. McNary of Oregon as their vice presidential candidate.[41]

Nye's attitude toward Willkie's candidacy was partly dependent upon the course followed by the Democrats at their Chicago convention in July. Previously Nye had said that Senator Burton K. Wheeler of

Montana "would get a lot of Republican votes" if he were the Democratic nominee. Wheeler was a western liberal who had supported Roosevelt and the New Deal until he led the fight against court packing in 1937. Unlike Nye, he had not been particularly active in foreign policy controversies until 1939 when he added his voice to the Senate isolationist bloc.[42]

On June 21, 1940, the day before France signed the armistice imposed by the victorious Hitler, Senator Nye made a sensational proposal in the Senate. Choosing his words with care, he urged Roosevelt to resign and turn the office of the presidency over to Vice President John Nance Garner. Nye feared that dictatorship might be developing in the United States, and charged that America's policy of "any-and-all-steps-short-of-war in aid of a European cause" was formed "by one who was elected President as a noninterventionist, even as an isolationist." The main theme in his indictment, however, was that Roosevelt had "promised military support to France," expecting the Allies to hold out long enough for the President to lead America to declare war on Nazi Germany. The speed of Hitler's successes upset the President's timetable. Nye suspected that Roosevelt "on his own responsibility, by private assurances, may have encouraged a great and friendly power to ruin," and speculated that he might now do the same thing to England. The senator insisted that no one but the Vice President could now "restore the national unity and national confidence in governmental leadership." He emphasized that his proposal was not inspired by any sympathy for the Fascist dictators. "I have in my heart but one wish, one cause to serve, that is, the cause of keeping my country out of this war, on this lone theory that when the war shall have ended there will be nothing of democracy, there will be nothing of stability, left for any country which permits itself to participate in the war." He predicted that no matter who won or lost the European war, there would "be victory in store for only one ideology" – communism. Coming in the midst of the fall of France, the Battle of Britain, and national political conventions, Nye's speech was buried on page six of the *New York Times*.[43] The President was not shaping his actions to please Nye, and the Democratic party obviously was not influenced by the senator's recommendation: it nominated Roosevelt for an unprecedented third term on July 17.

With Roosevelt seeking a third-term and William Langer running for the United States Senate in North Dakota, Nye's work was cut out for him in the fall of 1940. He had serious reservations about Wendell Willkie, but since his two most formidable political adversaries were running for office, Nye was obliged to hit the hustings against them. He did so aggressively in numerous campaign speeches in the Middle West.

Nye charged that there was "a million times larger chance that America can stay out of war with Wendell Willkie and Charles McNary at the helm and Mr. Roosevelt a private citizen." The emergency confronting the United States in foreign affairs, he said, was created by the President. Nye believed that "the real emergency" was "not in the danger of attack upon us by any foreign power or group of powers. The threat to our democracy lies within our own borders. It is largely economic. It grows primarily out of the changed economy and the great burden of debt and cost which became ours as a result of our last participation in a foreign war." He was referring to the problems "of unemployment, farm help, relief for those in distress and with the debt." Nye charged that Roosevelt had "appealed to the hates, the fears and the deepest prejudices of our people, all to the end that we might abandon sight of these problems at home which continue to constitute a dire threat to the one remaining democracy upon this earth—our own." He said Willkie and McNary would "tackle" these "home problems" and "solve them." He also alleged that the Roosevelt administration was "exercising dictatorial powers without the consent of the people" in foreign affairs. He feared that Roosevelt's foreign policies were leading the United States "into a world conquest with the one goal, the dominance of the United States over all the world, the creation of a far-flung empire." Roosevelt, he said, "talks sweetly of peace, but his acts for the past two years have been acts taking us ever closer to war." In answer to the admonition that it was dangerous to change horses in the middle of a stream, Nye said, "when you have leaders and horses that don't know how, or have not the will, to keep out of the middle of dangerous streams, or who don't know how to get back to shore from such dangerous streams, it is high time that we changed leaders and changed horses if we care a snap about our country."[44] A listener in South Dakota wrote Nye lauding his criticisms of the President, but asked if the senator could count on Willkie being any better than Roosevelt. The writer questioned whether Willkie might not "out-Roosevelt Roosevelt" if he were elected.[45] Undoubtedly Nye shared these fears, but in a choice between evils the North Dakota senator certainly would not choose Roosevelt in 1940.

While both Langer and Roosevelt were victorious at the polls on November 5, the President failed to carry North Dakota. Though they had given their electoral votes to Roosevelt in 1932 and 1936, North Dakota voters in 1940 apparently shared Nye's view of the President, and Willkie easily carried the state. Farmers and farm states, however, no longer determined the outcome of presidential elections. Even more than in 1936, the cities re-elected Roosevelt, beat Willkie, and rebuffed Nye.[46]

In the two months between the election and the next session of Congress Nye continued his speaking engagements, but found time to remarry. In an uncontested action, Mrs. Nye had quietly divorced the senator in March 1940.[47] On December 14, 1940 – five days before his forty-eighth birthday – he married Miss Marguerite Johnson in her home town of Iowa Falls, Iowa. Marguerite, over fifteen years younger than her husband, was a graduate of Iowa State College and had taught school a number of years in Iowa and Illinois. They met by chance a few years before their marriage when Nye had assisted Marguerite and her companion with the repair of an automobile tire. The new Mrs. Nye was attractive, blonde, unpretentious, and socially poised and charming. She became and remained her husband's most loyal supporter. The couple eventually had three children – Gerald, Richard, and Debra. After a honeymoon in Florida, they returned to Washington where the senator prepared for the final phase of his long, losing battle against intervention.[48]

⁂ 11 ⁂

America First

TWO EPISODES stand out prominently in Gerald P. Nye's career. The first was the Senate munitions investigation that he headed from 1934 to 1936. The second was his participation in the America First Committee's battle against intervention in 1941. The America First Committee was the most powerful noninterventionist pressure group in the United States during the fifteen months before the Japanese attacked Pearl Harbor. Senator Nye addressed scores of rallies under its auspices — including its very last public meeting on the afternoon of December 7.

In his almost desperate efforts in 1941 to prevent American involvement in World War II, Senator Nye re-emphasized in ever more strident terms themes he had developed earlier. Over and over again he charged that the administration's steps to aid Great Britain short of war were actually steps *to* war. He repeatedly voiced the fear that United States intervention would destroy American democracy and the American way of life. Increasingly he denounced war propaganda and propagandists for arousing the emotions of the American people in order to overcome their aversion to war. And through it all, the senator saw Franklin D. Roosevelt as the principal villain. In his view the President was building a dictatorship at home on the pretext of opposing dictatorship abroad. He was leading the nation to war, Nye believed, while professing to be working for peace.

Numerous pressure groups (local, state, and national) designed to influence public opinion on foreign policy and to affect American policies toward the war participated in the Great Debate of 1941. On the interventionist side in this "Battle of the Committees," two organizations were particularly important. Both of them (like all interventionists) emphasized that a victorious Axis would constitute an extremely serious threat to American peace, security, and vital interests.

The Committee to Defend America by Aiding the Allies was organized in May 1940 with William Allen White, a respected Republican newspaper editor from Emporia, Kansas, as national chairman, and Clark Eichelberger as executive director. It was partly a response to an appeal by President Roosevelt to White for help "to get the American people to think of conceivable consequences [of the war in Europe and Asia] without scaring the people into thinking that they are going to be dragged into this war." Like the President, leaders and members of the White Committee were convinced that defeat of the Axis was essential for American security and favored aid to Britain short of war to accomplish that objective. They were active in marshaling public opinion in support of the destroyer deal and of the Lend-Lease Act. They believed that it was more important for the United States to assure defeat of the Axis than it was to stay out of the European war, but they, along with other interventionists, were divided on the question of how much aid was necessary to that end. The growing restiveness of those who favored more drastic steps partly accounted for White's resignation as national chairman in January 1941, and the committee never found a wholly satisfactory successor. The Roosevelt administration gradually became less accessible to leaders of the Committee to Defend America, and increasing difficulty was encountered in raising the funds essential for its activities.[1]

In April 1941 a second major interventionist committee was organized called Fight for Freedom, Inc. Drawing support from many who had backed the White Committee, it contended that aid short of war was not enough, and urged the United States to enter the European war as a full belligerent. Its national chairman was Henry W. Hobson, Episcopal bishop of southern Ohio. The Fight for Freedom Committee reflected the attitudes of Stimson and Knox in the President's Cabinet and a growing and powerful segment of the interventionist camp in general. It won its greatest support in states along the Atlantic seaboard.[2]

The America First Committee was the most formidable adversary of the interventionist organizations from September 1940 until December 7, 1941. It grew out of an earlier student group at Yale University led by R. Douglas Stuart, Jr., a twenty-four-year-old law school student and son of the first vice president of Quaker Oats Company in Chicago. This student group had tried unsuccessfully to persuade Senator Nye to speak under its sponsorship at Yale in the fall of 1939. During the summer of 1940 the personable young Stuart won the support of prominent middle western business and political leaders for a national organization. On September 4, the formation of America First was formally announced, with headquarters in Chicago. General Robert E. Wood, chairman of the board of Sears Roebuck and Company, was national chairman and Stuart was national director. Its seven-member executive committee included Wood; Stuart; General Thomas S. Hammond, president of the Whiting Corporation; William H. Regnery, president of the Western Shade Cloth Company; Hanford MacNider, Iowa manufacturer and former national commander of the American Legion; Clay Judson, a Chicago attorney; and Jay C. Hormel, president of Hormel Meat Packing Company. In the spring of 1941 Mrs. Janet Ayer Fairbank, a former national Democratic committeewoman from Illinois, replaced Hormel on the executive committee. All were from the Middle West and most were Republican businessmen from the Chicago area. A larger America First national committee included prominent men and women from many walks of life, among them John T. Flynn, Mrs. Bennett Champ Clark, Mrs. Burton K. Wheeler, George N. Peek, Chester Bowles, Kathleen Norris, Alice Roosevelt Longworth, the Reverend John A. O'Brien, Robert Young, Lillian Gish, Mrs. Ruth Hanna McCormick Simms, and Sterling Morton. In April 1941, Charles A. Lindbergh became a member of the national committee as well as the organization's most popular and controversial speaker. Though it drew support from persons with widely varying social and economic views, its leadership and financial backing came predominantly from the conservative wing of the noninterventionists. It was a more conservative group than Nye had ever been prominently associated with before.[3]

In the fall of 1940 the America First Committee placed full-page advertisements in the newspapers of widely scattered cities and sponsored noninterventionist radio addresses. By the end of the year, like the White Committee, it began to organize local chapters and sponsor public meetings. Its greatest growth occurred from December 1940 through May 1941; at its peak the loosely knit organization had approximately 450 local chapters and a total membership of 800,000 to 850,000. The committee won adherents in every state and chapters were formed in most of them. About one-fourth of its members were in the Northeast, but nearly two-thirds were within a three-hundred-mile radius of Chicago. Although many people in rural areas (outside of the South) shared the views represented by America First, the organized membership of the committee was largely urban. America First won very little support in the South and encountered particularly vehement and effective opposition there.[4]

Like all noninterventionists, the leaders and members of America First believed it was more important for the United States to stay out of the European war than to assure a British victory over the Axis. They feared that the administration's moves to aid Britain short of war would lead to war itself. It was not a pacifist organization and it advocated construction of "an impregnable defense for America." The committee was charged with harboring pro-Fascists, but its leaders made earnest efforts to bar such persons from its ranks.[5]

Senator Nye was never an officer of America First and he was not a member of either its executive or national committee. Furthermore, he was not active during the early months of its history. The noninterventionist radio addresses sponsored by America First in the fall of 1940 were delivered by General Hugh S. Johnson, Senator Henry Cabot Lodge, Senator Robert M. LaFollette, Jr., General Wood, Senator Arthur Capper, Senator David I. Walsh, Senator Burton K. Wheeler, and others. Nye was not included. In November, Stuart sought his suggestions for persons to form America First chapters in North Dakota, and in January he was consulted for advice in forming the America First research bureau in Washington, D.C. In both instances he was sympathetic but not particularly helpful.[6]

In 1941, however, he and Burton K. Wheeler were the most active senators in the America First Committee's campaign. Nye cooperated with its major effort to defeat the administration's lend-lease proposal. After lend-lease became law, he conducted an almost continuous round of speaking engagements at public meetings sponsored by America First. He was, of course, discouraged by the reverses suffered by noninterventionists on specific issues, and he was pained by the mounting criticism directed at him and America First. But he was intensely in earnest and thoroughly convinced of the righteousness and vital importance of the noninterventionist cause. And the senator enjoyed the excitement, acclaim, and drama of the crusade. Even after Pearl Harbor, Nye was proud of the role he had played in the America First battle against intervention in 1941.

As Nye had predicted in 1939, repeal of the arms embargo and re-enactment of the cash-and-carry law were followed by proposals to modify the "cash" requirement and later to repeal the "carry" provisions. After the election of 1940 the question of America's course when Britain was no longer able to pay cash in the United States came increasingly under debate. Late in November the British ambassador, Lord Lothian, warned of the seriousness of his country's financial situation. In a long letter to President Roosevelt on December 8, Prime Minister Winston Churchill described Britain's needs and warned that the time was coming when England would "no longer be able to pay cash." He also pointed out that if Great Britain were "divested of all saleable assets" it would cause "cruel privations" in Britain and "widespread unemployment in the United States" after the war. Reminding the President "that the defeat of the Nazi and Fascist tyranny is a matter of high consequence to the people of the United States and to the Western Hemisphere," Churchill expressed confidence that Roosevelt would find the "ways and means" to cope with the crisis. At his press conference on December 17, 1940, President Roosevelt described his plan "to eliminate the dollar sign" in aiding Great Britain. In his fireside chat on December 29, he vividly portrayed the disastrous consequences to American security if Britain fell or agreed to a negotiated peace. He called upon Americans to make the United States "the great arsenal of democracy." In his message on January 6, 1941, the President urged Congress to pass legislation to implement his lend-lease idea.[7]

The America First Committee threw all its energies against lend-lease – and so did Senator Nye. Immediately after Lothian's statement in November, Nye called for an investigation by the Senate Foreign Relations Committee of British holdings in the United States. He believed these holdings were greater than the British or interventionists would admit. England should spend what she had, Nye contended, before getting any financial aid from the United States.[8]

During the two months following Roosevelt's message to Congress on January 6, Senator Nye attacked the lend-lease proposal repeatedly and at length in the Senate, in committee hearings, in radio addresses, and at public meetings. Over and over again he charged that lend-lease would be a major step toward American involvement in the European war, and that it would give the President dictatorial powers. In the Senate Foreign Relations Committee hearings on H. R. 1776 he tried the patience of witnesses with his prolonged questioning. When Wendell Willkie testified for lend-lease, Nye asked him if he still believed, as he had said in the 1940 campaign, that America might be at war by April 1941 if Roosevelt were elected. Willkie replied that his statement had been "a bit of campaign oratory." Many noninterventionists had been unenthusiastic about Willkie before, but this statement infuriated them. The senator rejected many speaking engagements outside the Washington area so he could be close at hand during the melee. He listed seventeen drastic powers he believed the President would have under lend-lease, including the power "to give away the United States Navy," "to junk all the laws for the protection of labor," and "to govern through administrative proclamation." Supporters of lend-lease denied that Roosevelt would ever use all the powers that conceivably could be exercised under the bill. Nye then asked at an America First meeting why such broad powers should be granted if there was no intention to use them. He denied that American defense was dependent upon the British navy. "Fear and hate have obsessed us, blinded us, fooled us," he said, and urged letting "reason play a more substantial part in our American consideration once again." He charged that it was "only the Hitlers, the Mussolinis, the Stalins, and, I regret to say, the ambitious leaders in our own country, who clamor for war and for the steps leading to war." He was "more alarmed by the encroachments upon our constitutional status, and the impairment of the regular processes of our Government by the forces within the Government itself, than about possible aggressions against us by potential, but not necessarily probable, foreign foes." The twelve hours Nye spoke against lend-lease in the Senate chamber amounted to nearly one-fifth of the time devoted to the debate in the upper house.[9]

The efforts of noninterventionist legislators were supplemented by the fervent activities of the America First Committee and other noninterventionist and pacifist groups. Nye first addressed a major America First rally in the midst of the lend-lease furor, in New York City on

February 20. The committee used standard pressure group methods to arouse and marshal public opposition to the bill. One result was a flood of letters received by the President and congressmen. The White House received much more mail opposing lend-lease than supporting it.[10]

At the same time, administration leaders, their supporters in Congress, the Committee to Defend America by Aiding the Allies, and other groups were equally vigorous in their defense of the proposal, and public opinion polls indicated that most Americans followed the President on this issue. With senators clamoring for a vote on March 8, Nye said he would filibuster all alone if he thought it would defeat lend-lease, but he realized that it would be futile. The Senate adopted H. R. 1776 by a vote of 60 to 31. The negative votes were cast by seventeen Republicans (including Nye), thirteen Democrats, and one Progressive. More significant, however, was the fact that most of those voting against lend-lease were from agricultural and mining states in the Middle West, Great Plains, and Far West. Voting with Nye against the measure were most of the western progressives including LaFollette, Wheeler, Shipstead, Langer, Johnson, Capper, Clark, and Bone. The measure, signed into law by Roosevelt on March 11, 1941, authorized him to "sell, transfer title to, exchange, lease, lend, or otherwise dispose of" any "defense article" to "the government of any country whose defense the President deems vital to the defense of the United States." Nye also opposed the lend-lease appropriations in March and again in October but, as usual, he was beaten.[11]

After enactment of lend-lease, both Nye and the America First Committee resolved to continue their battle against intervention. America First took over the responsibility for the senator's speaking engagements (previously arranged by private lecture bureaus, largely by Redpath's), and paid his expenses for speeches delivered under its auspices. Mrs. Nye nearly always accompanied her husband on these trips. From March 28 onward, when he left Washington for the Pacific coast to begin his first tour for America First, he and his wife traveled many thousands of miles and he addressed approximately one hundred and sixty America First meetings and made numerous radio broadcasts. He almost never turned down an America First request to speak if he could possibly make the engagement. Thousands upon thousands heard him, and millions more read the newspaper reports of his speeches and interviews. There were complaints that he and other America Firsters sometimes spoke too long (occasionally over two hours), but even his critics conceded that he was an effective and powerful orator. His appearance (like that of Lindbergh, Wheeler, Clark, and others) almost invariably resulted in an increase of America First membership where he spoke.[12]

While his greatest contribution to America First was as a speaker, he also cooperated in other ways. For example, like Wheeler and others, Nye let committee representatives go through letters he received to prepare mailing lists of noninterventionists for use by America First.[13] He made available at cost noninterventionist material reprinted from the *Congressional Record.* When ordered by America First chapters and others, these materials were sent in franked, sealed envelopes that could then be mailed without postage. Thousands of pieces of noninterventionist literature were distributed in this way.[14]

One proposal backed by Senator Nye and America First in 1941 was a food relief plan for distressed peoples in occupied Europe. Former President Herbert Hoover, who had played the key role in Belgian relief in World War I, was the leading proponent of the idea. An America First Committee principle stated: "Humanitarian aid is the duty of a strong free country at peace. With proper safeguard for the distribution of supplies, we should feed and clothe the suffering and the needy people of England, the other democracies, and the occupied countries." Nye was one of thirty-seven senators who sponsored a resolution in June 1941 urging the administration to extend "relief for all stricken and hungry countries, beginning with Belgium," but under rigid safeguards "so that no military advantage whatever may accrue to the civilian populations or armed forces of the invading nations." Genuine humanitarian considerations were undoubtedly involved. But it was probably more than a coincidence that Nye and most of the other senators sponsoring the resolution were from agricultural states that would benefit from the operation of the plan, while relatively few senators from urban areas endorsed it. Secretary of State Cordell Hull said that Germany was responsible for the hardships in Europe, and the Foreign Relations Committee never acted on the resolution.[15]

The original Selective Service Act of 1940 had prohibited sending selectees outside the Western Hemisphere and provided that they should serve only twelve months. In the summer of 1941 the Roosevelt administration wanted both of these limitations removed. America

First opposed authorizing the President to send selectees outside the hemisphere, but the national organization did not take an official stand on extension of service beyond one year. Nye flatly opposed both changes. He said that authorizing use of selectees overseas would be like looking for a fight. He denied that defeat of draft extension would cripple the armed forces, pointing out that as men were released after their year of service they would be replaced by new draftees. He considered the proposals an "indication of plans to put American troops onto the European battlefields." The administration did not press for authority to send selectees outside the hemisphere after it learned that it did not have the necessary votes in Congress. Extension of the draft was certain of approval in the Senate, but the vote was expected to be close in the House of Representatives. Nye and other noninterventionist senators actively opposed the proposal partly to encourage opposition to it in the House. As expected, it carried easily in the Senate, but was adopted by a margin of only one vote in the House of Representatives. The close vote encouraged noninterventionists to hope that stepped-up efforts might enable them to win their battle against intervention.[16]

Senator Nye repeatedly urged more democratic control of foreign affairs and denounced war propaganda for misleading the public by arousing emotions. Implicit in Nye's whole public career (both in his editorial crusades as a newspaperman and in his speaking tours as a senator) was a faith in the capacity of "the people" (if not corrupted by the propaganda of "selfish interests") to decide wisely on public issues. Nye did not favor formulation and control of public policies by an "elite"—unless by a reverse pattern of reasoning his attitudes toward the farmer and "the common man" be portrayed as elitist. He never abandoned his faith in democracy even when he was rejected later at the polls by the voters of North Dakota.

His speaking tours on foreign policy issues reflected this faith, as did his support for the Senate version of the Ludlow amendment. He expressed this same attitude when he led America First in supporting the principle of advisory referendums on foreign policy in 1941. The leading pacifist groups, including the Keep America Out of War Congress, the National Council for the Prevention of War, and the Women's International League for Peace and Freedom, had urged an advisory referendum on war or peace long before America First took up the idea. Nye, too, had long favored variations of the idea, and immediately after enactment of lend-lease he advocated such a referendum. He had the encouragement and cooperation of pacifist leaders, and Ruth Sarles, head of the America First research bureau in Washington, assisted Nye on the project. As a result, on March 27, Senators Nye, Wheeler, Capper, LaFollette, D. Worth Clark of Idaho, and Shipstead (all progressives from agricultural states) sponsored a concurrent resolution calling for an advisory referendum on the question of whether Congress "under existing conditions" should "approve the use of land, naval, and air forces outside the Western Hemisphere." It was referred to the Foreign Relations Committee. In June, Congressmen James Oliver of Maine and Knute Hill of Washington introduced a similar resolution in the House of Representatives. At the same time America First endorsed the idea and urged its local chapters to bombard Congress with letters supporting an advisory referendum. America First leaders did not have any real expectation that Congress would adopt the resolution, but they hoped it might dramatize noninterventionist sentiment and put the interventionists on the defensive. Nye and the others who favored an advisory referendum were confident that the American people would vote overwhelmingly against entry into the war. The resolution was opposed by Secretary of State Cordell Hull and was never reported out of committee or voted on in either house.[17]

Somewhat paradoxically, Nye's faith in "the people" was combined with a fear of war propaganda and propagandists. At the America First rally he addressed during the lend-lease debate, he denounced the "Hate and fear planted by the Lippmanns and the Lawrences and the Winchells and the Dorothy Thompsons and the Roosevelts and the Knoxes and the Stimsons and the Morgenthaus." "The most dangerous column a nation of free people" had ever known, he charged, was "that column of American columnists feeding us daily with the fear of what is going to be our lot if Britain loses this war." In May he introduced a resolution calling for a Senate investigation of public opinion polls on the ground that their conclusions about public attitudes on foreign affairs did not seem accurate – at least on the basis of his own observations.[18]

On August 1, 1941, Nye and Bennett Champ Clark stirred up a hornet's nest on this issue when they proposed a Senate investigation of interventionist propaganda in motion pictures and radio broadcasts.

This was not a wholly new idea for Nye. A dozen years earlier he had introduced a bill for the establishment of government-owned radio stations to assure equal opportunity for all political parties to reach voters. In 1934 he urged creation of a federal motion picture commission to inspect and classify movies. He also wanted to prevent restraints on free competition in the industry.[19] Since in the 1930's the motion picture industry produced many anti-war pictures, the senator's proposals were not inspired by foreign policy considerations. By 1940–41, however, the industry was overwhelmingly interventionist. The Roosevelt administration and interventionist pressure groups had won enthusiastic support in Hollywood. America First, on the other hand, found it almost impossible to get support there and encountered vigorous opposition from leading figures in the industry.[20]

The Nye-Clark resolution, drafted largely by John T. Flynn, called motion pictures and radio "the most potent instruments of communication of ideas." It wanted the Senate Committee on Interstate Commerce "or any duly authorized subcommittee" to make a thorough investigation of propaganda in motion pictures and radio broadcasts designed "to influence public sentiment in the direction of participation by the United States in the present European war."[21]

The same day the resolution was introduced, Senator Nye delivered a major radio address in St. Louis on the subject. He contended that motion picture companies had "become the most gigantic engines of propaganda in existence to rouse the war fever in America and plunge this Nation to her destruction." He named the men and companies that he believed dominated the industry: "There is Harry and Jack Cohn, of Columbia Pictures. There is Louis B. Mayer, of Metro-Goldwyn-Mayer. There is George J. Schaefer, of R. K. O. There is Barney Balaban and Adolph Zukor, of Paramount. There is Joseph Schenck and Daryl Zanuck, of Twentieth Century Fox, dominated by Chase National Bank. There is Murray Silverstone, of United Artists, and the great Sam Goldwyn, of Samuel Goldwyn, Inc. There are the three Warner brothers, Arthur Loew, Nicholas Schenck, Sam Katz, and David Bernstein, of Loew's Inc." In part he blamed Hollywood's interventionism on "refugees" and British actors working there. But he emphasized particularly economic explanations, charging that foreign markets (especially in Britain and the Commonwealth countries) accounted for most of the profits realized from American motion pictures.

In his opinion the industry had "a stake of millions of dollars annually in Britain winning this war." He also suspected that the federal government encouraged production of interventionist films. War propaganda in motion pictures was particularly "insidious," he said, because viewers expected to be entertained and were not on guard against it.[22]

The preparations for the proposed investigation were almost wholly in noninterventionist hands. Nye and Clark, of course, were leading isolationists. John T. Flynn, using funds provided by one of the larger contributors to America First, directed most of the research for the probe. The chairman of the Senate Interstate Commerce Committee was Burton K. Wheeler, a leading speaker for America First. The subcommittee he appointed to "consider" the Nye-Clark resolution was headed by D. Worth Clark, a Democrat from Idaho who spoke frequently at America First meetings, and included Homer T. Bone, Democrat from Washington; Charles W. Tobey, Republican from New Hampshire; C. Wayland Brooks, Republican from Illinois; and Ernest W. McFarland, Democrat from Arizona, all active noninterventionists except McFarland. The America First Committee supported the whole project, which was launched in an atmosphere of much noninterventionist enthusiasm.[23]

It was promptly subjected to an avalanche of criticism and abuse, however, on the grounds that it, and Senator Nye, were anti-Semitic. Nye was accustomed to criticism. He could give it and he could take it. Many simply criticized what they considered inadequacies in Nye's foreign policy views. They charged that he underestimated the Axis threat to American security, the importance of Britain to the United States, and the difficulties in dealing with victorious Fascist dictators, and exaggerated the capacity of the United States to defend itself in the Western Hemisphere. But in 1941 the criticisms often were pitched on much lower levels. The controversy between isolationists and interventionists became an unusually rugged affair with no holds barred on either side. The senator and other noninterventionists became increasingly aggressive and virulent in their attacks on Roosevelt, the interventionists, and the British; the attacks upon Nye, America First, and isolationists became equally extreme and even more effective. The name-calling, mud-slinging, and smearing on both sides made the foreign policy debate a poor place for the sensitive or fainthearted. Each side welcomed almost any chance to discredit the opposition. And the proposed investigation of motion pictures and radio provided an opportunity that interventionists seized quickly and effectively.[24]

Nye and Clark were convinced that motion pictures constituted a dangerous source of war propaganda, and they were inspired by sincere noninterventionist convictions when they called for the investigation. But Jews controlled considerably more than half of the motion picture industry,[25] and most of the persons named by Nye in his address on August 1 were of the Jewish faith. Interventionists immediately charged that the probe was anti-Semitic and even Fascist. Nye, of course, denied the charge, insisting that his only objective was to prevent American intervention in foreign war. He said that the men he named in his address did in fact control the motion picture industry and that it was only a coincidence that most of them were Jews. It was their war propaganda he objected to, he said, not their religion.[26]

The senator had had a good record on religious toleration. In 1933 he helped raise funds for the George Washington Memorial Forest in Palestine. In that same year he addressed the National Jewish Congress and denounced "the lash being used to persecute" Jews in Germany. He urged educating people "away from prejudices," and advocated reducing the economic distress that fanned "dormant fires of hate." In 1938 while opposing admission of large numbers of Jewish refugees from Germany, he criticized Nazi persecution of Jews. In August 1940 he denounced anti-Semites and emphasized that there was "no such thing as a united Jewry, or a united body of international Jews."[27]

The senator had, to be sure, lauded Father Charles E. Coughlin's monetary proposals in the 1930's, although he did not endorse the anti-Semitism that infected the Coughlin movement late in the decade. In 1939 when he refused to approve a petition supporting Jewish interests in Palestine, he based his refusal on a determination "to avoid mixing in any foreign entanglement which might later prove embarrassing." In February 1941, he addressed a "No Foreign Wars" rally in Detroit under the auspices of Gerald L. K. Smith's "Committee of 1,000,000," and later spoke at a noninterventionist meeting in Jamaica, New York, even after Rabbi Stephen Wise charged that its sponsors were anti-Semitic. Reprints of Nye's noninterventionist addresses were sold to explicitly anti-Semitic organizations that shared his foreign policy views.[28]

It is impossible to know with certainty the inner thoughts and feelings of any person, but the senator repeatedly rejected and denounced anti-Semitism. Neither in public addresses nor in private correspondence that is available did he embrace the doctrines of professional anti-Semites. Nye poured out his feelings on the issue in a letter to William Stern, a Jewish banker in Fargo, North Dakota. Stern was a personal friend of the senator's and had been best man at Nye's marriage in 1940. In this long letter he denied that either he or America First was anti-Semitic and complained that there was "an over-sensitiveness on the part of some Jewish people" on the issue. He pointed out that Jews had been prominent in interventionist pressure groups but rarely supported America First. He conceded that because of Nazi persecution the interventionist inclinations of Jews were "quite understandable," and he suspected that if he were Jewish he would probably "feel as they do about giving larger help to Britain." He insisted, further, that in his St. Louis speech he had criticized "the motion picture industry, not Jews." He wrote: "It would have made no difference to me if the gentlemen named had all been Methodists or Catholics or Mormons. I am distinctly uninterested in their religions. I am emphatically interested in what they are doing in a way which might contribute to our entry into another futile foreign war."[29]

He elaborated his views on September 9, when he testified before Senator D. Worth Clark's subcommittee. Nye contended that those charging him with anti-Semitism were doing so "to cover the tracks of those who have been pushing our country on the way to war with their propaganda." He said that however much his patience might be tried by such attacks he remained, "as yet at least" — this phrase disturbed his critics — "bitterly opposed to the injection of anti-Semitism as a cause or issue in our American thinking and acting." He said that despite their understandable desire to end Nazi persecution, Americans of Jewish faith would better serve their interests by supporting noninterventionist foreign policies. If America entered the war Jews might be blamed and suffer persecution. In that event, Nye promised to battle against racial prejudice and anti-Semitism.

In his testimony he complained that motion pictures portrayed "a lot of glory for war" and exaggerated "the glory of certain peoples engaged in that war." He said the movies were "not revealing the sons of mothers writhing in agony in trench, in mud, on barbed wire, amid scenes of battle or sons of mothers living legless, or lungless, or brainless, or sightless in hospitals. These alleged propaganda pictures are not showing us the disemboweled sons of fathers and mothers, lying upon fields of battle."[30]

The motion picture industry did not go on the defensive in the face of the proposed investigation. Wendell L. Willkie (now a vigorous interventionist) served as its legal counsel, and with enthusiastic backing from the industry and from interventionists, he made the hearings more embarrassing for the noninterventionists than for the movie industry. The charge that the probe was anti-Semitic probably encouraged an early adjournment of the hearings in the fall of 1941. They were never renewed. The subcommittee made no report before Pearl Harbor, and on December 18, recommended that "in the interest of national unity" it would not be desirable to submit a detailed report on its findings. The Nye-Clark resolution and the subcommittee hearings did not change the character of motion pictures, but they did identify America First and Senator Nye with anti-Semitism in the minds of many Americans.[31]

In the midst of the furor surrounding the proposed investigation, Charles A. Lindbergh, on September 11, 1941, told an America First audience in Des Moines, Iowa, that the "three most important groups who have been pressing this country toward war are the British, the Jewish and the Roosevelt administration." This statement provoked impassioned attacks on Lindbergh and America First. While some America First leaders criticized the speech, the committee did not repudiate him, and Senator Nye came to his defense.[32] The senator said he had recently spent an afternoon with Lindbergh and concluded that there was "not a shred of anti-semitism in a single fibre of the being of this courageous American." Nye agreed "that the Jewish people are a large factor in our movement toward war." He denounced interventionists in general and Willkie in particular for "dragging this red herring" into the foreign policy debate to blind the people to the "real issues" and to weaken the noninterventionist movement.[33]

The charges of anti-Semitism were disturbing enough, but interventionists expanded their indictment by alleging that Nye, Lindbergh, and America First were pro-German and even pro-Nazi. Nye braved such charges when he addressed a banquet of the Steuben Society of America in New York City, on September 20. The Steuben Society was not pro-Nazi or anti-Semitic, but it was composed of German-

Americans and it supported noninterventionist foreign policies. Before addressing the group Nye conferred with its national leader and obtained written assurances that the society did not believe in "Fascism, Nazi-ism, Communism or British Imperialism, or any other foreign ism." In his address he urged the society not to confuse the words "unity" and "loyalty." He insisted that until Congress actually declared war one could be wholly loyal to America without uniting behind the administration's interventionist policies. He said that he detested communism, fascism, and naziism and lauded the Steuben Society for rejecting "bundism." By the fall of 1941, however, even his appearance at this respectable German-American gathering elicited criticisms from interventionists.[34]

Senator Nye received numerous plaudits and thousands of letters commending him for his noninterventionist efforts. He was lauded for bringing "reason and sane thinking into the minds of a now confused public," for his "noble stand against the forces that strive to involve our nation in a foreign war," for his "knowledge and wisdom," and for his "courageous fight in preserving America." The appeal "For God's sake keep up your great work so we can save our boys" was echoed in countless letters, cards, and earnest personal encounters.[35]

Nevertheless, in 1941 Nye was criticized more than he was praised. An organization called "Friends of Democracy, Inc.," published and distributed a pamphlet that called America First "a transmission belt by means of which the apostles of Nazism are spreading their antidemocratic ideas into millions of American homes!" It included a statement by Nye criticizing British imperialism that was printed next to a similar statement by Hitler, and suggested that "Hitler's arguments" were being transmitted "through the mouths of America First Committee spokesmen." In September the interventionist New York newspaper *PM* vehemently attacked Nye's anti-Semitism. A periodical called *Film Bulletin* said Nye's criticisms of the motion picture industry were blows "below the belt in the best storm trooper fashion." Fight for Freedom, Inc., of New York City sponsored advertisements in several North Dakota newspapers which announced that there was growing resentment against the senator in North Dakota protesting his "appearance at a Steuben Society meeting in New York City and his injection of the racial issue into the debate on foreign policy." The Council against Intolerance in America charged Lindbergh and Nye with "injecting the poison of racial and religious prejudice into American life" and with "seeking to destroy liberty through bigotry."[36] Abusive letters accused the senator of "making a shoddy imitation of Hitler's Goebbels," and called him "a German Nazi parading as an American citizen." One writer said Nye had "the same murderous instincts as your friend Hitler possesses," and recommended that "Men like you and Hitler should be wiped off the face of the earth." On October 1, the Reverend Henry W. Hobson, head of Fight for Freedom, in a telegram called Nye "the fuehrer from North Dakota" and said he spoke for Berlin but not for North Dakota. A writer from Brooklyn told America First headquarters that Lindbergh, Wheeler, and Nye were "arch traitors who would have sold out their country."[37]

The interventionist tactic before Pearl Harbor of associating noninterventionists with Nazi Hitler was essentially the same as the effort made after World War II by conservative nationalists to discredit liberal internationalists by associating them with Communist Russia. The method was very successful against Nye in 1941. In the minds and emotions of many people then and since, Nye was little better than a Fascist. His reputation never recovered from the beating he received; the stereotype created by his assailants contributed to his defeat three years later. The portrait was, however, a gross distortion regardless of what one thinks of his views on foreign policy. Nye never abandoned his faith in democracy or his abhorrence of totalitarianism. He never embraced the militarism implicit in fascism. And he did not endorse the doctrines of professional anti-Semites. Insofar as he became critical of Jews, his attitude was due largely to what he considered unfair attacks on him by Jews and by interventionists who professed to be defending Jews.

Anti-Semitism and criticism of Jews are found in both urban and rural populations. But such hostility as Nye felt against Jewish interventionists was in tune with his agrarian background, just as criticism of Baptists and Methodists is socially acceptable in many urban circles. Most people of Jewish faith lived in cities, particularly in the Northeast. Indeed, it is at least conceivable that the interventionist inclinations of American Jews were nourished by their urban social and economic status as well as by their hostility to Hitler following persecution of their fellow religionists. In any event, Nye's criticism of Jewish influences on foreign affairs was as consistent with his agrarian frame of reference as was his earlier hostility to international bankers and munitions makers and his newly developing opposition to urban labor and unions.

The avalanche of abuse that engulfed Senator Nye and America First in the last half of 1941 diverted public attention somewhat from the steps the administration was taking to aid Britain short of war. These moves essentially followed the general pattern predicted by Nye earlier. Revision of the Neutrality Act in 1939 enabled Britain and her allies to buy American goods (including munitions) on a cash-and-carry basis. The financial problems resulting from the "cash" requirement were resolved with the enactment of lend-lease in March 1941. Then much of the foreign policy controversy from March through November focused on the "carry" provision. Lend-lease materials would not help Britain's struggle against the Axis if they were sent to the bottom of the ocean by German submarines. The Roosevelt administration considered, proposed, and implemented various actions to assure delivery of the goods to Britain. In every instance the administration had to contend with noninterventionist opposition from Senator Nye and the America First Committee.

As early as November 1939, Nye had objected unsuccessfully to the transfer of American merchant ships to Panamanian registry. He charged that this was simply a device for by-passing the "carry" requirement and enabling the vessels to enter combat areas.[38] In the spring of 1941 Secretary of War Henry L. Stimson and other interventionists urged the President to use the American navy to escort British convoys. Nye and America First, convinced that such a move would put the United States into the European war, quoted Roosevelt's earlier statement that convoys would mean shooting and "shooting comes awfully close to war." Senator Charles W. Tobey of New Hampshire carried the main burden of the opposition in the Senate to convoying, but he had the backing and cooperation of Nye and America First. Tobey's joint resolution to prohibit use of the American navy to escort convoys to belligerents was, of course, opposed by the administration. The resolution was never voted on in the Senate—partly because noninterventionist leaders (including Nye) feared the administration might interpret a vote against the anti-convoy measure as permission to convoy. The aid-short-of-war formula had an irresistible attraction, and by May 1941 public opinion polls available to the President showed that over half of the American people favored convoys. Nevertheless, the White House mail on the issue, partly reflecting the efforts by Nye, Wheeler, and others in America First, overwhelmingly opposed the use of the American navy for convoys to England. The strength of the opposition persuaded Roosevelt not to seek positive congressional authorization for convoys. Instead, he ordered naval "patrols" designed to render maximum aid, short of actual convoys, to Britain against Axis raiders in the western Atlantic. In April 1941, American warships began to trail German submarines outside the war zones and report their positions to British convoys and airplanes.[39]

In that same month the United States occupied Greenland and declared that the Red Sea was no longer a war zone. Nye denounced these moves as "steps toward war." He cited data from the United States Maritime Commission to demonstrate that the British and the Roosevelt administration exaggerated the magnitude of shipping losses due to submarines. The senator, of course, objected to American occupation of Iceland in July.[40]

No ship flying the American flag was sunk by a German submarine until May 21, 1941. On that date the *Robin Moor*, an American merchant vessel, was sent to the bottom of the South Atlantic with no loss of life. After he was convinced of German responsibility for the sinking, Nye said it was no more than might have been expected. The administration's policies in the Atlantic, he charged, were "engraved invitations for this sort of incident." To prevent such sinkings he urged the United States to "abandon any assertion of freedom of the seas . . . and adopt a mind-our-own business policy." If this reduced or stopped aid to Britain, he thought that was "Britain's worry."[41]

Nye told newsmen in April that the British Empire was doomed anyway and that its destruction should not cause the United States "undue alarm." He thought a Nazi victory in Europe would require the United States to devote more resources to defense, but if American defense efforts were limited to the Western Hemisphere it might not be terribly costly. In May he told an America First audience that "even with our help, England cannot win the war if winning the war means driving the Germans back across the continent."[42]

In the last half of 1941 the number of shooting incidents involving Americans on the high seas increased. On August 17, 1941, the *Sessa*, an American-owned merchant ship under Panamanian registry, was torpedoed near Iceland. One of the casualties was an American. On September 4, 1941, the *Greer*, an American destroyer, was missed by two torpedoes fired by a German submarine. The *Steel Seafarer*, flying the American flag, was bombed in the Red Sea on September 5, with no loss of life. Three other American-owned ships flying the flag of Panama were torpedoed later in September and on October 17, the *Kearny*, an American destroyer, was torpedoed near Iceland with the loss of eleven lives.[43]

On September 11, 1941, President Roosevelt delivered his famous "shoot-on-sight" address. He accused the German submarine of firing on the *Greer* first "without warning, and with deliberate design to sink her." He labeled this "piracy legally and morally." He denounced the sinking of the *Sessa* and the *Steel Seafarer* and warned of Hitler's plan to control the oceans. The President ordered the American navy to attack German and Italian ships wherever found within the patrol zones without waiting for them to attack first.[44]

This speech was delivered on the same night as Lindbergh's controversial address in Des Moines, and while the noninterventionists were facing attacks on all sides. Nevertheless, Nye, Lindbergh, Wheeler, and America First fought against the administration's policy. They did not condone the sinking of American ships but insisted that the attacks were being provoked by the United States. Nye called Roosevelt's speech "a declaration of war by presidential proclamation." He said this action was taken "at a time when the Congress of the United States would vote by large margins against a declaration of war." If the President believed there were just grounds for hostilities, Nye thought he should forthrightly ask Congress to declare war. The senator charged that the *Greer* and *Kearny* incidents were "very largely of our own making and our own inviting. We cannot order our ships to shoot to destroy the vessels of certain belligerent nations and hope at the same time that the ships of those nations are not going to seek to destroy our ships." He, of course, pointed out that the *Greer* had been trailing the German submarine for several hours before the submarine finally fired upon its pursuer.[45]

On October 9, 1941, President Roosevelt urged Congress to repeal the "crippling provisions" of the Neutrality Act. Specifically, he wanted to permit arming of American merchant ships and to allow them to enter combat zones. This meant repeal of the "carry" part of cash-and-carry. The President said the changes would "not leave the United States any less neutral than we are today, but will make it possible for us to defend the Americas far more successfully, and to give aid far more effectively against the tremendous forces now marching toward conquest of the world."[46]

The America First Committee threw its whole weight against the President's proposals and so did Gerald P. Nye. The senator's major address in the Senate on October 29 against revision of the Neutrality Act dramatized his shift of emphasis since he had presided over the Munitions Investigating Committee in the mid-1930's. He denied that anyone had "ever argued that the production of munitions was anything more than a small part of the causes that enter into the making of war." Instead, in this speech he centered his attack on the President for leading the nation to the brink of war. He said he despised "Hitler and Hitlerism," but he urged Americans to control their hatred and "not entirely abandon our solicitude for the welfare of our own country." Defending himself and other noninterventionists, he declared: "We have been condemned as pro-Hitler and pro-Nazi, as British haters and as plotters of a Fascist regime for the United States. Our sin, of course, was that we wanted and still want to keep America out of war." He charged that if merchant ships were armed and permitted to enter war zones it was "pretty certain that we will be involved in the European war," for arming merchant ships "invites attack" and "strips them of whatever possible immunity they might enjoy as unarmed craft." The America First Committee never worked harder than it did in its efforts to block revision of the Neutrality Act in the fall of 1941.[47]

As usual, however, Nye and America First were beaten and the short-of-war formula prevailed. According to public opinion polls, a majority of Americans was persuaded of the wisdom of the President's proposals. Both houses of Congress adopted the revisions and they became law with Roosevelt's signature on November 17, 1941. Nye was among the thirty-seven senators who voted nay. Most of those who voted with him had substantial rural constituencies.[48]

This defeat discouraged noninterventionists, but they had demonstrated rather striking strength even in defeat. The vote against the administration in both houses of Congress was larger than it had been on lend-lease. A shift of ten votes in the House of Representatives would have meant defeat for the administration on the issue. Several legislators who had generally supported Roosevelt on foreign affairs broke from the fold this time. Senator Nye summed up his view of the vote in a letter to the leader of an America First chapter on November 22: "The Administration and the War Party are finding no comfort on the vote on the neutrality bill. The vote demonstrates how utterly lacking is anything resembling unity on this business of going further into the war, and this is a time to be fighting back at every turn to the end that there can be continued demonstration of the overwhelming sentiment of the people." In this same letter, the senator pointed to the dangers of getting into the war by way of the Far East. He warned that there was "larger animosity in the United States toward Japan than there is toward even Germany." He feared that America might enter the war "through the back door of Japan with Britain negotiating the plays for us."[49]

Like America First and most of the rest of the nation, Senator Nye had concentrated his attention on Europe much more than on Asia. Nevertheless, he opposed American war against Japan before Pearl Harbor just as he opposed war against Germany and Italy. From the beginning of the Sino-Japanese war in 1937 he had favored banning shipment of arms to the Asiatic belligerents and he criticized Roosevelt's failure to invoke the neutrality law in the Far East. As negotiations between the United States and Japan neared the breaking point late in November 1941, Nye said he believed the United States could end the Asiatic war satisfactorily if it would "help Japan save her face" by making relatively minor concessions in China. He thought that if Japan were permitted to maintain two or three air bases in China and if the United States resumed trade with her, Japan might agree to end the fighting and withdraw her troops from China. He was convinced, however, that the Roosevelt administration really did not want to settle the Far Eastern crisis peacefully.[50]

Sunday, December 7, 1941, witnessed Japanese bombs and torpedoes shattering American naval and military installations at Pearl Harbor, Hawaii, and in the Philippines. It also saw Senator Gerald P. Nye in Pittsburgh, Pennsylvania, addressing the last public rally of the America First Committee. Even while the senator spoke, flames roared in the debris left by the surprise air attack on Pearl Harbor, and medical personnel scurried about tending the wounds of those who survived. Approximately two thousand American victims—members of the armed forces and civilians—were already dead.

Contemporary newspapers and subsequent historical accounts of the Pittsburgh meeting implied that the sponsors and principal speaker at the America First rally on December 7 were little better than traitors. One Pittsburgh newspaper called it the most "disgraceful meeting in all Pittsburgh's history," and said that those who participated "should forever hang their heads in shame."[51] There is no denying, of course, that Senator Nye and the America First Committee vigorously opposed intervention up to the very moment they learned reliably that Japan had attacked. But their noninterventionist crusade was not inconsistent with loyalty and democracy—assuming that foreign policy is a legitimate object for public discussion and debate.

Under the able leadership of attorney John B. Gordon, the America First chapter in Pittsburgh was one of the finest in the country. A sizable audience crowded into Soldiers and Sailors Memorial Hall for the afternoon meeting on December 7. The program scheduled talks by former state Senator C. Hale Sipe and Irene Castle McLaughlin, but Nye was the main speaker. A few minutes before three o'clock, while they were preparing to go on the stage, a reporter told them that the White House had announced a Japanese attack on Hawaii and the Philippines. At that moment Japanese planes were actually in the midst of the last of their three assaults on Hawaii. Nye and the others, however, were skeptical of the report. Recalling the *Greer* incident, when the first reports were misleading, Nye suspected a hoax or at least exaggeration in the report. In any event, he told the reporter that he would need more reliable information. He then put the incident out of his mind, and, with the others, began the meeting.

While Sipe was speaking, an army colonel in civilian clothes rose in the audience to ask if they knew that Japan had attacked. Those around him noisily drowned out the colonel and he was ejected from the hall. From Nye's position on the platform the disturbance appeared like others that hecklers had caused at previous meetings he had addressed. In the hubbub he could not hear the colonel's statements and did not know his identity. Nye began his own address shortly before five o'clock, approximately two hours after the meeting began and nearly an hour and a half after the last Japanese planes had left Pearl Harbor. As he was commenting on the role of British propaganda in

American relations with Japan, a reporter laid a note before him that said: "The Japanese Imperial Government in Tokyo at 4 P.M. announced a state of war against the United States and Great Britain." He was taken aback and flustered by the information and still not certain whether to believe it or not. He finished the point he was making at the moment by citing England's Liddell Hart to the effect that the only way the United States might be brought into another British war would be through war with Japan. He then told the audience of the attack and quickly closed his remarks and the meeting – still somewhat doubtful about the truth of the report.[52]

After the meeting the senator told newsmen: "If Japan attacked, there is nothing left for Congress to do but declare war." He added that this did not change his "non-interventionist opinions materially on the European war." This was essentially the approach taken by the national leadership of the America First Committee.[53] Nye voted for the declaration of war against Japan on December 8, and, after Germany and Italy declared war, he joined in voting for war against these European members of the Axis.

On December 9, Senator Nye wrote that as a result of the Japanese attack there was "but one thing an American can want to do – win the war and win it with the greatest possible dispatch and decisiveness. It is not time to quibble over what might have been done or how we got where we are. We know only that the enemy chose to make war against us. To give our Commander in Chief unqualified and unprejudicial backing in his prosecution of the war is an obligation which I shall gladly fulfill. Differences over matters of foreign policy up to this hour are abandoned and unity should be accorded in every particular."[54]

He and other noninterventionists in Congress, though urging support for the war effort, hoped that America First would be kept intact to function on different foreign policy issues later. General Wood, Stuart, and most other committee leaders disagreed. On December 11, 1941, the America First national committee voted to dissolve the organization and promised its full support to the war effort. At the same time, it maintained that its "principles were right" and that if they had been followed "war could have been avoided."[55] Stuart wrote Nye a month after Pearl Harbor that "If the Government had followed the policy we advocated, war could have been avoided and America and the world would have benefited." Of the America First battle against intervention Stuart wrote that the country had "rarely witnessed a finer fight for a better cause." He also lauded Nye: "Your contribution was immense. Without your tireless energy and your wonderful courage, such a great fight could not have been made. I often marvelled at your stamina and the way in which you carried on night after night, meeting after meeting. Your rallies were political phenomena. It will be a long time before this country sees such crowds or such genuine enthusiasm."[56]

Like America First officers, Nye remained unrepentant. He viewed American involvement in the war as proof of his contention that aid short of war would lead to war. He was confident that history would demonstrate the wisdom of the noninterventionist position. The America First crusade, he wrote, was "the outstanding demonstration of public opinion known in all American history." He believed that if it had not been for "the extreme folly of the Japanese on December 7th, this effort would have accomplished that thing for which we were fighting, namely, freedom from involvement in these wars by the United States." He predicted that soon there would "be terrific demand for rebirth of the America First Committee" to oppose the Union Now movement. "While everyone wants to contribute to the winning of the war," he wrote, "it doesn't necessarily follow that everyone is willing to see our country sold out while engaged in winning the war." In a speech in Fargo, North Dakota in August 1942, the senator summed up his reaction to American involvement in the war: "The task before us is tremendous. We do not properly meet the challenge by raking through words of what might have been. I opposed the Roosevelt administration of foreign policy step by step because I believed it was leading us to war. I believed then, and I still believe, that the alternative policy which I and many others advocated was sounder and that it would have kept us out of this war. That alternate policy was in no sense or degree a policy of non-defense, however much some sources may try to confuse the question of non-intervention with the question of defense. But all of that need not now concern us. At war as we are, so far as I am concerned, there will be support of every measure and every purpose advanced which has as its purpose the successful prosecution of our great cause in the winning of the war." Speaking in the Senate in November 1943, he defied "any American to find a more honorable lot of Americans than those who gave their names to the founding of the America First movement."[57]

Nye's evaluation of the noninterventionist movement was not shared by most Americans during and after World War II. The Japanese attack on Pearl Harbor destroyed the America First Committee and virtually ended Senator Gerald P. Nye's public career. More than three years remained of his Senate term, but the causes he represented on both domestic and foreign affairs were beaten and discredited. His desperate efforts later to win vindication at the polls were doomed to defeat. He was not quite forty-nine years old when war came to America on December 7, still a young man in comparison with most of his Senate colleagues. But the world had passed him by and he faced the scorn, abuse, and political oblivion commonly reserved for leaders of lost causes.

12

The Lonely Road

PEARL HARBOR abruptly changed Gerald P. Nye's pattern of living. There were no colorful and exciting America First rallies to address any more. Speakers' bureaus found little demand for his services. The press paid scant attention to him, except to criticize occasionally. Under Tom Connally's leadership the Foreign Relations Committee was not a receptive forum. Of course, neither the President nor the Department of State sought or accepted his advice. Though he continued to work hard, for the first time in years he had leisure. He supervised the construction and landscaping of his comfortable new home in Chevy Chase, Maryland. Marguerite guided him to membership and activity in the Lutheran Church. She thought he looked younger as he relaxed from the strains of the battle against intervention and enjoyed the children that were born to their marriage.[1] But he knew that he faced a fight for his political life in the elections of 1944. And a combination of personal conviction and political necessity drove the North Dakota senator to continue his efforts on behalf of the farmer during World War II.

True to his promises, Nye supported the war effort and generally refrained from emphasizing "what-might-have-been" — though he never abandoned his conviction that the noninterventionists had been right. During the year following Pearl Harbor he rarely commented on foreign affairs publicly except to urge unity for winning the war. Still, he was not prepared to remain silent while others implemented domestic and foreign policy innovations under the guise of winning the war.

Specifically, on the domestic scene he was unwilling to sacrifice the farmer or freedom of expression on the altar of the war effort. And he insisted that support for winning the war did not require his silence on plans for postwar peace settlements. He charged that "globalists" took advantage of the war to discredit isolationism and to urge "policing the world" when the conflagration came to an end.

Nye spoke vigorously on behalf of the farmer in the war economy. In January 1942, he was the only senator to vote against the price control bill. He complained that it did not control "the largest item entering into the price structure – namely, wages." He contended that the bill would hurt farmers and "deny them a chance to hold their own in the mighty battle raging to determine who shall control the economy of America." He objected that it put "the farmer in a price strait jacket, without doing the same with all other factors entering into price making." Nye cited statistics to demonstrate the high profits enjoyed by industrial corporations and ridiculed criticism of "the profiteering farmer." Agriculture would not add to inflation, he said, "until that farm one-quarter of our population is receiving something approximating one-quarter of the national income." After the price control law was adopted, he feared that administration officials might try to prevent farm prices from reaching the levels permitted by the law. He continued his crusade on this issue in the fall of 1942 when he supported the Thomas-Hatch amendment to include farm labor costs in determining parity prices. Nye's general attitude was shared by the American Farm Bureau Federation and the Grange (relatively conservative farm organizations), but it was opposed by the more liberal Farmers' Union. The Farmers' Union was the strongest of the three organizations among North Dakota farmers, but after spending several weeks among his constituents Nye was convinced that they did not share the Farmers' Union and administration views on price controls. He said North Dakota farmers were "greatly angered by the fact that industrial wage earners were not brought under stabilization rules as was the farmer." He insisted that the high food prices were due largely to increased industrial wages, farm labor costs, and profits of middlemen handling and processing farm products. In his opinion the farmer got "virtually none of the increased prices being collected from the consumer."[2]

During the war the senator unsuccessfully opposed lowering the draft age to eighteen, expanding the armed forces to 11,000,000 men, and drafting married men with children born before Pearl Harbor. One of the factors affecting his thinking on the manpower problem was the need for farm workers. In a moving address to the Senate on October 26, 1942, in which he opposed lowering the draft age from twenty to eighteen as unnecessary, he said: "Until last Friday morning I was quite uncertain in my own mind as to how I should vote on the proposal to draft 18- and 19-year-olds. . . . But while I pondered these things on my drive from home to my office on that morning I found myself slowed by traffic at the intersection adjacent to one of our Washington high schools. I was struck by what was before my eyes in a way that caused me to pull up to the curb, shut off my motor, and watch this surge of boys and girls on their way to school. . . . One cannot see in these youngsters what is needed in the military ranks these days. . . . I have a son in the 18- and 19-year category. He is giving his second year to college work and Naval Reserve training. I expect him to be ready any day to give an account of himself in the naval ranks. I am proud of what he is making himself ready to do. But he has an advantage not known to these boys I watched going to high school the other morning. I hark back to the days when that boy of mine was approaching and turning the 18-year marker, and shudder when I think he might then have been forced into the military ranks. Then something within me cries out: 'Do not do to the 18-year-old sons of other parents that which you would not willingly do to your own.'" In his speech Nye neglected to mention that his second son was 18 years old. Actually, both of his sons from his first marriage served in the American armed forces.[3]

In opposing enlargement of the military forces to 11,000,000 men in the spring of 1943, the senator protested that military manpower would be ineffective without "plenty of food," and warned that this expansion would draw farm workers who were needed to produce essential food supplies. American military strategy must be cut "from the cloth at hand, even though it means possibility of a longer war but surer victory." He urged deferments for all remaining farm workers and returning to the farms many who were already in the armed forces. He also said farm workers should be honored for "doing a service quite as important as any other service being performed in the winning of the war." And, finally, he recommended paying higher farm wages so workers would be less attracted by the high pay and short hours in urban industry. He denied that farmers were being selfish: there were "positive limitations upon them and upon their machines and upon their lands."[4]

In the fall of 1943 Nye supported an amendment proposed by Senator Burton K. Wheeler that would have continued military exemptions for pre-Pearl Harbor fathers. Nye insisted that there was much wasted manpower in industry and government, and that these men should be drafted before fathers. Again he emphasized the "shortage of farm manpower."[5] In each of these controversies Nye was, as usual, on the losing side.

He also battled for the farmer on other issues during the war. In line with his growing conservatism, Nye complained in 1943 that the Farm Security Administration had contributed "to collectivism and regimentation" and had caused some "to abandon initiative and resign themselves to a dependence upon government." But he believed the "faults and failures" of the F.S.A. were "insignificant by comparison with the great services rendered deserving individuals," and urged that it be continued. The senator also supported crop insurance and appropriations for soil conservation.[6] In each of these instances he was undoubtedly inspired partly by the desire to win votes from North Dakota farmers in the election of 1944, as well as by a genuine concern for the welfare of American farmers.

In July 1942, Nye supported study of postwar problems – particularly economic problems – and from December 1942 onward he often spoke on the subject of postwar peace settlements. He repeatedly warned against utopian expectations and urged Americans to be "realistic." He pointed out that the United States could not shape the postwar world in its own image, that America's allies (including the Soviet Union) would have much to say about peace terms, that her allies would be moved by self-interest, that their attitudes would be different from those of the United States, and that the United States ought to look out for its own interests and sovereignty. He objected to efforts by internationalists to "smear" the isolationists and their foreign policy views while the latter were prevented by the war environment from freely expressing their views. On December 2, 1942, Nye said: "I am sure we approach the exceedingly difficult problem before us most wisely when we devote ourselves in this hour to the saving of our Nation and the saving of our way for our own at least, just as other nations allied with us are saving, so far as they can, their nations and their ways for their own. If we will pursue such a course, however selfish it might appear to be, we shall find that in the end we have contributed far more to the well-being of the world than would be the case were we to go on shutting our eyes to reality and painting wonderful and grandiose pictures of a future that just will not, and cannot, prevail." Early in 1943, he wrote: "To take care of our own first will be the Number One American obligation." He denied that such an approach would be "narrow isolation." Nye did not believe that the United States "should take no interest whatever in the affairs of our neighbors, to abandon all trade and all social intercourse." Nevertheless, the destiny of this nation is not "either to reform or to police the world. . . . Americans must have first consideration by the American government, never left-overs. To pursue any other course is not noble in purpose, but on the contrary short-sighted reasoning."[7]

He recognized that "no one would have a larger right to dictate terms of peace than would Russia, in the light of the extreme sacrifices which the Russians have made in this war." American policies toward Russia, according to Nye, "would depend upon the kind of co-operation that was prevalent at the peace table. It should be on a perfectly normal basis, as it is with other countries irrespective of the differences in ideologies." He did not "have any fear of a Russian Communistic bogey as long as we maintain our own sovereignty."[8]

In a major address in Chicago on May 20, 1943, Nye tried to arouse Republicans to "come out of their corner swinging and clubbing" against "globalism." He contended that their silence since Pearl Harbor did not mean that critics of the administration's foreign policies had abandoned their opinions or theories. "It meant only that we were ready to concede that the Nation had its hands full with the winning of the war." He objected to efforts by "interventionists who have now become globalists" to destroy "all who had tied to the noninterventionist cause" and lamented the "element of terror" that caused Americans "to stand in fear that if they dare to speak what is in their minds there will be retaliations of serious consequences." As long as there was the "threat that unanswered global thinking is going to accomplish its purpose for want of opposition" Nye urged Republicans to speak up on foreign affairs. The senator hinted at the agrarian base for his objections to internationalism when he said that since "agricultural production is largely the only thing that many nations have to offer us on a trade basis, it seems to follow that a first essential in global thinking is that American agricultural interests will be completely surrendered, put on the block, so to speak." He predicted that Americans would "never tolerate any such policing job as globalists seem to contemplate," and warned that "this international policeman isn't going to be the most popular fellow on earth."[9] Despite his appeal, however, in the urbanized America of World War II neither national political party shaped its foreign policy positions to conform to the wishes of Middle West and Great Plains agriculture as interpreted by Gerald P. Nye.

On November 5, 1943, the Senate adopted the Connally resolution urging that "the United States, acting through its constitutional processes, join with free and sovereign nations in the establishment and maintenance of international authority with power to prevent aggression and to preserve the peace of the world." The resolution explicitly endorsed American cooperation "with its comrades-in-arms in securing a just and honorable peace." It recognized the necessity for establishing "at the earliest practicable date a general international organization, based on the principle of the sovereign equality of all peace-loving states . . . for the maintenance of international peace and security." Senator Nye was one of the eighty-five senators who voted for the resolution. President Roosevelt was delighted with the resolution, but in his letter congratulating Senator Connally he asked facetiously: "But why, oh, why did you let Nye vote for it?"[10] Was Nye embracing internationalism?

The North Dakota senator had explained his views in a long address to the Senate on November 4. He pointed out that the Connally resolution also stated that "any treaty made to effect the purposes of this resolution . . . shall be made only by and with the advice and consent of the Senate of the United States, provided two-thirds of the Senators present concur." Nye said this paragraph might "ultimately prove to be the only part of the resolution that has real and direct meaning and force." He defended America First and isolationists in his address and denied that isolationism was dead. He was skeptical about postwar cooperation by America's allies, including Britain and Russia. But he was "not ready to close the door to whatever might develop in the way of a chance to win and enjoy the cooperation of the world. . . . If we can not isolate ourselves from these experiences of war, then at least we might try, with the hope of preventing them, cooperative undertakings with the rest of the world, but undertakings, mind you, that do not create some super-super-government that shall dictate our own destiny, undertakings that will not jeopardize our own sovereignty as a nation, undertakings of a purely cooperative nature that will not challenge our identity or our sovereignty any more than does cooperation with our allies in winning the war." Senator Nye then summarized his recommendations for the peace settlement. They included an emphasis on self-determination and anti-imperialism reminiscent of some of Woodrow Wilson's views on peace a quarter of a century earlier. "To me a just and honorable peace is one that will go further than merely to punish the leaders who have been responsible for the catastrophe that is upon the world. . . . To me, a just and honorable peace means one . . . that will –

"Undertake seriously the elimination of the factors making for war;

"Afford liberation and sovereignty to all the peoples of the world wanting it;

"Deny to the victors the acquisition of any territory without the consent of the people of the proposed newly acquired territory;

"Give every nation equal access to commercial lanes and ports;

"Withhold aid and encouragement from imperialistic and world domination ambitions;

"Deny undertakings to preserve unpopular monarchies or their reign over others;

"Restore and maintain the identity and sovereignty of lands like Finland, Poland, Norway, and Sweden, unless the peoples of those lands find an association or a partitioning to their own liking;

"Refrain from undertaking to force a race of people to live forever under foreign masters.

"Deny extraterritorial rights for any power in other lands unwilling voluntarily to grant such rights.

"Refrain from subjecting any people or their resources to the profit or advantage of any other power."

The tenor of these recommendations was determined partly by the senator's continuing hostility to the British Empire and British imperialism. He warned that a peace settlement "which ignores the cardinal causes for war is a peace which could not possibly be successfully maintained with a league of nations, a world court, an international police force, a union now with Britain, and a superworld government all combined." He said Americans must never "subscribe to the theory that any definite order that grows out of this war must be or can be forever maintained." Though he voted for the Connally resolution, he thought the United States might eventually "be more definitely and overwhelmingly isolationist in its determination to avoid involvement in more foreign wars than has ever been true in the past."[11]

It was virtually inevitable that noninterventionists would be criticized and smeared in the emotional and intolerant war atmosphere. The fact that some noninterventionists (including Nye) faced elections during the war increased the certainty of attacks. Nye's forthrightness stripped him of any immunity that timorousness and obsequiousness might have provided.

The Washington federal grand jury investigation of foreign propaganda and the indictments and trials growing out of that investigation from 1941 through 1944 were aimed at foreign agents in the United States. They also provided, however, convenient weapons for discrediting noninterventionists who had no ties or sympathies with the Axis powers or for fascism. The tactics used against loyal noninterventionists during World War II were somewhat similar to those used by McCarthyites against loyal internationalists in the Cold War after World War II. In both cases patriotic Americans were assailed on the grounds that their foreign policy proposals were similar to those urged by agents of a hated and feared totalitarian adversary in world affairs. In both cases they were denounced for being too "soft" and "unrealistic" in their attitudes toward the evil and dangerous enemy. And in both cases they were attacked either as conscious agents of the enemy (Nazi Germany in World War II and Communist Russia in the Cold War) or as "dupes" being "used" by the ruthless leaders of those countries.

For example, Ralph Townsend, a former American Foreign Service officer and writer, was convicted in 1942 on charges of failing to register as a Japanese agent. Townsend wrote Nye that the charges against him were based on books by Townsend that were bought and circulated in the United States by foreigners in 1938–39. He insisted in his letter that he was moved exclusively by patriotic noninterventionist motives and not by any desire to aid any foreign government or cause, and he invited the senator to write a letter on his behalf if he was convinced that Townsend was "a sincere American and a defender of our form of traditional representative government." As a result, on April 11, 1942, Nye, who had known him for some time, wrote the probation officer of the federal District Court in Washington, stating that he had never heard Townsend "make any reference or drop any remark that was not in complete keeping with everything that could be expected of a loyal and patriotic American citizen" and was convinced that before Pearl Harbor Townsend was moved simply by the desire to keep the United States out of war. He discounted "any conclusions which would reflect upon Mr. Townsend or his Americanism."[12] The senator's endorsement of Townsend was roughly comparable to Dean Acheson's later reference to Alger Hiss. Both Nye and Acheson suffered for their candor and courage.

In January 1943 the grand jury indicted thirty-three persons and one corporation on charges of conspiracy to undermine the morale of the armed forces. A few days after the indictment Drew Pearson in his column in the *Washington Post* wrote that Nye had "been active behind the scenes in aiding the appeal of George Sylvester Viereck, convicted for failure to register as a foreign agent and now indicted for sedition." The senator took the floor of the Senate the next day and called Pearson's charge "a deceitful falsehood" and "a lie." Nye said he had talked with Viereck "only once or twice" and that Viereck had been "abruptly rebuffed" when he had last visited the senator's office more than a year before Pearl Harbor. (Nye was undoubtedly referring to the unsuccessful effort by Viereck in the spring of 1940 to purchase six or seven million copies of a speech by the senator on "Propaganda in the Next War.") Nye also denied charges by Pearson and others that he had inserted Nazi propaganda in the *Congressional Record* to be sent out later under his frank. (There had been an acknowledged misuse of his frank by the Steuben Society involving a speech by the head of the society, but Nye insisted the speech was explicitly anti-Nazi.) Pearson also charged Nye and Wheeler with working "feverishly for an investigation of the Justice Department and its prosecution of Hitler's stooges in the United States of America," partly to prevent disclosures affecting them. Nye admitted that he had "grave doubts concerning the merit of the charges" growing out of the sedition investigation and he worried about "the issue of personal liberty." "I would hold no brief in any quarter for anyone guilty of contributing to the undermining of our defense, or undermining the morale of our armed forces, but I submit that with respect to the indictments returned against most of those involved in this alleged conspiracy they are no more guilty of conspiracy than I am."[13] For many of his critics this statement tended to confirm their suspicions of Nye rather than clear those under indictment.

In February 1943, O. John Rogge became special assistant to Attorney General Francis Biddle with responsibility for the sedition case. Under his direction a more narrow superseding indictment was returned in January 1944. It attempted to distinguish between sincere isolationists and foreign agents by charging the thirty persons named with conspiracy "with officials of the Government of the German Reich and leaders and members of said Nazi Party." This was the only sedition indictment that was brought to trial and it ended in a mistrial when the judge died in November 1944. The case was never retried, but Rogge continued his probe and submitted a report to the Justice Department in September 1946. He listed congressmen who, he said, collaborated with Viereck in his German-financed propaganda activities. Nye was not on this list. Rogge also named twenty that he said Viereck "used" in his propaganda activities before Pearl Harbor. Nye was included on this second list. According to Rogge, at least 95,000 copies of reprints from the *Congressional Record* were purchased and distributed under Nye's frank by Viereck through Prescott Dennett's Make Europe Pay War Debts Committee. Over half of these consisted of two speeches by Nye. Others who were used by Viereck, according to Rogge, included Usher L. Burdick, D. Worth Clark, Robert M. LaFollette, Jr., Robert R. Reynolds, Henrik Shipstead, and Burton K. Wheeler. Rogge concluded that there was "no evidence that any of those Viereck used had knowledge of the fact."[14]

Five days before the North Dakota primary election on June 27, 1944, in which Nye was a candidate for renomination, the senator's name was again publicized in connection with the sedition trial. A defense attorney charged in an affidavit filed in the United States District Court that Nye had failed to keep a promise to provide evidence for the defense. Nye promptly wrote a blistering letter to Attorney General Biddle denouncing the Justice Department for "using the pending trials as a stage from which to insinuate that I might be involved in incriminating relations with those now being tried on charges of sedition and to so stage the proceedings as to bring me under a cloud of suspicion just five days before a primary election in which I am seeking renomination to the Senate." He complained of "an uncanny timing" by the Justice Department "in developing a smear against me at the very hour when the voters of North Dakota are asked to pass judgment upon my candidacy for re-election to the senate." Nye complained that none of the sedition indictments was brought to trial until 1944 – an election year. A month after the primary, Judge Edward G. Eicher denied the defense attorney's plea that Nye be summoned for questioning on the ground that the senator said he had no evidence bearing on the sedition charges.[15]

Nye had cause to worry about the political effects of this episode. He had been one of the most successful campaigners in North Dakota's political history. But he had neglected to keep his political fences in repair and he faced impressive opposition in his efforts to win renomination and re-election in 1944. William Langer, Nye's old political adversary, was spearheading the attack. After election to the United States Senate in 1940, Langer had been subjected to a lengthy probe by the Senate Committee on Privileges and Elections, which sustained charges of "moral turpitude" against him, although he was finally seated anyway. Nye officially remained neutral on the issue, but he obviously had no sympathy for Langer and did not raise a hand to defend him.[16] In any event, Langer and his Nonpartisan League vigorously opposed Nye and supported Usher Burdick for senator in the Republican primary on June 27.

Willkie Republicans (largely urban and internationalist) supported attorney Lynn U. Stambaugh of Fargo in the primary. By splitting the non-League Republican votes Stambaugh's candidacy conceivably could help beat Nye and nominate Burdick. But Stambaugh insisted he was in the race to win, and the fact that he had been national commander of the American Legion in 1941–42 probably won support for him from many former servicemen. Many who had voted for Nye in 1938 only because he opposed Langer now shifted to Stambaugh. In his aggressive campaign Stambaugh denounced the senator's isolationism and charged that Nye "would wrap the United States in a blanket and deny it relationships with any other nation. He hates the British and has contempt for our Allies. He believes the Nazis should be permitted to continue their government of hatred and oppression if they want to. He thinks the United States invited attack by our enemies. Had he succeeded in his efforts to defeat lend-lease, selective service, neutrality revision and other last minute preparedness measures, German and Jap forces might be converging on Bismarck tonight."[17] Those in the Farmers' Union who supported President Roosevelt generally opposed Nye. Substantial opposition to the senator originated outside the state – particularly from the Roosevelt administration, internationalists, and the East. Nye had won labor support in his earlier campaigns, but in 1944 organized labor actively opposed him, particularly the C.I.O. Political Action Committee. During the campaign the opposition distributed in the state many copies of John Roy Carlson's book *Under Cover*, a sensational account of "the Nazi Underworld of America" which was highly critical of Nye and other isolationists. The senator's divorce hurt him politically among Scandinavians, Roman Catholics, and others. Some suspected that he was so busy being a "big shot" out East that he no longer had much time for the "little fellow" in North Dakota. Nye had virtually no chance for victory if his opponents united behind a single candidate. In the June primary, however, they unintentionally opened the door for his renomination by scattering their support among Burdick, Stambaugh, and the Democratic candidate, John Moses.[18]

Moreover, Nye campaigned aggressively and won substantial support in and out of North Dakota. The Republican state convention endorsed his candidacy. He aroused sympathy by charging that "Willkieites," "New Dealers," Jews, Communists, and eastern newspapers and columnists were out to "get" him. In effect, he asked whether the people of North Dakota were going to choose their own senator or let easterners determine their choice. Like his opponents, however, Nye won support outside the state. Edwin S. Webster, Jr., of New York City, a former member of the America First national committee, helped solicit funds for the senator's campaign. Numerous former America Firsters and isolationists contributed funds for his campaign, including, among others, General Robert E. Wood, William H. Regnery, Sterling Morton, and J. M. Patterson. On June 18, the *Chicago Sunday Tribune* prominently carried a laudatory feature article by Walter Trohan on "Gerald Nye—Man of Courage." This article was widely distributed in North Dakota.[19]

In his campaign Nye, as usual, emphasized his efforts on behalf of agriculture. He also pointed out that if Republicans gained a majority in the Senate, he would become chairman of the important Appropriations Committee. In striking contrast to the progressive tenor of his previous campaigns, Nye's speeches in 1944 were distinctly conservative. For example, in a radio address on April 18, he said he believed:

"That we cannot lift up the wage-earner by pulling down the wage-payer;

"That we cannot further the brotherhood of man by inciting class hatred and jealousy;

"That we cannot build character and courage by destroying rewards for initiative and independence;

"That government cannot permanently help men by doing for them what they could do for themselves; and

"That we've got a great job to be done after winning this war if we are going to save the kind of America our forefathers gave us."

In an address on May 24, he denounced "bureaucratic control operating from Washington upon everyone," and objected to "the planning and scheming to impair the rights of farmers and businesses." Though he had criticized Calvin Coolidge's reactionary policies earlier, in 1944 Nye said that "the time has come to force more of business into government and less government in business."[20]

Perhaps the senator was simply growing conservative as he got older, but there were other possible explanations as well. He may have believed that with Langer Nonpartisans supporting Burdick, Willkie Republicans backing Stambaugh, and Roosevelt New Dealers backing Stambaugh or Moses, his only chance for victory lay with the conservatives. Further, there was a rather widely held belief that wartime prosperity had made the North Dakota electorate less receptive to agrarian radicalism than it had been earlier.[21] Partly, however, his conservatism was a product of the basic attitudes he had held all along: Like Jefferson, Nye had never really believed in continuous, positive participation by the federal government in the economy, particularly when that government was controlled by urban America. Except for emergencies, he wanted to do little more than end the special privileges of urban groups so the farmer would have equal economic opportunities.[22] His opposition to government favoritism to urban business put Nye in the radical or progressive camp earlier. By the 1940's, however, his views helped move him into accord with conservatives who denounced favoritism to urban labor, particularly by the executive branch of the government. He did not plan it that way, but these patterns of thought and action drove him into the arms of conservatives — partly because he had nowhere else to go. And he gradually made their "folklore" his own.

Nye won renomination on June 27, but it was an extremely close contest. He received less than thirty-four per cent of the votes cast for senator in the Republican primary and carried only twenty-one of the state's fifty-three counties. Stambaugh ran an impressive second—only 972 votes behind Nye—and carried most of the more prosperous and urbanized Red River Valley of eastern North Dakota. Burdick led in the Nonpartisan strongholds of western North Dakota and his followers complained that heavy rains on election day prevented many of his rural supporters from reaching the polls. Nye's greatest strength was in the central part of the state.[23]

The campaign before the general election in the fall was fought as bitterly as the primary had been. One pamphlet opposing his re-election warned that Nye offered "continued obstruction and isolationism, hate and prejudice—the certain way to WORLD WAR III." It charged that "Consciously or unconsciously, Senator Nye has done a lot for the Nazis and their sympathizers in this country."[24] By 1944 the term "isolationist" had become such a derogatory label that it hurt Nye even among people who had shared completely his specific views on foreign policy.[25] To protect himself against the damning charge of isolationism, in October 1944 he summarized his foreign policy views in terms somewhat out of tune with much he had advocated earlier:

"(1) When this war is won we must maintain a military force sufficiently strong to defend ourselves against any possible combination of forces that might be brought against us or against which we might possibly find ourselves having to contend.

"(2) We must find the way to curb and hold in check those nations which prove themselves to be threats to the peace of the world, aggressor nations.

"(3) We must invite the cooperation of other nations and give to other nations our cooperation to the end that jointly we can maintain the peace of the world; remembering always that there must be more than America concerned if there is to be cooperation; remembering, too, that so long as our Constitution remains with its present provisions, there can be no power given any cooperative international body or force that would let that body or force take our country to war without Constitutional consent."[26]

Nye also continued the conservative economic emphasis in his campaign.

In a two-man contest with the Democratic candidate, John Moses, Nye might have been re-elected on November 7. But Stambaugh ran for the Senate as an independent in the fall, thus splitting the Republican vote between himself and Nye. This obviously pleased (and may have been encouraged by) the Democrats. Langer's followers in the League backed Stambaugh in their determination to beat Nye. Stambaugh and Nye combined got more votes than Moses, but the Democrat got more votes than either of them individually and was elected. Stambaugh carried only one county, but he took enough votes away from Nye to help beat the senator. In the final tabulation Moses got 95,102 votes to 69,530 for Nye and 44,596 for Stambaugh. When the Democratic administration appointed the Republican Stambaugh to a post on the board of the Export-Import Bank in 1945, many interpreted this as his political reward for helping defeat Nye. Stunned by this repudiation by the voters, Senator Nye returned to Washington and prepared to move out of his office.[27]

On December 19, 1944, his fifty-second birthday, Nye delivered his "Farewell Address" to the Senate. In this long speech he complained of the methods that were used to defeat him. "Propaganda sponsored by irresponsible forces outside the State, plus propaganda the source and responsibility for which could not be traced to anyone, had many honest North Dakotans convinced that if I was not actually on Hitler's pay roll, I should have been." He devoted most of his talk, however, to a discussion of American foreign relations during his nearly two decades in the Senate and to his views on the future. He said he brought "to the Senate a prejudice against involvement in another foreign war, against the terrible economic condition which the last war had brought to our country, particularly the agricultural sections of our country . . . against the propaganda which had been fed to us during that war. . . . [and] against the countries which had found us so easy in and after the last war." He proudly traced his role in the munitions investigation, in the enactment of the neutrality laws, and in opposing American involvement in World War II. He complained that under Roosevelt's leadership the neutrality laws were "whittled away, until there was no neutrality law left." He lamented that isolationism was identified with "everything that was bad, terrible, un-American, and indecent. The attempt to keep our country out of war had become an unforgivable sin."

Nye emphasized that the United States "must prosecute the war to a victorious end, and we must have these allies with us if we are to do it. No other way is open to us." Whether he would go back to the original neutrality legislation was, he said, "an academic question, for we never can go back. History moves on; what has been done cannot be undone." But he ridiculed the idea that World War II would be "followed by the golden age for America, when there will be 60,000,000 jobs paying the same kind of wages that the war has brought; when everyone will be protected against all the perils of sickness, old age, unemployment, and death; when we will find the seven seas with our American ships crammed with American goods to flood every export market." He said "wars are not followed by great advances," but rather "by let-downs." He thought postwar disillusionment might lead to a new wave of isolationism in the United States.

The senator said the preliminary plans for a world organization that had been drafted at Dumbarton Oaks called for "a military alliance between the great powers to rule the world by means of regional understandings." He said it would only "work against the little fellows" and was "not expected to work against any state that might be a real threat to world peace." He predicted that after World War II Europe would be "divided into two great blocs, a Russian bloc and a British bloc" and that there would be "another attempt to rule Europe by the old balance-of-power system — a system that has never worked in the past, but has always led at last to war." He believed Russia would "build up her bloc and run her bloc with complete ruthlessness in the gaining of her ends" and that Britain would do the same thing. Where would the United States fit in? He was convinced, "knowing the power of British propaganda, that within 20 years from now — perhaps within 10 years — we shall be told that we must go into another European war to keep Russia from seizing control of the world." (A *New York Times* editorial interpreted this statement as a "reckless" prediction that could "serve no other purpose than sow mutual suspicions and division.") In Asia Nye saw "a revived imperialism . . . with the United States held responsible by all Asiatics for having wiped out the one nonwhite empire and having restored all the white, European empires." Nye also predicted: "Our people will be staggering under a debt that may even go beyond the $300,000,000,000 mark. We shall have a standing army that will fill this capital with an officer cast with insatiable appetites for power and that will militarize the whole educational system of our Nation. We shall have the most enormous Navy that ever covered the seas, with all the enormous costs that such a Navy entails.

We shall be involved in every quarrel between our partners in this new world order, for they will know how necessary it is for them to be able to count on using our power to win their quarrels, and there will be other quarrels directly between them and us. And when World War No. 3 comes along, as it certainly will as a result of this attempt to divide up Europe and the Near and Middle East between Russia and England, we will be in it from the first day." He said the only way the United States could keep out of World War III was "By minding our own business. By keeping out of these entangling alliances. By developing our own markets here in this hemisphere and devoting our strength honestly and solely to the defense of our own territory."

He denied that American prosperity was dependent upon protection of "our commercial interests all over the globe." Appropriately, he cited in laudatory terms historian Charles A. Beard's book *The Open Door at Home* to support the contention that "it is quite possible for us to find, in our own domestic market and in the trade which we can easily develop on friendly terms with our neighbors in this hemisphere, all the prosperity we need for our American people."

Senator Nye believed it was "the Congress of the United States, and particularly the Senate of the United States which stands between these plain people and a future of misery and ruin, through being dragged into one world war after another." He did not repudiate or apologize for any part of his career in the Senate. He closed his speech with an expression of "faith in the good purpose and patriotic spirit of the plain people of America and in what I have come to know, during 20 years, to be the purpose and spirit of the Senate. . . ."[28]

His address got little attention in the press. The *New York Times* buried it in a half-column on page sixteen and, in a short editorial, declared that the only "good effect" of the talk was that it would "prove to the complete satisfaction of the voters of North Dakota how right they were when they rejected him in the last election."[29]

Less than a month later Nye's career as a United States senator formally ended, more than nineteen years after he was first appointed to that post. Still hurt by his defeat, he was uncertain what course to follow next. Gerald L. K. Smith wanted to arrange a lucrative speaking tour for him, presumably to attack "the Internationalists and the Jews." Nye declined the proposal with thanks. He wrote Smith: "I couldn't in good conscience undertake a hand in any stirring of class strife against the Jewish race or any other race of people. I don't suppose anyone has larger cause than I have to entertain a spirit of revengefulness against the Jews for they were a pretty solid lot in opposition to me in my late campaign. But, somehow, I'm not so much blaming them as I am blaming the New Deal propagandists who, in my estimation, are wholly responsible for stirring up the prejudices of the Jews and must stand responsible for the day when retaliation will doubtless be undertaken. Incidentally, that day will find me doing whatever I can to bring America back to sanity, with highest regard afforded the cause of freedom of worship."[30] Instead, there were three alternatives that Nye seriously considered: becoming a newspaper editor again, trying a political comeback, and going into business. He explored the first alternative, unsuccessfully attempted the second, and eventually followed the third.

His thoughts first turned to editing a magazine or newspaper in North Dakota, possibly as a steppingstone to an eventual political comeback. There were rumors about various newspapers he might purchase including the *Bismarck Tribune*. But the *Tribune* was not for sale and no other comparable possibility materialized.[31]

Running for the Senate again became a possibility after an unusual sequence of events. His successor, John Moses, died soon after taking office. The new Republican governor of North Dakota, Fred Aandahl, had authority to appoint a successor until a special election was held. Aandahl had run for office on the same ticket with Nye and had had friendly relations with him. Moses, too, had had Nye's support when he ran for governor in 1938. Nye was passed over, however, and the governor appointed Milton R. Young to the Senate. Ironically, Young had been Nye's campaign manager in 1944. Nye's comment was: "This is a hell of a way to run an election campaign for the United States Senate. The candidate is licked and his campaign manager gets the job."[32]

If he ran for the Senate in 1946, there were two alternatives available. He could oppose William Langer for Republican nomination for the long term in the primary on June 25. Or he could run in the special election for the unexpired portion of Moses' term. The special election was on the same day as the primary. Nye's political position, damaged seriously by the abuse and beating he had taken in 1944, was made more difficult because he did not have the backing of any major state political organization. In 1944 he had won votes from some anti-

Langer Nonpartisans and from many in the Republican Organizing Committee (R.O.C.), but he did not control either organization. Endorsement by or affiliation with either in 1946 would have hurt him in the other camp. Furthermore, he could not get the official endorsement of either group. Langer controlled most of the Nonpartisan wing of the Republican party, and in March 1946 Governor Aandahl's appointee, Milton R. Young, was endorsed for the short term by the Republican state convention controlled by the R.O.C. Nye had neglected his political "homework" in North Dakota after his re-election in 1938 and he paid for that neglect in 1944–46.[33]

Probably because he considered Langer a more formidable adversary, Nye finally decided to run as a Republican in the independent column against Young for the short term. He had no difficulty getting enough signatures on petitions to place his name on the ballot. The League did not endorse Nye, but neither did it endorse anyone else for the short term and he believed this would make it possible for him to win the votes of many Nonpartisans. In addition to Young, Nye was opposed in the election by P. W. Lanier, Jr., a Fargo Democrat and Marine combat veteran. As in 1944, groups and individuals from outside North Dakota opposed Nye, but he also got outside support, particularly from former America Firsters.[34]

As always, Nye campaigned aggressively and he enjoyed the battle. As he had throughout his political career, he emphasized his interest in the welfare of farmers, declaring that "there can be no real and lasting prosperity unless there is a prosperous, progressive agricultural industry at the base." While he urged continuation of the Farm Security Administration and gave qualified support to certain price controls and to the Missouri Valley Authority, he spoke in essentially conservative terms on most economic and political issues. He boasted that for years he had "fought against the enlarging controls the federal government was fastening on our economy," and warned that government controls "could result in destruction of the American way." Paraphrasing Jefferson, he said he had "always entertained the conviction that the government that governs least is the government that governs best." At the same time, however, he favored legislation to put more restrictions on labor and strikes.[35]

In foreign affairs he defended his noninterventionist course before Pearl Harbor, but he said that in 1946 there was "no alternative to the

United Nations as an instrument through which to strive to attain and keep peace." He urged doing "everything within our power" to make the United Nations successful. He also believed the United States must keep itself "as powerful as any other nation, ready to meet any emergency which could arise." In the nuclear era, however, he believed peacetime conscription was not necessary. He opposed loans by the United States government to Britain, France, or Russia.[36]

In personal letters written during the campaign Nye was extremely optimistic about his chances for victory. But on June 25, 1946, he came in a very weak third behind Young and Lanier.[37] With this defeat Gerald P. Nye's political career in North Dakota ended forever.

His careers as newspaper editor and as politician behind him, Nye set out in new directions as a businessman. One of his committee assignments in the Senate during the war had been concerned with the preservation and disposal of rapidly accumulating government records and files. The feasibility of microfilming to conserve space was one of the alternatives his committee explored. His activities on this committee led him to organize a business in Washington, D.C., that he headed from 1946 to 1960. It was first called Records Engineering, Incorporated, and later was reorganized as Nye-Mahan Associates, management consultants. Nye's firm advised business and government units on the reorganization, microfilming, and disposing of their files and records. As other larger corporations saw the possibilities of the service, they added it to their activities and provided Nye with growing competition. His business finally folded in the winter of 1959–60.[38] In April 1960 the former senator was appointed special assistant in the Federal Housing Administration. He thoroughly enjoyed his responsibilities as he traveled all over the country promoting housing programs for elderly people.[39]

During the postwar years he also found leisure to spend with his family, caring for his flowers and garden, and in church activities. He played golf regularly twice a week at the Burning Tree Country Club, visited with old friends from North Dakota and Wisconsin, and reminisced with associates from his Senate days.[40]

Nye rarely gave speeches after his political defeats, but he remained interested in public issues. He liked the Taft-Hartley Act of 1947 with its controls on labor unions, and he also approved the Landrum-Griffin Labor Act of 1959. While his affection for the farmer survived during the generation he had lived in comfortable suburban Chevy Chase, agricultural matters faded into the background in his thinking. He opposed permanent subsidies to agriculture and generally approved the farm programs of President Eisenhower's conservative secretary of agriculture, Ezra Taft Benson.[41]

Nye approved of Senator Joseph McCarthy's attacks on Communists in America. Since McCarthy used the guilt by association technique in attacking fellow travelers and liberals, one might have expected Nye to be critical of methods comparable to those used against him in a different context earlier. This was not Nye's reaction, however. Instead, he felt McCarthy's probes were being subjected to the same sort of smears that Nye had suffered in his investigations earlier and at the hands of many of the same people. Consequently, Nye sympathized with the Wisconsin senator and felt he was doing a job that needed to be done. Nye, who had earlier denounced charges of "bolshevism" leveled against him and his fellow agrarian radicals, was alarmed about the power of Communists in the government, schools, and churches of America. In this connection, Nye liked the vigor with which the Roman Catholic Church opposed communism. He conceded that McCarthy sometimes spoke before he had the facts, went on "fishing expeditions" in his questioning, and was blunt, but Nye believed he was on the right track.[42]

In the Cold War Nye considered Communist Russia a terrible threat to American peace and security and believed the United States should be tough in dealing with the Soviet Union. He regretted that the United States had not simply sat back and let Communist Russia and Nazi Germany fight it out by themselves in World War II. Nye could have viewed such a war between the two dictatorships without misgivings. Sometimes he almost felt that the United States might as well get the fighting with Russia over—on the Berlin issue, for example. But he realized the terrible consequences of any such war and wanted the United States to remain militarily powerful until some binding agreement with the Soviet Union might become possible. In 1953 he favored international control of atomic materials. As he had earlier, Nye considered air power more essential to American security than naval or land forces.[43]

His views on the Cold War were interventionist in contrast to his noninterventionist attitudes toward Axis aggression twenty years earlier. Nye regretted American involvement in World War II, but believed it was not possible to withdraw from world politics once the United States was caught up in the Cold War. America must, he said, keep its "international commitments wherever on this globe there develops a stomach ache that might lead to more war. We've no other choice." He hoped, however, that the United States no longer believed it could make "all parts of the world over in our own American image." He was highly critical of most American foreign aid programs. In 1959 he joined with others (including Sterling Morton, Samuel B. Pettengill, Burton K. Wheeler, Robert E. Wood, Clarence Manion, and other former isolationists) in a Citizens Foreign Aid Committee opposing large foreign aid programs.[44]

He thought President Dwight D. Eisenhower's policies were not sufficiently different from those urged by the Democratic opposition. He much preferred Richard Nixon to John F. Kennedy, but was fearful of Nixon's tendency to take the expedient course. He looked with favor on Senator Barry Goldwater's conservative nationalist movement within the Republican party.[45]

While Nye never abandoned his faith in democracy and in the capacity of the people, when adequately informed, to decide wisely on public issues, he was disturbed by what he considered the failure of the press and news media to provide full and balanced information on which the people could intelligently base their decisions.[46]

As Nye reached the age of seventy he mellowed, was more relaxed, and less aggressive. He retained his earnestness, generosity, and graciousness. Though ailments common to his age obliged him to undergo repeated surgery, he continued to look younger than his years. He still hated Franklin D. Roosevelt and the policies he represented, but he was not cynical or disillusioned. He was able to recognize with equanimity that the interests and ideas he represented had faded in the memories of most — that he was not even a familiar name to young men and women who were born or reared in World War II and the Cold War, eras vastly different from those that produced him and different from those he had hoped to preserve.

EPILOGUE

❧ 13 ❧

The Decline of Agrarian Isolationism

THE MIDDLE DECADES of the twentieth century (World War II and the Cold War) witnessed a striking decline of isolationism in American attitudes and policies on foreign affairs. The explanations for the decline may be found in both international and domestic developments. In varying degree both categories of explanations are related to the rise of the city and to the accompanying growth of industry.

On the world scene, part of the explanation may be traced to changing power relationships that undermined the comfortable security enjoyed by the United States earlier. The balance of power that prevailed in the middle of the nineteenth century, and the dominant position of the British, helped provide a relatively stable, secure, and peaceful environment in world affairs in which the United States could accomplish its continental territorial expansion with relatively little serious opposition, and could even suffer the agonies of civil war without destroying its national security. At the same time Americans persuaded themselves that the Monroe Doctrine, unilateralism, and nonintervention in European affairs—that is, isolationism—were responsible for the security they enjoyed.

The gradual erosion of the relative power of Great Britain and France, plus emergence of the increasingly powerful and ambitious states of Germany in Europe and Japan in Asia, upset the old nineteenth-century security arrangements. World Wars I and II not only dramatized the deteriorating power positions of Britain and France, but (despite the ultimate victories of the Allies) contributed to their decline (and to the lessening of American national security). After World War II, the weakened condition of Britain and France, the temporary destruction of German and Japanese power, and the emergence of Communist Russia as a major world power presented the American people with an extremely disturbing international situation in which the security taken for granted in the nineteenth century was gone.

This alarming state of affairs was made literally terrifying in the middle of the twentieth century by the destructive capabilities of weapons created by science and industry and commanded by the leading adversaries in the Cold War. Science and technology not only perfected nuclear and thermonuclear weapons capable of mutilating and destroying the human race, but also developed intercontinental bombers, submarines, and missiles capable of delivering bombs and warheads to targets anywhere on the earth.

The first atomic bomb was not set off until after Gerald P. Nye had been retired from public life in 1945, and intercontinental bombers (even with conventional bombs) were not a practical reality during his years in the United States Senate. Nevertheless, the changes in power relationships on the world scene and the destructive capabilities of weapons were developing rapidly during his later public career. The disintegration of the old balance of power, the rise of aggressive challenges from the Central Powers, from the Axis, and later from the Communist bloc, the creation of fantastically destructive weapons—all these developments on the world scene combined to threaten American national security and to help defeat American isolationism.

The role of urbanization in all this must not be overlooked. Urban commerce, industry, science, technology, and finance helped make the world community more closely knit and interdependent. Germany, Japan, and Russia developed the power to challenge old security arrangements as they built urban industrial economies. Both fascism and communism were, in part, totalitarian efforts to grapple with opportunities and problems created or intensified by industrialization. And the unbelievable destructiveness of modern war would be impossible without the complex weapons manufactured, financed, and delivered by urban industrial economies.

The developments and conditions that doomed isolationism were not, however, limited to other parts of the world. In addition to external influences, forces within the United States that helped shape

American reactions to world affairs also contributed to the decline of isolationist attitudes. For example, isolationism attracted less support from German-Americans in the Cold War with the Soviet Union than it won when Germany was America's principal adversary. Samuel Lubell illustrated this point when he asked: "If Germany is overrun, will the German-Americans vote 'isolationist'?" He concluded: "The same turn of the strategic wheel which has left America the only great power in the world other than Russia has robbed 'isolationism' of its ethnic base."[1]

Although Roman Catholics in the United States tended to be more isolationist than the population as a whole before World War II, the vigorous opposition of Catholicism to communism probably encourages interventionist rather than noninterventionist attitudes toward the Cold War. For that matter, communism's explicit atheism and materialism make it easy for leaders and members of most religious groups to add their weight to the struggle against the Soviet bloc. The Calvinist clergyman who said that the Cold War was fundamentally a struggle between Christianity and atheism probably was voicing a view shared by millions.

Furthermore, myriad developments in transportation, communication, and education have reduced the significance of geographic remoteness and inadequate information as bases for isolationism. Television has been added to such older media as books, newspapers, radio, and motion pictures. For all its trivia, television brings into the living rooms of remote farmers intimate views of moving and dramatic events and explosive tensions in every part of the world. It permits the most provincial villager to sit in on probing interviews and discussions of top political, diplomatic, and military officials from the United States and abroad. Furthermore, the combination of improved transportation facilities and economic prosperity enables growing numbers to visit not only all sections of the United States but foreign lands as well. The North Dakota farmer or small businessman making the "grand tour" of Europe is neither so unusual nor so incongruous as he would have been a generation ago. Thirst for knowledge, drive for economic gain, a high level of prosperity, and the belief that "it is the thing to do" lead a growing proportion of young people to continue their formal education beyond levels achieved by their parents. Opportunity and exposure to broader horizons do not assure immunity to provincialism for farmers, for townspeople, or for urban dwellers, but they do contribute to its decline.

In addition to these influences, there were other fundamental socio-economic changes within the United States that help to account for the eclipse of isolationism. These changes were related to the rapid urbanization of American society that accompanied the phenomenal growth of American business, industry, finance, and labor. The foreign policy views represented by Thomas Jefferson, William Jennings Bryan, and Gerald P. Nye fell into disfavor partly as a result of the rise of the city and the decline and urbanization of the farmer in the United States.

At the time of the first census in 1790 (when Jefferson became secretary of state), ninety-five per cent of Americans were classified as rural and most of them were farmers. Only about five per cent were urban, and these lived in relatively small communities by European or twentieth-century standards. America had a debtor status in international finance, an unfavorable balance of trade, and little commercial manufacturing. Most exports were farm products and most imports were manufactured goods. In economic terms the United States still had essentially a colonial relationship to Britain.[2]

Throughout the history of the United States, however, the urban population has nearly always increased at a more rapid rate than rural population. By the middle decades of the twentieth century the population and economic patterns of 1790 were reversed. Even before Nye was appointed to the Senate in 1925, the total urban population exceeded rural population – though not in North Dakota. According to the 1960 census nearly seventy per cent of Americans were classified as urban (i.e., lived in cities of 2,500 or more). North Dakota still had a rural majority in 1960, but urban population and income exceeded rural in three-fourths of the states including such traditionally farm states as Iowa and Nebraska. More than seventeen per cent of the American people lived in the "supermetropolis" extending almost continuously for nearly five hundred miles along the northeastern seaboard. That huge concentration of people, talent, industry, and capital exerted an influence on American thought, taste, education, national politics, and foreign policy that far exceeded its proportion of the population.[3]

This urbanization was both a cause and an effect of fundamental economic developments. When Nye became a senator, the United States was already the leading industrial and financial center of the world. By 1960 less than nine per cent of the American people were farmers, and many of these obtained part of their incomes from non-farm sources. As a reflection of this urban economy, most American exports consisted of manufactured goods and many imports were raw materials and tropical and semitropical food products. The United States had a favorable balance of trade and a creditor balance in international finance.[4]

Farmers and farms not only declined in numbers, they also changed greatly. The impact of science and technology revolutionized farming methods just as they affected urban manufacturing. Commercial farms grew strikingly in size, capitalization, mechanization, and production. The enlarged operations, in addition to marketing difficulties, inspired sophisticated managerial and organizational innovations that often gave the producer, processor, and distributor a community of interest cutting across rural-urban lines. Furthermore, the modes of living for twentieth-century commercial farmers often differed little from those of persons on comparable social and economic levels in the cities. Automobiles, highways, radio, television, mass-circulation newspapers and magazines, schools and universities, commercial recreational facilities, and mass-produced consumer goods were available to farmers as they were to city people. The urbanization of American agriculture did not wholly eliminate differences between rural and urban interests and views on domestic and foreign affairs, but it did reduce many of those differences.[5]

The rise of the city affected both major political parties in the United States. The combination of a number of factors – the tenacity of rural values among large segments of the population, advantageous institutions, the cooperation between agrarian and business interests on particular issues, the political skill of the agrarian spokesmen – served to delay urban political triumphs, particularly on the state level and in Congress. The ultimate outcome was inevitable, however, and urban groups obtained control of both parties on the national level in the twentieth century. Business and its spokesmen generally dominated the Republican party. The nomination of Wendell Willkie by the Republicans in 1940 was a victory for urban groups and they never relinquished their control. The Democratic party traced its ancestry and some of its principles back to Jefferson's Republican party which was rooted largely in agriculture, and in 1932 Franklin D. Roosevelt relied heavily on the West. Nevertheless, under Al Smith's leadership in the 1920's urban influence in the Democratic party increased greatly, and the new political coalition Roosevelt developed in the middle of the 1930's was predominantly urban. From 1936 onward the cities reigned in the Democratic party in the North. *Insofar as they reflected urban interests and values*, President John F. Kennedy and his Democratic administration had more in common with Federalist Alexander Hamilton than with Thomas Jefferson. Kennedy and Hamilton differed in many important respects, of course, but they (and their foreign policy views) shared an urban orientation that contrasts sharply with the agrarianism of Thomas Jefferson, William Jennings Bryan, and Gerald P. Nye.[6]

In a speech opposing extension of the reciprocal trade agreements program in 1940, Senator Nye vividly indicated his reaction to some of these social and economic changes and their implications for foreign policy. He complained that the reciprocal trade agreements had "put American exports of agricultural products on the downgrade and the importation of foreign agricultural production on the upgrade." He said the agreements had "not stopped wars," but while farmers were "cooperating to eliminate surpluses in production . . . they must stand and watch trainloads and shiploads of that reduced commodity entering the country from foreign fields to add to the surpluses and deny them the fullness of their own market." Some Americans believed, Nye feared, that "agriculture must cease to be the American economic base and must give way to an industrial base; that American prosperity and trade growth are dependent upon our ability to find a foreign outlet for the production of our mills and factories, and that this outlet can be found only as America may take foreign agricultural production in exchange for the manufactured articles of the United States. In other words, there is some feeling that we must change from an agricultural dependence to an industrial dependence." He charged that this pattern was encouraged by the trade agreements program "which finds in so many instances the interests of the American farmer being traded in the interests of American manufacturers." "If this is to be the American policy," Nye said, "then let us prepare as we have never thought of preparing before in a military way, to defend those channels of trade on the high seas which are to be so essential if we are to keep a stream of food flowing to feed ourselves in time of war. Two- or three-billion-dollar military programs annually will never begin to provide a sufficiency if we are to let agriculture become a secondary consideration." As he had many times before, Nye objected to reliance on "war trade" as a basis "for American prosperity and economy." He did not favor abandoning foreign trade, but he did urge "abandonment of our continuing dependence upon foreign trade as a leading source for our prosperity." He emphasized the importance of farm purchasing power to the prosperity of industrial and urban America, and belittled the contributions of foreign markets to the economy. He wanted trade agreements subject to approval in the Senate, where (though he did not say so) agricultural representation was more substantial than in the executive branch of the government.[7]

Nye's analysis in 1940 was perceptive and accurate in some ways, but fundamentally it was many years behind actual economic, political, and foreign policy developments in the United States. By 1940 agriculture had already ceased to be the primary base for the American economy; industry and finance had taken over that role long before. He underestimated the importance of foreign markets to the farmer and overestimated the capacity of the domestic market to absorb the tremendous output of American farms. Furthermore, by 1940 rural purchasers, though still important, could not begin to absorb all the goods and services that the cities had to sell in order to achieve prosperity. Substantial urban and foreign markets (including tremendous military preparedness programs) have seemed essential to absorb the phenomenal production of urban America. Nye's worry that "Two- or three-billion-dollar military programs annually" would be insufficient if agriculture became "a secondary consideration" grossly underestimated the fifty-billion-dollar military budgets of mid-century America. His explanation for military preparedness programs overemphasized economic influences and neglected national security considerations. Nevertheless, the huge expenditures for national defense have helped to sustain an effective demand for American goods and services—predominantly urban and industrial. The economic benefits derived from exports and defense programs extend into every state. But agricultural North Dakota's share of defense contracts was still at the bottom of the list in 1960.[8]

Since North Dakota remained largely rural, Nye's agrarianism did not, by itself, doom him to defeat there. Indeed, some of his opponents in the state criticized him for not doing more to help the farmer. With more skilled handling of his political lines in North Dakota it is at least conceivable that he might have been returned to the Senate in spite of urban dominance elsewhere. But even if he had managed to get re-elected, his influence in Washington on foreign policy matters could only have remained negligible. The reverses he had already suffered on the national level symbolized the erosion of the agricultural base for isolationism. Insofar as isolationism was rooted in the interests and values of agriculture in the upper Missouri-Mississippi-Ohio River valley, the relative decline of agriculture virtually assured its defeat. The surprising thing is not that Nye and the views he represented were defeated, but that they won so much support as they did in the 1930's. This is *not* to say that isolationist views grew out of only economic influences or that the economic bases were only agricultural. But the decline and urbanization of the farmer in America reduced the political power that isolationists could command. The views Nye represented were overwhelmed partly by an urban society based on commerce, industry, finance, and labor.

In a sense, the struggle between agrarian isolationists and urban internationalists has been transferred from the United States to the world scene since World War II. The United States, Great Britain, and Western Europe evolved into a huge metropolis with a community of interests in both security and economic matters. This industrial-financial complex has a role in the world economy roughly comparable to the role of the Northeast in the United States. The economically underdeveloped areas of the Near and Middle East, Asia, Africa, and Latin America have a relationship to the North Atlantic metropolis or to the Soviet Union not unlike that of rural North Dakota to the urban Northeast during Nye's senatorial career. The foreign policy attitudes toward the Cold War of many people in these relatively weak agricultural and mineral-producing countries are roughly comparable to the views of Nye and his fellow agrarians toward World War II. For example, like agrarian isolationists before Pearl Harbor, neutralist states in the Cold War generally lack enthusiasm for large-scale military preparedness, fear that armaments may lead to war, are skeptical of the motives of both sides, object to imperialism by the industrial giants, and are preoccupied with their own internal economic problems. The North Atlantic metropolis, however, is as unresponsive to the views of the neutralist bloc in the Cold War as urban America was to agrarian isolationists before Pearl Harbor.

Isolationism is not completely dead in the United States and perhaps will not be in the foreseeable future. It is much weaker than it was a quarter of a century ago, however, and insofar as it depends on agriculture it cannot expect a significant revival. If isolationism ever becomes powerful in American attitudes again (which is unlikely), it will have to find other sources of sustenance to replace and supplement agriculture.

NOTES

Notes

Chapter 1. Agrarians and American Foreign Policy

[1] The best published description and analysis of the content of "isolationist" ideas is Albert K. Weinberg, "The Historical Meaning of the American Doctrine of Isolation," *American Political Science Review*, XXXIV (June 1940), pp. 539–47. See also Selig Adler, *The Isolationist Impulse: Its Twentieth-Century Reaction* (London and New York: Abelard-Schuman, 1957), pp. 26–29; Charles A. Beard, *A Foreign Policy for America* (New York and London: Alfred A. Knopf, 1940), pp. 12–35; William Worthington Cover, "Neo-Isolationism and Types of Military Policy" (Unpublished M.S. thesis, Iowa State College, 1956), pp. 33–63; Alexander DeConde, "On Twentieth-Century Isolationism," in Alexander DeConde, ed., *Isolation and Security* (Durham, N.C.: Duke University Press, 1957), pp. 3–32; and Arthur M. Schlesinger, Jr., "The New Isolationism," *Atlantic Monthly*, CLXXXIX (May 1952), pp. 34–38. For examples of Senator Nye's definitions of the term see Gerald P. Nye, "Should We Turn to 'Isolation'?" *New York Times Magazine*, January 14, 1940, pp. 1–2; *PM* (New York), February 2, 1943; and *Congressional Record*, 78 Congress, 1 session (1943), pp. 9087–89.

[2] Thomas A. Bailey, *The Man in the Street: The Impact of American Public Opinion on Foreign Policy* (New York: Macmillan Company, 1948), pp. 108–9; Ray Billington, "The Origins of Middle Western Isolationism," *Political Science Quarterly*, LX (March 1945), pp. 44–64; William G. Carleton, "Isolationism and the Middle West," *Mississippi Valley Historical Review*, XXXIII (December 1946), pp. 377–90; Wayne S. Cole, *America First: The Battle against Intervention, 1940–1941* (Madison: University of Wisconsin Press, 1953), pp. 30–31; Bernard Fensterwald, Jr., "The Anatomy of American 'Isolationism' and Expansionism," *Journal of Conflict Resolution*, II (June 1958), pp. 128–29; George L. Grassmuck, *Sectional Biases in Congress on Foreign Policy* (Baltimore: Johns Hopkins Press, 1951), pp. 14–15, 98–107, 141–70; Jeannette P. Nichols, "The Middle West and the Coming of World War II," *Ohio State Archaeological and Historical Quarterly*, LXII (April 1953), pp. 122–45; and Ralph H. Smuckler, "The Region of Isolationism," *American Political Science Review*, XLVII (June 1953), pp. 386–97.

[3] Bailey, *Man in the Street*, pp. 90–92; Cole, *America First*, pp. 167–75; Fenster-

wald, "Anatomy of American 'Isolationism,'" *Journal of Conflict Resolution*, pp. 133–34; Grassmuck, *Sectional Biases*, pp. 12–29, 92–112, 119–32, 134–41; Walter Johnson, *The Battle against Isolation* (Chicago: University of Chicago Press, 1944), pp. 10–11, 52, 222; Robert E. Sherwood, *Roosevelt and Hopkins: An Intimate History* (New York: Harper and Brothers, 1948), pp. 367–68; and Smuckler, "Region of Isolationism," *American Political Science Review*, p. 401.

[4] Bailey, *Man in the Street*, pp. 205–11; Billington, "Middle Western Isolationism," *Political Science Quarterly*, p. 53; Fensterwald, "Anatomy of American 'Isolationism,'" *Journal of Conflict Resolution*, pp. 136–37; Robert Moats Miller, *American Protestantism and Social Issues, 1919–1939* (Chapel Hill: University of North Carolina Press, 1958), pp. 317–44.

[5] Bernard Fensterwald, Jr., "The Anatomy of American 'Isolationism' and Expansionism. II," *Journal of Conflict Resolution*, II (December 1958), pp. 280–307.

[6] Samuel Lubell, "Who Votes Isolationist and Why," *Harper's Magazine*, CCII (April 1951), pp. 29–36. See also Adler, *Isolationist Impulse*, pp. 75–92, 175, 291–95; Bailey, *Man in the Street*, pp. 18–33; Billington, "Middle Western Isolationism," *Political Science Quarterly*, p. 52; DeConde, *Isolation and Security*, pp. 12–17; Fensterwald, "Anatomy of American 'Isolationism.' I," *Journal of Conflict Resolution*, p. 135; Smuckler, "Region of Isolationism," *American Political Science Review*, pp. 400–1; and Robert P. Wilkins, "Middle Western Isolationism: A Re-Examination," *North Dakota Quarterly* (Summer 1957), pp. 69–76. Most of these authors believe that Lubell overemphasized the importance of the ethnic base for American isolationism.

[7] Bailey, *Man in the Street*, pp. 134–39. See also Gabriel A. Almond, *The American People and Foreign Policy* (New York: Harcourt, Brace and Company, 1950), p. 134; Fensterwald, "Anatomy of American 'Isolationism.' I," *Journal of Conflict Resolution*, p. 137; and Smuckler, "Region of Isolationism," *American Political Science Review*, p. 399. Smuckler, using congressional voting records rather than public opinion polls for his basic data, arrived at conclusions quite the opposite of Bailey's.

[8] For analyses of the South's foreign policy attitudes before Pearl Harbor see Bailey, *Man in the Street*, pp. 109–14; Wayne S. Cole, "America First and the South, 1940–1941," *Journal of Southern History*, XXII (February 1956), pp. 36–47; Virginius Dabney, "The South Looks Abroad," *Foreign Affairs*, XIX (October 1940), pp. 171–78; Alexander DeConde, "The South and Isolationism," *Journal of Southern History*, XXIV (August 1958), pp. 332–46; Grassmuck, *Sectional Biases*, pp. 15, 41–42, 84, 152–54; John Temple Graves, "The Fighting South," *Virginia Quarterly Review*, XVIII (1942), pp. 60–71; John Temple Graves, *The Fighting South* (New York: G. P. Putnam's, 1943); and Paul Seabury, *The Waning of Southern "Internationalism"* (Princeton: Princeton University Center of International Studies, 1957).

[9] Of seminal importance for this interpretation is Charles A. Beard, *The Idea of National Interest: An Analytical Study in American Foreign Policy* (New York: Macmillan Company, 1934), *passim*, but see particularly pp. 50–60, 84–88, 166–68, 545–53. Among other accounts that point to agrarian bases for American isolationism are Almond, *American People and Foreign Policy*, pp. 132–34; Billington, "Middle Western Isolationism," *Political Science Quarterly*, pp. 50–51; Fensterwald, "Anatomy of American 'Isolationism.' I," *Journal of Conflict Resolution*, p. 129; Walter Johnson, *1600 Pennsylvania Avenue: Presidents and the People, 1929–1959* (Boston: Little, Brown and Company, 1960), p. 109; Smuckler, "Region of Isolationism," *American Political Science Review*, pp. 398–99; and Wilkins, "Middle Western Isolationism," *North Dakota Quarterly*, pp. 69–76.

[10] *Creston Daily Plain Dealer*, March 3, 1915.

[11] *Ibid.*, July 23, 1915.

[12] *Griggs County Sentinel-Courier*, May 6, 1920.
[13] *Ibid.*, June 21, 1923.
[14] Cole, *America First*, pp. 14–22, 32–33; Gilbert C. Fite, *George N. Peek and the Fight for Farm Parity* (Norman: University of Oklahoma Press, 1954), pp. 296–97; and R. Douglas Stuart, Jr., to J. Austin White, October 21, 1941, America First Committee Papers, Hoover Library, Stanford, California.
[15] *Fryburg Pioneer*, May 23, 1919.
[16] *Congressional Record*, 70 Congress, 1 session (1928), p. 10073.
[17] For example, see *Griggs County Sentinel-Courier*, January 5, 1922; *Fargo Forum*, February 11, 1937; and *Congressional Record*, 75 Congress, 2 session (1937), p. 1236.
[18] *Congressional Record*, 71 Congress, 1 session (1929), p. 1497, and 77 Congress, 1 session (1941), pp. 1108–21; and Citizens Foreign Aid Committee, *Foreign Aid and You: A First Report* (Washington, D.C., 1959).
[19] See below, Chapters 5, 6, and 9.
[20] See below, Chapter 7.
[21] See below, Chapter 8.
[22] The analysis of Jefferson in this chapter is based particularly on the following: Charles A. Beard, *Economic Origins of Jeffersonian Democracy* (New York: Macmillan Company, 1915), *passim*, but see particularly pp. 415–67; Beard, *Idea of National Interest*, pp. 50–56, 84–88, 166–68, 549–51; Wilfred E. Binkley, *American Political Parties: Their Natural History* (New York: Alfred A. Knopf, 1947), pp. 52–93; Gilbert Chinard, *Thomas Jefferson: The Apostle of Americanism* (2nd ed. rev.; Ann Arbor: University of Michigan Press, 1957); Alexander DeConde, *Entangling Alliance: Politics and Diplomacy under George Washington* (Durham: Duke University Press, 1958); Richard Hofstadter, *The American Political Tradition and the Men Who Made It* (New York: Alfred A. Knopf, 1948), pp. 18–43; and Louis M. Sears, *Jefferson and the Embargo* (Durham: Duke University Press, 1927).

The analysis of Bryan in this chapter is based particularly on Binkley, *American Political Parties*, pp. 315–20; Merle Eugene Curti, *Bryan and World Peace* (Northampton: Smith College Studies in History, 1931); Paul W. Glad, *The Trumpet Soundeth: William Jennings Bryan and His Democracy, 1896–1912* (Lincoln: University of Nebraska Press, 1960); Paxton Hibben, *The Peerless Leader: William Jennings Bryan* (New York: Farrar and Rinehart, 1929); and Hofstadter, *American Political Tradition*, pp. 183–202.

Documentation for the generalizations about Nye is provided in the chapters that follow.
[23] Hofstadter, *American Political Tradition*, pp. 30–39, 187–90.

Chapter 2. The Oldest Nye Boy

[1] [Irwin R. Nye] to Gerald P. Nye, December 19, 1913, Gerald P. Nye Papers, Chevy Chase, Maryland.
[2] Gerald P. Nye to P. I. Prentice, October 15, 1941, Nye Papers; *Wittenberg Enterprise*, March 4, 1909; *Weekly Review* (Hortonville, Wisconsin), August 9, 1923; interview with Gerald P. Nye, July 20, 1959.
[3] George Hyatt Nye and Frank E. Best, compilers, and David Fisher Nye, ed., *A Genealogy of the Nye Family* (Cleveland: O. S. Hubbell Printing Company, 1907), pp. 19–29, 41–43, 83–87, 131, 221, 353, 494–95, 580; interview with Nye, July 20, 1959.
[4] *Enterprise* (Wittenberg, Wisconsin), November 16, 1893; *Weekly Review*, August 9, 1923; interview with Nye, July 20, 1959.
[5] Beulah Folkedahl, *A Dream Come True: The Homme Homes at Wittenberg*

(Wittenberg, 1956), pp. 5–7, 13–15, 39–40; *Enterprise*, November 16, 1893, November 23, 1893.

[6] *Enterprise*, May 26, 1898; *Wittenberg Enterprise*, November 17, 1907; *Weekly Review*, August 9, 1923; interview with Nye, July 20, 1959.

[7] *Enterprise*, April 19, 1894, October 22, 1896, September 30, 1897, April 28, 1898, November 2, 1900, November 9, 1900, November 4, 1904. Gilbert C. Fite, "Republican Strategy and the Farm Vote in the Presidential Campaign of 1896," *American Historical Review*, LXV (July 1960), pp. 787–806, is an excellent study and makes it clear that many farmers supported McKinley against Bryan. On the Wisconsin vote in 1896 see p. 804n of Fite's article.

[8] Interview with Nye, July 20, 1959.

[9] *Wittenberg Enterprise*, December 12, 1907, January 16, 1908, September 17, 1908, September 24, 1908, October 22, 1908, November 5, 1908, November 19, 1908, December 10, 1908, February 11, 1909, April 15, 1909, September 23, 1909, January 6, 1910, January 13, 1910, January 20, 1910, March 3, 1910, March 17, 1910, March 31, 1910, May 5, 1910, September 15, 1910, October 6, 1910, November 3, 1910, June 15, 1911; interview with Nye, July 20, 1959.

[10] *Wittenberg Enterprise*, July 13, 1911, August 3, 1911; interview with Nye, July 20, 1959.

[11] *Weekly Review* (Hortonville, Wisconsin), December 19, 1912. [Irwin R. Nye] to Gerald P. Nye, December 19, 1913, Nye Papers, is a moving, touching letter from the father to his son on the latter's twenty-first birthday that provides a perceptive portrait of the young man at that time.

[12] *Weekly Review*, December 19, 1912, January 9, 1913.

[13] *Ibid.*, January 30, 1913, March 25, 1913, March 31, 1913, April 1, 1913; interview with Nye, July 20, 1959.

[14] [Irwin R. Nye] to Gerald P. Nye, December 19, 1913, Nye Papers; "Bills Payable on September 28, 1914," Nye Papers; *Weekly Review*, October 8, 1914; *Wittenberg Enterprise*, October 8, 1914, February 18, 1915, February 25, 1915; interview with Nye, July 20, 1959.

[15] *Wittenberg Enterprise*, February 18, 1915, February 25, 1915; *Creston Daily Plain Dealer*, February 23, 1915; interview with Nye, July 20, 1959.

[16] *Creston Daily Plain Dealer*, February 23, 1915.

[17] *Ibid.*, March 3, 1915, March 21, 1915, July 23, 1915.

[18] *Ibid.*, February 24, 1915, April 10, 1915, May 2, 1915, July 4, 1915.

[19] *Ibid.*, March 26, 1915, March 31, 1915, May 7, 1915, June 2, 1915.

[20] *Ibid.*, March 18, 1915.

[21] *Ibid.*, May 8, 1915.

[22] *Ibid.*, May 13, 1915, May 15, 1915, June 10, 1915, June 12, 1915.

[23] *Ibid.*, June 10, 1915.

[24] *Ibid.*, June 13, 1915, June 18, 1915, June 20, 1915.

[25] *Ibid.*, July 24, 1915.

[26] *Ibid.*, August 13, 1915, August 15, 1915.

[27] *Ibid.*, August 27, 1915.

[28] *Congressional Record*, 75 Congress, 3 session (1938), p. 5845.

[29] F. E. Sampson to Nye, July 24, 1919, Nye Papers.

[30] *Fryburg Pioneer*, July 28, 1916; unsigned typed manuscript headed "For Sale," undated but probably prepared in 1919, Nye Papers; interview with Nye, July 20, 1959.

[31] *Fryburg Pioneer*, May 25, 1916.

Chapter 3. North Dakota Newspaperman

[1] Ralph H. Smuckler, "The Region of Isolationism," *American Political Science Review*, XLVII (June 1953), p. 391.

[2] Melvin E. Kazeck, *North Dakota: A Human and Economic Geography* (Fargo: North Dakota Institute for Regional Studies, 1956), *passim*, but see particularly pp. 35–37; J. M. Gillette, *Social Economics of North Dakota* (Minneapolis: Burgess Publishing Company, 1942), *passim*, but see particularly pp. 68–74, 196–99; Federal Writers' Project of the Works Progress Administration, *North Dakota: A Guide to the Northern Prairie State* (Fargo: Knight Printing Company, 1938), *passim*, but see particularly pp. 78–93; Ross Talbot, "Wheat Politics and Election Predictions" (Unpublished paper delivered at Midwest Conference of Political Scientists, Purdue University, May 5–7, 1955). See also Elwyn B. Robinson, "The Themes of North Dakota History" (Mimeographed article originally presented as an address at Seventy-Fifth Anniversary Conference, University of North Dakota, November 6, 1958).

[3] Kazeck, *North Dakota*, pp. 135–49, 230; Gillette, *Social Economics*, pp. 86–122; Federal Writers' Project, *North Dakota*, pp. 59–71.

[4] Kazeck, *North Dakota*, pp. 150–95; Gillette, *Social Economics*, pp. 125–42; Federal Writers' Project, *North Dakota*, pp. 72–76, 111–65.

[5] Robert L. Morlan, *Political Prairie Fire: The Nonpartisan League, 1915–1922* (Minneapolis: University of Minnesota Press, 1955), pp. 3–51, 87; Theodore Saloutos and John D. Hicks, *Agricultural Discontent in the Middle West, 1900–1939* (Madison: University of Wisconsin Press, 1951), pp. 149–63; Russel B. Nye, *Midwestern Progressive Politics: A Historical Study of Its Origins and Development, 1870–1958* (East Lansing: Michigan State University Press, 1959), pp. 289–91.

[6] *Fryburg Pioneer*, May 25, 1916.

[7] Kazeck, *North Dakota*, pp. 121–35; Federal Writers' Project, *North Dakota*, pp. 297–300.

[8] Kazeck, *North Dakota*, pp. 142–43; *Fryburg Pioneer*, October 27, 1916; interview with Nye, July 20, 1959.

[9] Kazeck, *North Dakota*, pp. 142–43, 127–28.

[10] Kazeck, *North Dakota*, pp. 133–34; Federal Writers' Project, *North Dakota*, pp. 298–99.

[11] *Fryburg Pioneer*, September 22, 1916, October 6, 1916, October 13, 1916, October 27, 1916.

[12] Morlan, *Political Prairie Fire*, pp. 47–87; Saloutos and Hicks, *Agricultural Discontent*, pp. 163–68; Samuel P. Huntington, "The Election Tactics of the Nonpartisan League," *Mississippi Valley Historical Review*, XXXVI (March 1950), pp. 614–21.

[13] *Fryburg Pioneer*, June 29, 1916, August 24, 1916.

[14] Charles Liessman, ed., *Compilation of Election Returns: National and State, 1914–1928* [Bismarck, 1930], pp. 18–19; Morlan, *Political Prairie Fire*, pp. 87–90; *Fryburg Pioneer*, November 10, 1916; Huntington, "Election Tactics," *Mississippi Valley Historical Review*, pp. 621–22.

[15] *Fryburg Pioneer*, February 9, 1917, April 27, 1917.

[16] *Ibid.*, September 7, 1917, October 12, 1917, November 2, 1917. For a balanced account of the League meeting addressed by LaFollette see Morlan, *Political Prairie Fire*, pp. 142–46.

[17] *Creston Daily Plain Dealer*, July 19, 1916; *Fryburg Pioneer*, July 28, 1916.

[18] *Fryburg Pioneer*, June 15, 1917, July 20, 1917, May 3, 1918, May 10, 1918, May 18, 1918, June 7, 1918, August 9, 1918, September 13, 1918, September 27, 1918; W. L. Stoekwell to Nye, September 25, 1918, Nye Papers. The Nye Papers also contain his draft classification cards and various certificates indicating positions he had held in home-front activities.

[19] *Fryburg Pioneer*, October 18, 1918, November 29, 1918.

[20] *Ibid.*, February 28, 1919, March 14, 1919.

[21] *Ibid.*, April 11, 1919.

[22] *Ibid.*, June 27, 1919.

[23] *Ibid.*, July 4, 1919.

[24] Morlan, *Political Prairie Fire*, pp. 110–13, 136–46, 190.

[25] *Ibid.*, p. 90.

[26] *Fryburg Pioneer*, March 1, 1918, June 21, 1918; Huntington, "Election Tactics," *Mississippi Valley Historical Review*, p. 622; Morlan, *Political Prairie Fire*, p. 187.

[27] *Fryburg Pioneer*, August 2, 1918.

[28] *Ibid.*, August 16, 1918.

[29] *Ibid.*, November 1, 1918, November 22, 1918.

[30] *Ibid.*, January 10, 1919.

[31] *Ibid.*, May 23, 1919.

[32] *Ibid.*, June 20, 1919.

[33] *Ibid.*, July 25, 1919, August 1, 1919; Kazeck, *North Dakota*, p. 128.

[34] Agreement for Delivery of Bill of Sale to J. W. Brinton, November 22, 1918, Minutes of Organization Meeting of the Billings County Pioneer Press, November 22, 1918, Brinton to Nye, January 20, 1919, Brinton to Nye, February 11, 1919, Brinton to Nye, March 18, 1919, January 19, 1920, undated typed manuscript headed "For Sale," Nye Papers; *Billings County Pioneer*, August 15, 1919, August 29, 1919; interview with Nye, July 20, 1959.

[35] Federal Writers' Project, *North Dakota*, pp. 308–10; Kazeck, *North Dakota*, pp. 77–120.

[36] Saloutos and Hicks, *Agricultural Discontent*, pp. 199–200; Morlan, *Political Prairie Fire*, pp. 113–14; *Griggs County Sentinel-Courier*, April 29, 1920, January 26, 1922; interview with Nye, July 20, 1959.

[37] *Griggs County Sentinel-Courier*, August 28, 1919, September 4, 1919, January 22, 1920; interview with Nye, July 20, 1959.

[38] *Griggs County Sentinel-Courier*, September 4, 1919, January 22, 1920, April 29, 1920, July 1, 1920; interview with Nye, July 20, 1959.

[39] *Griggs County Sentinel-Courier*, June 17, 1920, June 24, 1920, July 1, 1920, August 5, 1920.

[40] *Ibid.*, June 3, 1920.

[41] *Ibid.*, October 28, 1920, November 11, 1920. For general accounts of the primaries and election in North Dakota in 1920 see Morlan, *Political Prairie Fire*, pp. 292–94, 298–300; Huntington, "Election Tactics," *Mississippi Valley Historical Review*, pp. 622–23; Saloutos and Hicks, *Agricultural Discontent*, pp. 200–1.

[42] *Griggs County Sentinel-Courier*, November 25, 1920, May 5, 1921, August 18, 1921, September 22, 1921; letter to Nye, July 25, 1921, C. F. Knause to Griggs County Sentinel Courier, September 22, [1921], Nye Papers.

[43] *Griggs County Sentinel-Courier*, May 12, 1921, November 3, 1921, December 3, 1921; Morlan, *Political Prairie Fire*, pp. 315–29; Saloutos and Hicks, *Agricultural Discontent*, pp. 203–6.

[44] *Griggs County Sentinel-Courier*, January 12, 1922.

[45] *Ibid.*, March 2, 1922, March 9, 1922, March 23, 1922, July 13, 1922, August 17, 1922; interview with Nye, July 20, 1959.

[46] Morlan, *Political Prairie Fire*, pp. 342–46; Huntington, "Election Tactics," *Mississippi Valley Historical Review*, p. 629.

[47] Nye to George Heinze, September 24, 1923, Heinze to Nye, September 30, 1923, Nye to William Langer, January 29, 1924, Nye Papers; *Griggs County Sentinel-Courier*, September 27, 1923.

[48] Printed Resolution by the Temporary Nye for Congress Club, November 5, 1923, Nye to J. W. Hempel, January 28, 1924, Hempel to Nye, January 31, 1924, Usher Burdick to Nye, January 29, 1924, John Andrews to Nye, January 29, 1924, Nye to Andrews, January 30, 1924, Nye Papers.

[49] *Griggs County Sentinel-Courier*, February 14, 1924, June 5, 1924; interview with Math Dahl, March 1, 1960.

[50] *Compilation of Election Returns: National and State, 1914–1928*, p. 62; *Griggs County Sentinel-Courier*, July 3, 1924.

[51] *Griggs County Sentinel-Courier*, July 26, 1923.

[52] *Ibid.*, December 6, 1923.

[53] *Ibid.*, January 17, 1924, January 31, 1924, March 27, 1924; Saloutos and Hicks, *Agricultural Discontent*, p. 356; *Compilation of Election Returns*, p. 56.

[54] *Griggs County Sentinel-Courier*, July 3, 1924, July 31, 1924; A. G. Sorlie to Nye, July 7, 1924, Nye to Fred J. Engel, July 22, 1924, C. A. Fislie to John L. Mikkelthun, August 4, 1924, David C. Poindexter to Nye, August 6, 1924, Nye Papers.

[55] Nye to John N. Hagen, August 6, 1924, Nye to Vannie A. Hall, August 28, 1924, E. F. Ladd to Nye, September 4, 1924, printed circular to its North Dakota members put out by the Order of Railroad Telegraphers, October 24, 1924, Nye Papers; *Labor* (Washington, D.C.), October 25, 1924; *Griggs County Sentinel-Courier*, August 7, 1924, September 25, 1924, October 30, 1924.

[56] Nye platform printed on letterhead stationery of LaFollette-Nye Club of Griggs County, Nye to E. S. Elliott, October 15, 1924, Nye Papers; *Griggs County Sentinel-Courier*, September 13, 1923.

[57] *Griggs County Sentinel-Courier*, November 6, 1924, November 13, 1924; *Compilation of Election Returns*, pp. 66–67; Nye to John Bloom, November 8, 1924, Nye to Edward Voigt, November 8, 1924, Nye Papers.

[58] *Griggs County Sentinel-Courier*, June 25, 1925, July 2, 1925.

[59] Nye to A. G. Sorlie, June 23, 1925, Sorlie to Nye, June 29, 1925, Nye to Sorlie, July 6, 1925, Nye to James Sinclair, July 6, 1925, Sinclair to Nye, August 3, 1925, Nye Papers; *Griggs County Sentinel-Courier*, July 9, 1925.

[60] *Griggs County Sentinel Courier*, July 30, 1925.

[61] Alton G. Sorlie to the author, September 23, 1960.

[62] *Griggs County Sentinel-Courier*, August 27, 1925, September 3, 1925, November 12, 1925; Nye to Sorlie, September 21, 1925, Nye Papers.

[63] *Griggs County Sentinel-Courier*, November 12, 1925.

[64] *Ibid.*

[65] F. J. Graham to Nye, October 22, 1925, Graham to Nye, October 26, 1925, and carbon list headed "*Invited to Conference* Nov. 13th," Nye Papers; interview with Nye, July 20, 1959; interview with Math Dahl, March 1, 1960; Elmer W. Cart to the author, September 18, 1960; *Fargo Forum*, November 15, 1925; *Bismarck Capital*, November 19, 1925; *New York Times*, July 25, 1934. The descriptions of this hotel meeting vary considerably in specific details, but the developments described seem well established by the available evidence.

[66] Interview with Nye, July 20, 1959; *New York Times*, July 25, 1934; Official Appointment of Nye to the United States Senate signed by Sorlie and Robert Byrne, secretary of state, November 14, 1925, Nye Papers.

[67] *Bismarck Tribune*, November 14, 1925; *Bismarck Capital*, November 19, 1925; *Griggs County Sentinel-Courier*, November 19, 1925; Alton G. Sorlie to the author, September 23, 1960.

[68] *Griggs County Sentinel-Courier*, November 26, 1925.

[69] *Ibid.*, December 2, 1920, November 17, 1921, January 5, 1922, January 25, 1923, April 17, 1924, August 14, 1924, December 11, 1924, April 16, 1925, July 9, 1925, August 20, 1925.

Chapter 4. Young Senator Nye

[1] *Congressional Record*, 69 Congress, 1 session (1925–26), pp. 376, 904, 1408–9, 1479, 1615–34, 1680–1700, 1737–54, 1814–40, 1884–93; U.S. Congress, Sen-

ate, Committee on Privileges and Elections, *Report on the Right of Gerald P. Nye to a Seat in the Senate as a Senator from the State of North Dakota*, Senate Report 3, 69 Congress, 1 session (Washington, D.C.: Government Printing Office, 1925); *Griggs County Sentinel-Courier*, November 26, 1925, December 7, 1925, January 14, 1926; *Washington Post*, December 15, 1925; *North Dakota Nonpartisan*, December 16, 1925; *Boston Herald*, January 13, 1926; *New York Times*, January 13, 1926; interview with Nye, July 20, 1959.

[2] G. P. Nye to the author, March 11, 1960; Oswald Garrison Villard, "Issues and Men," *Nation*, CXLVI (February 26, 1938), p. 245.

[3] This sketch of the young senator's personal traits is based largely on the following sources: *Knoxville News-Sentinel*, May 5, 1935; "Sharpshooters into Arms Trade," *Literary Digest*, 121 (January 18, 1936), pp. 32–33; *Williston Daily Herald*, April 21, 1936; *Tampa Daily News*, March 18, 1939; Walter Trohan, "Gerald Nye – Man of Courage," *Chicago Tribune*, June 18, 1944; miscellaneous unidentified newspaper clippings in the Nye Papers; interviews with Mrs. Marguerite Nye, August 7 and 8, 1959; and numerous visits and conversations with Nye in 1956, 1958, and 1959.

[4] *Washington Post*, February 12, 1926.

[5] *New York Times*, July 2, 1926; *Bismarck Capital*, undated clipping in Nye Papers.

[6] *Congressional Record*, 69 Congress, 1 session (1926), pp. 5997–6003.

[7] *Ibid.*, p. 7716.

[8] *Ibid.*, pp. 9926–27.

[9] *Labor* (Washington, D.C.), June 12, 1926; *Chicago Tribune*, July 1, 1926; *Griggs County Sentinel-Courier*, July 1, 1926; *New York Times*, July 2, 1926; *Recorder-Post* (Dickinson, North Dakota), undated editorial; *Fargo Forum*, July 3, 1926; *Bismarck Capital*, undated clipping; County Executive Committee of the Nonpartisan League of Griggs County, *The Nyepartisan League of Griggs County, N.D. "How Come?"* [Cooperstown, 1926]; Charles Liessman, ed., *Compilation of Election Returns: National and State, 1914–1928* [Bismarck, 1930], pp. 70–76.

[10] Typed copy of a speech delivered by Nye before the Chamber of Commerce, October 18, 1927, Nye Papers.

[11] *Ibid.*; *Congressional Record*, 69 Congress, 2 session (1927), pp. 3406–8; *Stanley Sun*, March 10, 1927.

[12] *Congressional Record*, 69 Congress, 2 session (1927), pp. 3830–34. An excellent general analysis of Nye's economic and political views is in E. Francis Brown, "The Crusading Mr. Nye," *Current History*, XLI (February 1935), pp. 521–27.

[13] *New York Herald Tribune*, September 20, 1927.

[14] *Bismarck Tribune*, November 24, 1927; *New York Times*, December 11, 1927, January 12, 1928, March 24, 1928; *Milwaukee Journal*, February 14, 1928; *St. Louis Star*, March 15, 1928; *World* (New York), March 18, 1928, May 24, 1928, May 30, 1928; *Chicago Tribune*, March 18, 1928; *Baltimore Sun*, March 18, 1928; *Christian Science Monitor*, March 20, 1928; *New York Herald Tribune*, May 30, 1928; *Congressional Record*, 71 Congress, 1 session (1929), pp. 1707–9.

[15] *Mandan Daily Pioneer* (North Dakota), April 28, 1927; *World* (New York), January 29, 1928; *New York Times*, May 15, 1928; *Congressional Record*, 70 Congress, 1 session (1928), pp. 10,072–75.

[16] *Detroit Times*, November 30, 1926; *New York Times*, September 15, 1927, November 8, 1930, December 14, 1934; *New York Herald Tribune*, September 20, 1927; *Star* (Washington, D.C.), January 12, 1930; *Washington Daily News*, February 27, 1933, March 9, 1934.

[17] *Bottineau Courant* (North Dakota), September 22, 1927; *New York Times*, November 4, 1927; *Jamestown Sun* (North Dakota), November 4, 1927; *Devils*

Lake Journal (North Dakota), June 20, 1928; *Washington Post*, August 23, 1928, September 6, 1928; *Bismarck Capital*, October 19, 1928; *Wells County Free Press* (Fessenden, North Dakota), November 1, 1928; Gilbert C. Fite, *George N. Peek and the Fight for Farm Parity* (Norman: University of Oklahoma Press, 1954), pp. 203–20; *Compilation of Election Returns*, p. 86; interview with Nye, July 20, 1959.

[18] *Bismarck Tribune*, January 11, 1929; *Fargo Forum*, April 27, 1929, June 11, 1929; *Mandan Pioneer*, June 11, 1929; *Williston Herald*, June 29, 1929; *Jamestown Sun*, July 1, 1929; *Amidon Post*, June 29, 1929; Fite, *George N. Peek*, pp. 160–61, 221–26.

[19] *Chicago Daily Times*, May 8, 1930; *Star* (Washington, D.C.), September 2, 1930; *Baltimore Sun*, September 25, 1930; *New York Times*, January 16, 1931; *Literary Digest*, CVI (September 20, 1930), pp. 5–7; J. L. Sayre, "Gerald P. Nye 'Essentially Negative,'" in J. T. Salter, ed., *Public Men in and out of Office* (Chapel Hill: University of North Carolina Press, 1946), pp. 131–34; Nye to John L. Cable, May 13, 1931, Nye Papers.

[20] *Congressional Record*, 71 Congress, 1 session (1929), p. 5004.

[21] *Grand Forks Herald*, June 8, 1931.

[22] *Congressional Record*, 72 Congress, 1 session (1932), pp. 10,890, 12,769–71.

[23] *Ibid.*, p. 12,770.

[24] *World* (New York), June 16, 1931.

[25] *New York Times*, March 28, 1932.

[26] *Center Republican*, May 12, 1932; *Labor* (Washington, D.C.), June 21, 1932; *Sargent County News* (Forman, North Dakota), June 23, 1932; *Stanley Sun*, June 30, 1932; *North Dakota Progressive* (Bismarck), July 5, 1932; *Fargo Forum*, July 1, 1932; Thomas Hall, Secretary of State, *Compilation of Election Returns: National and State, 1930–1944* [Bismarck, 1945]; James P. Curran to Nye, July 1, 1932, Nye Papers.

[27] *Devils Lake Journal*, October 25, 1932, October 31, 1932, November 2, 1932.

[28] Hall, *Compilation of Election Returns, 1930–1944*; *Richland County Farmer* (North Dakota), January 6, 1933.

[29] Among the histories that develop most clearly the distinction between a First and a Second New Deal are Basil Rauch, *The History of the New Deal, 1933–1938* (New York: Creative Age Press, 1944), pp. v–viii; Arthur M. Schlesinger, Jr., *The Politics of Upheaval* (Boston: Houghton Mifflin Company, 1960), pp. 385–443; Raymond Moley, *After Seven Years* (New York: Harper and Brothers, 1939), *passim*. Each of these volumes takes a different approach in its analysis. Moley does not refer explicitly to two New Deals, but clearly sees different patterns in the earlier and later phases of the New Deal.

[30] Unidentified clipping from a Toledo, Ohio, newspaper, October 29, 1933, Nye Papers.

[31] *St. Paul Pioneer Press*, July 25, 1934; *World-News*, October 7, 1934.

[32] *New York Times*, June 27, 1933.

[33] *St. Louis Post-Dispatch*, November 25, 1933; *New York Times*, November 26, 1933; *Congressional Record*, 73 Congress, 2 session (1934), pp. 1442–44, 9234–35, 12,046–51; Gerald P. Nye, "Squeezing the Consumer," *Current History*, XL (June 1934), pp. 291–95; *World-News*, October 7, 1934.

[34] *Washington Post*, December 27, 1933, April 19, 1934; *New York Times*, December 27, 1933, August 4, 1934; Transcript of Franklin D. Roosevelt's Press Conferences, December 29, 1933, Nye to Roosevelt, May 16, 1934, Roosevelt to Nye, May 18, 1934, President's Personal File 1614, Franklin D. Roosevelt Papers, Franklin D. Roosevelt Library, Hyde Park, New York; *Congressional Record*, 73 Congress, 2 session (1934), pp. 9234–40, 12,046–51; Schlesinger, *The Coming of the New Deal* (Boston: Houghton Mifflin Company, 1959), pp. 131–35.

[35] *Congressional Record*, 73 Congress, 1 session (1933), pp. 2550–51, 3327–29; *New York Times*, May 12, 1933.

[36] *Congressional Record*, 73 Congress, 2 session (1934), pp. 12,046–51; *World-News*, October 7, 1934.

[37] *St. Paul Pioneer Press*, July 25, 1934.

[38] *Progressive*, IV (September 2, 1933), p. 2.

[39] *New York Times*, April 17, 1934, July 25, 1934; *Star* (Washington, D.C.), January 7, 1937; John M. Holzworth, *The Fighting Governor: The Story of William Langer and the State of North Dakota* (Chicago: Pointer Press, 1938), pp. 1–16.

[40] *Congressional Record*, 73 Congress, 2 session (1934), pp. 3497–98; *Minot News*, March 7, 1934; Holzworth, *Fighting Governor*, pp. 57–59; interview with Nye, July 20, 1959.

[41] *Kalispell Interlake* (Montana), March 9, 1934; *New York Times*, April 17, 1934; Holzworth, *Fighting Governor*, pp. 60–62.

[42] *Devils Lake Journal*, April 23, 1934; *Mandan Pioneer*, June 26, 1934; *New York Times*, July 24, 1934, August 3, 1934; Holzworth, *Fighting Governor*, pp. 64–82; Hall, *Compilation of Election Returns, 1930–1944.*

[43] *Bismarck Tribune*, August 2, 1934; *Devils Lake Journal*, August 10, 1934; *New York Times*, August 3, 1934.

[44] *Mandan Pioneer*, August 3, 1934; *Fargo News*, August 10, 1934; *Griggs County Sentinel-Courier*, August 9, 1934.

[45] *Devils Lake Journal*, October 8, 1934; *Minneapolis Star*, October 30, 1934; Hall, *Compilation of Election Returns, 1930–1944*; Holzworth, *Fighting Governor*, pp. 86–90.

Chapter 5. International Bankers and Munitions Makers

[1] *Griggs County Sentinel-Courier*, January 14, 1926.

[2] Gerald P. Nye to the author, March 11, 1960.

[3] *Congressional Record*, 69 Congress, 1 session (1926), pp. 2643–47.

[4] *Ibid.*, pp. 2795–2825; *New York Times*, February 10, 1927.

[5] *Congressional Record*, 69 Congress, 1 session (1926), pp. 7716, 9926–27; A. W. Mellon to Reed Smoot, May 17, 1926, in papers supporting S. J. Res. 95, 69 Congress, Record Group 46, National Archives, Washington, D.C.

[6] *Wisconsin News*, July 7, 1931; *Congressional Record*, 72 Congress, 1 session (1932), pp. 1086–89.

[7] Typed copy of a speech by Nye in Boston, Massachusetts, November 27, 1927, Nye Papers; *Congressional Record*, 70 Congress, 1 session (1928), pp. 933–34; *Philadelphia Enquirer*, February 6, 1928.

[8] *Congressional Record*, 69 Congress, 2 session (1927), pp. 2588, 4022.

[9] *Ibid.*, 71 Congress, 1 session (1929), p. 1497; *McClusky Gazette*, June 7, 1929; *New York Times*, August 15, 1931.

[10] *New York Times*, August 29, 1929; *New York American*, June 17, 1929; *Fargo Forum*, June 16, 1930; *Congressional Record*, 71 Congress, 1 session (1929), pp. 5887–88, 73 Congress, 2 session (1934), p. 10,395.

[11] *Congressional Record*, 73 Congress, 1 session (1933), pp. 4971–74.

[12] *Ibid.*, 71 Congress, 1 session (1929), pp. 666–67.

[13] *Ibid.*, 71 Congress, 2 session (1930), pp. 1724–28.

[14] *Ibid.*, 73 Congress, 2 session (1934), pp. 3780–85.

[15] Dorothy Detzer to Franklin D. Roosevelt, with enclosure, May 29, 1933, Franklin D. Roosevelt Papers, Official File 178, Franklin D. Roosevelt Library, Hyde Park, New York; Dorothy Detzer, *Appointment on the Hill* (New York: Henry Holt and Company, 1948), pp. 151–52; Roscoe Baker, *The American*

Legion and American Foreign Policy (New York: Bookman Associates, 1954), pp. 124–25; Cordell Hull, *The Memoirs of Cordell Hull* (2 vols.; New York: Macmillan Company, 1948), p. 398; Russell J. Clinchy, "The Plight of the Du Ponts," *Christian Century*, LI (October 3, 1934), pp. 1234–35; Paul Hutchinson, "The Arms Inquiry," *Christian Century*, LII (May 15, 1935), pp. 643–44; *Washington Daily News*, February 26, 1934; "Hucksters of Death," *New Republic*, LXXVIII (March 7, 1934), pp. 88–89; "Arms and the Men," *Fortune*, IX (March 1934), pp. 53ff; and numerous letters and telegrams to President Roosevelt in Roosevelt Papers, Official File 178.

[16] Detzer, *Appointment on the Hill*, pp. 151–54; *Chicago American*, January 6, 1936; *Washington Herald*, September 4, 1934; Russell J. Clinchy, "Plight of the Du Ponts," *Christian Century*, pp. 1234–35.

[17] *Griggs County Sentinel-Courier*, August 14, 1924.

[18] Detzer, *Appointment on the Hill*, pp. 154–56.

[19] *Ibid.*, pp. 156–57.

[20] *Congressional Record*, 73 Congress, 1 session (1933), p. 4183.

[21] *Ibid.*, 73 Congress, 2 session (1934), p. 2153; Detzer, *Appointment on the Hill*, pp. 157–58.

[22] Detzer, *Appointment on the Hill*, pp. 159–60; *Congressional Record*, 73 Congress, 2 session (1934), pp. 3783–84, 4228–29.

[23] "Arms and the Men," *Fortune*, pp. 53ff; H. C. Engelbrecht and F. C. Hanighen, *Merchants of Death* (New York: Dodd, Mead and Company, 1934); Detzer, *Appointment on the Hill*, p. 161; Clinchy, "Plight of the Du Ponts," *Christian Century*, p. 1234; and various letters in Roosevelt Papers, Official File 178.

[24] Detzer, *Appointment on the Hill*, pp. 160–61.

[25] *Ibid.*, pp. 161–63; *Congressional Record*, 73 Congress, 2 session (1934), pp. 6472–85; *Washington Post*, April 13, 1934.

[26] United States Senate, *Hearings before the Special Committee Investigating the Munitions Industry*, 73 Congress, 2 session (Washington, D.C.: Government Printing Office, 1934–37), Part 1, pp. 1–2.

[27] Interview with Gerald P. Nye, July 20, 1959.

[28] Jonathan Mitchell, "Mass Murderers, in Person," *New Republic*, LXXX (September 26, 1934), pp. 178–80; "Morrow's Successor," *Outlook and Independent*, CLIX (December 16, 1931), p. 488; *Time*, XXXII (November 7, 1938), pp. 2, 4; Jack Alexander, "Missouri Dark Mule," *Saturday Evening Post*, CCXI (October 8, 1938), pp. 5–7, 32–36; *Newsweek*, XVI (November 25, 1940), pp. 16–17; "Back in the Fold," *Scholastic*, XXXVIII (February 3, 1941), p. 16; *Literary Digest*, CXX (September 7, 1935), p. 27; Jonathan Mitchell, "Vandenberg: Heroes' Child," *New Republic*, CII (April 8, 1940), pp. 461–63; Ray Tucker, "Marked Man," *Collier's*, XCV (March 9, 1935), pp. 26, 38.

[29] Interview with Nye, July 20, 1959; Homer T. Bone to the author, September 24, 1959; *Star* (Washington, D.C.), April 23, 1934; *Fargo Forum*, April 24, 1934.

[30] Hull, *Memoirs*, pp. 398–400; Cordell Hull to Nye, April 27, 1934, Department of State Records, File No. 811.113 Senate Investigation/7, National Archives.

[31] *Congressional Record*, 73 Congress, 2 session (1934), p. 9095; Hull, *Memoirs*, p. 400.

[32] *Grand Forks Herald*, May 22, 1934.

[33] Detzer, *Appointment on the Hill*, pp. 164–70; *Grand Forks Herald*, May 22, 1934; *Washington Post*, September 23, 1934; *Congressional Record*, 74 Congress, 1 session (1935), pp. 10,131–43; *Time*, XXVII (January 20, 1936), p. 16; Stephen Raushenbush to Nye, August 10, 1934, Records of the Special Committee Investigating the Munitions Industry, General Subject File, Record Group 46, National Archives, Washington, D.C.; John Edward Wiltz, "The Nye Committee Revisited," *Historian*, XXIII (February 1961), pp. 216–17.

[34] *Washington Post,* September 23, 1934; Raushenbush to Homer T. Bone, August 9, 1934, Munitions Investigating Committee Records, Administrative File, National Archives; Raushenbush to Nye, August 18, 1934, Nye Papers.

[35] *Hearings before the Special Committee Investigating the Munitions Industry,* Parts 1 through 8; *News-Week,* IV (September 15, 1934), pp. 7–8; Jonathan Mitchell, "Mass Murderers, in Person," *New Republic,* LXXX (September 26, 1934), p. 178; Clinchy, "Plight of the Du Ponts," *Christian Century,* p. 1234.

[36] Clinchy, "Plight of the Du Ponts," *Christian Century,* pp. 1234–35.

[37] *Foreign Relations of the United States: Diplomatic Papers, 1934* (5 vols.; Washington, D.C., 1950–52), I, 428–48.

[38] Nancy Harvison Hooker, ed., *The Moffat Papers: Selections from the Diplomatic Journals of Jay Pierrepont Moffat, 1919–1943* (Cambridge, Mass.: Harvard University Press, 1956), pp. 113–14.

[39] *Foreign Relations, 1934,* I, 437–38; *Baltimore Sun,* September 12, 1934.

[40] Douglas MacArthur to Nye, August 8, 1934, Munitions Investigating Committee Records, General Subject File, National Archives.

[41] Hooker, *Moffat Papers,* pp. 114–15; *Star* (Washington, D.C.), September 14, 1934.

[42] *Star* (Washington, D.C.), September 14, 1934; *Washington News,* September 15, 1934; *New York Herald Tribune,* September 17, 1934.

[43] *Washington Post,* September 22, 1934; *Star* (Washington, D.C.), September 27, 1934; Clinchy, "Plight of the Du Ponts," *Christian Century,* p. 1235; *New York Times,* November 13, 1934; *Foreign Relations, 1934,* I, 447; *Hearings before the Special Committee Investigating the Munitions Industry,* Part 5, pp. 1136–38.

[44] *Hearings before the Special Committee Investigating the Munitions Industry,* Part 8, pp. 2035–36.

[45] *Washington Post,* September 30, 1934; hundreds of letters and clippings in the files and folders relating to Nye's speaking engagements, Nye Papers; various conversations with Nye and Mrs. Nye, July and August 1959.

[46] Gerald P. Nye, "Should Governments Exercise Direct Control of Munitions Industries," *Congressional Digest,* XIII (November 1934), pp. 266–70; Gerald P. Nye, "Munitions" (Address given before Empire Club of Canada in Toronto, November 15, 1934).

Chapter 6. The Nye Committee and Presidential Power

[1] United States Senate, *Hearings before the Special Committee Investigating the Munitions Industry,* 73 Congress, 2 session (Washington, D.C.: Government Printing Office, 1934–37), Parts 9 through 39. Part 40, published in 1943, consists of an index of the hearings and reports. Citations for the reports may be found in later footnotes in this chapter.

[2] Brent Dow Allinson, "Senator Nye Sums Up," *Christian Century,* LII (January 16, 1935), p. 80; *Congressional Record,* 74 Congress, 1 session (1935), p. 460.

[3] *Congressional Record,* 74 Congress, 1 session (1935), pp. 460–61; 75 Congress, 1 session (1937), pp. 121–22, 1798; *Hearings before the Special Committee Investigating the Munitions Industry,* Part 9, p. 2170.

[4] *Mandan Daily Pioneer,* April 28, 1927.

[5] The author spent the summer of 1958 in Hyde Park, New York, doing research in Roosevelt's papers in a setting in which Roosevelt was reared and lived. Later the author spent some weeks in Nye's home in Chevy Chase, Maryland, doing research in the senator's papers. The author also visited areas of Wisconsin, Iowa, and North Dakota in which the boy and man developed. These experiences in research and observation provided important bases for the comparison and contrast of the two men in this paragraph.

[6] *Congressional Record*, 74 Congress, 1 session (1935), pp. 1905–6.

[7] Transcript of Franklin D. Roosevelt's Press Conferences, December 12, 1934, Roosevelt Papers.

[8] *News-Week*, IV (December 22, 1934), pp. 3–4; "Nationalize the Arms Industry!" *Nation*, CXXXIX (December 26, 1934), p. 726; "Roosevelt and the Munitions Inquiry," *New Republic*, LXXXI (December 26, 1934), pp. 178–79; memorandum by Joseph C. Green, December 26, 1934, Department of State Records, File No. 811.113 Senate Investigation/185, National Archives; Lyn Smith to Roosevelt, December 14, 1934, F. E. Davison to Roosevelt, December 19, 1934, and many other letters to the President in December, 1934, in Roosevelt Papers, Official File 178; Bernard M. Baruch, *Baruch: The Public Years* (New York: Holt, Rinehart and Winston, 1960), pp. 267–68.

[9] *Foreign Relations of the United States: Diplomatic Papers, 1935* (4 vols.; Washington, D.C., 1952–53), I, 360–73; William C. Potter to Cordell Hull, March 5, 1935, Nye to Hull, March 6, 1935, Hull to Nye, March 15, 1935, Hull to Potter, March 9, 1935, memorandum of conversation between Hull and Sir Ronald Lindsay, March 14, 1935, memorandum from Joseph C. Green, March 20, 1935, memorandum on cooperation with the Nye committee, April 11, 1935, memorandum by William Phillips, April 18, 1935, Department of State Records, File No. 811.-113 Senate Investigation/214, 215, 216, 226, 237A, 247; Minutes of meetings of Senate Committee Investigating the Munitions Industry, March 22, 1935, Records of the Special Committee Investigating the Munitions Industry, Executive File, Record Group 46, National Archives; Cordell Hull, *The Memoirs of Cordell Hull* (2 vols.; New York: Macmillan Company, 1948), pp. 401–3.

[10] Memorandum by Green, August 14, 1935, Hull to Nye, August 15, 1935, Department of State Records, File No. 811.113 Senate Investigation/288; Minutes of meeting of Senate Committee Investigating the Munitions Industry, August 14, 1935, Records of Munitions Investigating Committee, Executive File.

[11] *Congressional Record*, 74 Congress, 1 session (1935), pp. 4726–27.

[12] United States Senate Special Committee on Investigation of the Munitions Industry, *Munitions Industry: Naval Shipbuilding*, Senate Report 944, Part 1, 74 Congress, 1 session (Washington, D.C.: Government Printing Office, 1935), *passim*, but see particularly pp. 1–9.

[13] *Ibid.*, pp. 11–14.

[14] Stephen Raushenbush to Senators on Munitions Committee, March 15, 1935, Records of Munitions Investigating Committee, General Subject File; *Congressional Record*, 73 Congress, 2 session (1934), pp. 6472–75.

[15] *Foreign Relations of the United States, 1935*, I, 318–23, 332–33, 363–64; *Washington Post*, March 20, 1935; Transcript of Roosevelt's Press Conferences, March 20, 1935, Roosevelt Papers.

[16] *Hearings before the Special Committee Investigating the Munitions Industry*, Part 22, pp. 6259–6423, but see especially 6267–69, 6280, 6423; Part 24, pp. 7078–85.

[17] Raushenbush to Nye, February 8, 1935, Records of Munitions Investigating Committee, General Subject File; Nye to William T. Stone, August 24, 1935, Nye Papers; United States Senate Special Committee to Investigate the Munitions Industry, *To Prevent Profiteering in War*, Senate Report No. 577, 74 Congress, 1 session; printed copy of H. R. 5529 as amended (Report No. 889), Nye Papers; *Star* (Washington, D.C.), February 27, 1936.

[18] United States Senate Special Committee on Investigation of the Munitions Industry, *Munitions Industry: Preliminary Report on Wartime Taxation and Price Control*, Senate Report 944, Part 2, 74 Congress, 1 session (Washington, D.C.: Government Printing Office, 1935), *passim*, but see particularly pp. 3–7.

[19] Nye to Stone, August 24, 1935, Nye Papers; *Star* (Washington, D.C.), Feb-

ruary 27, 1936, April 3, 1936; *Washington Post*, April 3, 1936; *New York Times*, April 4, 1936, April 20, 1938; *Congressional Record*, 75 Congress, 1 session (1937), pp. 674–75, 75 Congress, 3 session (1938), p. 5824; F. M. Johnston to H. F. Swanson, March 15, 1940, Papers supporting S. 1885, 76 Congress, Record Group 46, National Archives.

[20] *New York Times*, October 17, 1935, October 24, 1935; Raushenbush to Nye, December 13, 1935, Records of Munitions Investigating Committee, Neutrality File.

[21] Memorandum by Joseph C. Green, August 14, 1935, Nye to Hull, August 13, 1935, Hull to Nye, August 15, 1935, Hull to Nye, January 6, 1936, Department of State Records, File No. 811.113 Senate Investigation/288, 285, 371; Minutes of Munitions Committee Meeting, August 14, 1935, Executive File, Raushenbush to Homer T. Bone, November 11, 1935, Administrative File, Records of Munitions Investigating Committee.

[22] *New York Times*, February 10, 1936. The testimony and documents of the committee's probe of the House of Morgan are in *Hearings before the Special Committee Investigating the Munitions Industry*, Parts 25–35, pp. 7477–11,831.

[23] Nye to C. E. Backman, January 10, 1936, January 14, 1936, Nye Papers.

[24] *Hearings before the Special Committee Investigating the Munitions Industry*, Part 28, pp. 8509–12; Hull, *Memoirs*, p. 403.

[25] *Congressional Record*, 74 Congress, 2 session (1936), pp. 501–13; Tom Connally, *My Name Is Tom Connally* (New York: Thomas Y. Crowell Company, 1954), p. 214.

[26] *Congressional Record*, 74 Congress, 2 session (1936), pp. 562–70. Historical scholarship supports Nye's charge. See Thomas A. Bailey, *Woodrow Wilson and the Lost Peace* (New York: Macmillan Company, 1944), pp. 147–48; Robert H. Ferrell, "Woodrow Wilson and Open Diplomacy," in George L. Anderson, ed., *Issues and Conflicts* (Lawrence: University of Kansas Press, 1959), pp. 200–4.

[27] *Congressional Record*, 74 Congress, 2 session (1936), pp. 572–79, 650–57; Connally, *My Name Is Tom Connally*, p. 214; *New York Times*, January 18, 1936.

[28] Hull, *Memoirs*, p. 403; Memorandum by Joseph C. Green, January 18, 1936, Department of State Records, File No. 811.113 Senate Investigation/384.

[29] *Congressional Record*, 74 Congress, 2 session (1936), p. 567; Nye to Allen Dulles, January 23, 1936, Nye Papers.

[30] *Hearings before the Special Committee Investigating the Munitions Industry*, Part 28, pp. 8633–37.

[31] George W. Norris to Edward L. Novak, January 27, 1936, George W. Norris Papers, Library of Congress, Washington, D.C.

[32] *Congressional Record*, 74 Congress, 2 session (1936), p. 2616.

[33] *Hearings before the Special Committee Investigating the Munitions Industry*, Part 39, pp. 13,338–39.

[34] Nye to Backman, March 5, 1936, March 19, 1936, Nye Papers; *Star* (Washington, D.C.), March 6, 1936.

[35] *Congressional Record*, 74 Congress, 2 session (1936), pp. 5660–61; United States Senate Special Committee on Investigation of the Munitions Industry, *Report on Activities and Sales of Munitions Companies*, Senate Report 944, Part 3, 74 Congress, 2 session (Washington, D.C.: Government Printing Office, 1936), *passim*, but see particularly pp. 3–11.

[36] *Ibid.*, pp. 15–17.

[37] United States Senate Special Committee on Investigation of the Munitions Industry, *Munitions Industry: Report on War Department Bills S. 1716–S. 1722 Relating to Industrial Mobilization in Wartime*, Senate Report 944, Part 4, 74 Congress, 2 session (Washington, D.C.: Government Printing Office, 1936), *passim*, but see particularly pp. 1–5.

[38] United States Senate Special Committee on Investigation of the Munitions Industry, *Munitions Industry: Report on Existing Legislation*, Senate Report 944, Part 5, 74 Congress, 2 session (Washington, D.C.: Government Printing Office, 1936), *passim*, but see particularly pp. 1–9.

[39] *Ibid.*, p. 58. The entire Burns report is on pp. 11–87, and the Department of State documents on which it was based are on pp. 89–232. Miss Burns married Stephen Raushenbush in the midst of the investigation on January 25, 1936.

[40] United States Senate Special Committee on Investigation of the Munitions Industry, *Munitions Industry: Supplemental Report on the Adequacy of Existing Legislation*, Senate Report 944, Part 6, 74 Congress, 2 session (Washington, D.C.: Government Printing Office, 1936), *passim*, but see particularly pp. 1–7.

[41] *Congressional Record*, 74 Congress, 2 session (1936), p. 10,152; United States Senate Special Committee on Investigation of the Munitions Industry, *Munitions Industry: Report on Government Manufacture of Munitions*, Senate Report 944, Part 7, 74 Congress, 2 session (Washington, D.C.: Government Printing Office, 1936), *passim*, but see particularly pp. 121–23.

[42] Hadley Cantril, ed., and Mildred Strunk, *Public Opinion, 1935–1946* (Princeton, N.J.: Princeton University Press, 1951), p. 491.

[43] *Baltimore Sun*, February 22, 1937; *Congressional Record*, 75 Congress, 1 session (1937), p. 5408; David I. Walsh to Nye, August 18, 1937, and enclosed copy of letter from A. B. Cook, August 17, 1937, Nye Papers; *Foreign Relations of the United States, 1935*, I, 318–19.

[44] *Congressional Record*, 74 Congress, 2 session (1936), pp. 2616–19, 10,152; *ibid.*, 76 Congress, 1 session (1939), pp. 10,405–6.

[45] *Ibid.*, 78 Congress, 2 session (1944), p. 9686.

Chapter 7. Legislating Neutrality

[1] R. Walton Moore to Franklin D. Roosevelt, August 27, 1934, Roosevelt to Cordell Hull, September 25, 1934, Roosevelt Papers, Official File 1561; Cordell Hull, *The Memoirs of Cordell Hull* (2 vols.; New York: Macmillan Company, 1948), pp. 404–5. Since this chapter was written an excellent book on neutrality legislation has been published: Robert A. Divine, *The Illusion of Neutrality* (Chicago: University of Chicago Press, 1962).

[2] *Congressional Record*, 74 Congress, 1 session (1935), p. 461.

[3] Gerald P. Nye to Joseph Green, February 20, 1935, Green to Nye, February 23, 1935, Munitions Investigating Committee Records, Administrative Files, National Archives; *Foreign Relations of the United States: Diplomatic Papers, 1935* (4 vols.; Washington, D.C., 1952–53), I, 316–18; Hull, *Memoirs*, p. 405.

[4] Hull, *Memoirs*, p. 405; *Foreign Relations of the United States, 1935*, I, 318–21, 363–64; memorandum by Green, March 27, 1935, Department of State Records, File No. 811.113 Senate Investigation/242.

[5] *New York Times*, March 31, 1935.

[6] *Foreign Relations of the United States, 1935*, I, 323–25, 328–29; confidential memorandum Stephen Raushenbush to Nye, March 30, 1935, minutes of Munitions Investigating Committee meeting, April 1, 1935, Munitions Investigating Committee Records, General Subject File; *Congressional Record*, 74 Congress, 1 session (1935), p. 4726.

[7] Wayne S. Cole, "Senator Key Pittman and American Neutrality Policies, 1933–1940," *Mississippi Valley Historical Review*, XLVI (March 1960), pp. 644–49.

[8] *Ibid.*, pp. 647–48.

[9] *Foreign Relations of the United States, 1935*, I, 329–30; Key Pittman to Wallace S. Murray, April 11, 1935, Department of State Records, File No. 811.113 Senate Investigation/245.

[10] Hull, *Memoirs*, pp. 406–11; *Foreign Relations of the United States, 1935*, I, 331–36.

[11] Jack Alexander, "Missouri Dark Mule," *Saturday Evening Post*, CCXI (October 8, 1938), pp. 5–7, 32–37; "Sharpshooters into Arms Trade," *Literary Digest*, CXXI (January 18, 1936), p. 33; Ralph Coghlan, "Missouri – a Threat and a Promise," *Nation*, CXXXV (November 2, 1932), pp. 422–24.

[12] Printed copies of S. J. Res. 99, 100, and 120, Nye Papers.

[13] Printed copy of S. 2998, Cordell Hull to Nye, June 18, 1935, Hull to James P. Pope, June 18, 1935, Nye Papers.

[14] Hull, *Memoirs*, p. 410; Raushenbush to William T. Stone, June 26, 1935, Raushenbush to Lawrence Brown, June 26, 1935, Munitions Investigating Committee Records, Neutrality File.

[15] Raushenbush to Ed Villmoare, Jr., June 29, 1936, Bennett Champ Clark and Nye to Pittman, July 3, 1935, with enclosed memorandum, Munitions Investigating Committee Records, Neutrality File.

[16] Hull, *Memoirs*, p. 410; William Phillips to Hull, June 28, 1935, Department of State Records, File No. 811.04418/55.

[17] Hull, *Memoirs*, p. 410; telegram Raushenbush to Stone, July 10, 1935, Raushenbush to Stone, July 11, 1935, Munitions Investigating Committee Records, Neutrality File.

[18] Hull, *Memoirs*, pp. 410–11; Tom Connally, *My Name Is Tom Connally* (New York: Thomas Y. Crowell Company, 1954), p. 219; Raushenbush to Stone, July 10, 1935, July 16, 1935, memorandum (probably from Stone) to Raushenbush, July 18, 1935, memorandum on neutrality legislation by Raushenbush, July 30, 1935, confidential memorandum by Raushenbush, August 2, 1935, Raushenbush to Stone, August 9, 1935, Munitions Investigating Committee Records, Neutrality File; Pittman to Hull, July 17, 1935, memorandum from Green to Phillips, July 20, 1935, Phillips to Pittman with enclosure, July 31, 1935, Department of State Records, File No. 811.04418/58, 69, 68A; *Foreign Relations of the United States, 1935*, I, 343–45.

[19] Nye to Pittman, August 18, 1935, Senate Foreign Relations Committee Files, 74 Congress, Record Group 46, National Archives. A mimeographed copy of this letter over the names of Nye and Clark for release to the press on August 19 is in the Nye Papers.

[20] Hull, *Memoirs*, pp. 411–12; Hull to Roosevelt, n.d., Roosevelt to Pittman, August 19, 1935, Pittman to White House, August 19, 1935, Pittman to Stephen Early, August 19, 1935, Roosevelt Papers, President's Personal File 745.

[21] Hull, *Memoirs*, p. 412; Connally, *My Name Is Tom Connally*, pp. 219–20; unsigned, undated memo probably prepared by Raushenbush on August 19, 1935, Munitions Investigating Committee Records, Neutrality File.

[22] Telegram from Raushenbush to Stone, August 20, 1935, Munitions Investigating Committee Records, Neutrality File; *Congressional Record*, 74 Congress, 1 session (1935), pp. 13,775–93; *New York Times*, August 21, 1935; *New York Post*, August 21, 1935.

[23] *Congressional Record*, 74 Congress, 1 session (1935), pp. 13,951–56, 14,283, 14,430–34; Hull, *Memoirs*, pp. 412–13.

[24] Print of S. J. Res. 173, Nye Papers; *Congressional Record*, 74 Congress, 1 session (1935), pp. 14,535; *Foreign Relations of the United States, 1935*, I, 350–52.

[25] *Foreign Relations of the United States, 1935*, I, 350–52; Hull, *Memoirs*, pp. 413–15; Connally, *My Name Is Tom Connally*, pp. 220–21.

[26] Telegram from M. H. McIntyre to Nye, August 27, 1935, Roosevelt Papers, Official File 1561; Hull, *Memoirs*, p. 415; Samuel I. Rosenman, ed., *The Public*

Papers and Addresses of Franklin D. Roosevelt (13 vols.; New York, 1938–50), 1935 vol. (*The Court Disapproves*), pp. 345–46.

[27] *New York Times*, October 12, 1935, October 17, 1935, October 27, 1935.

[28] Hull, *Memoirs*, pp. 460–62; Raushenbush to Nye, November 23, 1935, undated radiogram Raushenbush to Nye, radiogram Nye to Raushenbush, December 10, 1935, Munitions Investigating Committee Records, Administrative File.

[29] Hull, *Memoirs*, pp. 462–65; *Congressional Record*, 74 Congress, 2 session (1936), p. 47; *Washington Post*, January 6, 1936; Pittman to Pat Harrison, January 4, 1936, Pittman to Hull, January 8, 1936, Pittman to Nye and Clark, January 24, 1936, Senate Foreign Relations Committee Files, 74 Congress.

[30] Hull, *Memoirs*, pp. 460–63; C. W. Y[ost] to Green, January 8, 1936, Department of State Records, File No. 811.04418/110; *Washington Post*, January 6, 1936.

[31] Hull, *Memoirs*, pp. 464–65; R. Walton Moore to Roosevelt, January 23, 1936, Roosevelt Papers, Official File 1561; Pittman to Raymond Moley, February 5, 1936, Senate Foreign Relations Committee Files, 75 Congress; Connally, *My Name Is Tom Connally*, p. 221.

[32] Connally, *My Name Is Tom Connally*, p. 222; *Washington Post*, February 12, 1936.

[33] *New York Times*, February 14, 1936; *Baltimore Sun*, February 14, 1936.

[34] *Washington Star*, February 14, 1936; telegram from Maury Maverick to Roosevelt, February 16, 1936, undated memo from Roosevelt to McIntyre, Roosevelt Papers, Official File 1561; *Washington Herald*, February 18, 1936.

[35] *Congressional Record*, 74 Congress, 2 session (1936), pp. 2291–2306; *Washington Herald*, February 19, 1936; *Washington Post*, February 19, 1936.

[36] Nye to C. E. Backman, February 21, 1936, Nye Papers; *New York Times*, February 19, 1936.

[37] *New York Times*, February 19, 1936; Hull, *Memoirs*, pp. 466–67; Connally, *My Name Is Tom Connally*, p. 222.

[38] *Washington Post*, June 30, 1936.

[39] Sumner Welles, *The Time for Decision* (New York and London: Harper and Brothers, 1944), pp. 57–61; Connally, *My Name Is Tom Connally*, pp. 222–23; Hull, *Memoirs*, pp. 490–91, 514–15; Dorothy Detzer, *Appointment on the Hill* (New York: Henry Holt and Company, 1948), pp. 213–17; Thomas A. Bailey, *The Man in the Street* (New York: Macmillan Company, 1948), p. 208.

[40] In addition to the items cited in the preceding note, see Harold L. Ickes, *The Secret Diary of Harold L. Ickes: The Inside Struggle, 1936–1939* (New York: Simon and Schuster, 1954), pp. 388–90.

[41] Telegram to Roosevelt from Elmer A. Benson, Nye, Fred Bierman, Guy Gillette, Fred Hildebrandt, Herman P. Kopplemann, Henry C. Luckey, Louis Ludlow, Bryon Scott, and Fred Sisson, August 14, 1936, Roosevelt Papers, Official File 1561. As he remembered it twenty-two years later, Nye believed that the Masonic Order and Senator Connally were most important in leading him to urge repeal of the Spanish embargo in 1938. Interviews with Nye, August 17, 1959, and August 21, 1959.

[42] *Congressional Record*, 75 Congress, 1 session (1937), pp. 76–80; *Washington Herald*, January 7, 1937; Hull, *Memoirs*, pp. 490–91.

[43] *Congressional Record*, 75 Congress, 1 session (1937), pp. 2737, 2865, 3315–17.

[44] Hull to Pittman, May 4, 1937, unsigned memo on S. J. Res. 120, Papers Supporting Senate Bills and Resolutions, 75 Congress, S. J. Res. 120, Record Group 46, National Archives; *Foreign Relations of the United States: Diplomatic Papers, 1937* (5 vols.; Washington, D.C.: Government Printing Office, 1954), I, pp. 870–71.

[45] Norman Thomas to Roosevelt, June 9, 1937, Roosevelt to McIntyre, June 16,

1937, President's Personal File 4840, Roosevelt to Hull, June 29, 1937, Official File 1561, Roosevelt Papers; Bowers to Pittman, June 26, 1937, Senate Foreign Relations Committee Files, 75 Congress.

[46] *Congressional Record*, 75 Congress, 3 session (1938), p. 6030; Gerald P. Nye, "America's Interest in Spain" (mimeographed copy of address over NBC, May 20, 1938), Nye Papers; Hull, *Memoirs*, pp. 516–17; Hull to Pittman, May 12, 1938, Papers Supporting Senate Bills and Resolutions, 75 Congress, S. J. Res. 288; *New York Sun*, May 14, 1938; *Philadelphia Record*, May 18, 1938.

[47] Mimeographed letter from Nye to Mrs. V. J. Larose, October 6, 1938, Nye Papers.

[48] *Congressional Record*, 76 Congress, 1 session (1939), pp. 742–43.

[49] Ickes, *Inside Struggle*, pp. 569–70.

[50] United States Special Committee on Investigation of the Munitions Industry, *Munitions Industry: Report on Existing Legislation*, and *Supplemental Report on the Adequacy of Existing Legislation*, Senate Report 944, Parts 5 and 6, 74 Congress, 2 session (Washington, D.C.: Government Printing Office, 1936), *passim*, but see particularly pp. 1–9 of each report; *Washington Post*, November 11, 1936.

[51] *Congressional Record*, 75 Congress, 1 session (1937), Appendix, pp. 120–22.

[52] Hull, *Memoirs*, pp. 506–8; Moore to A. Barr Comstock, February 25, 1937, Department of State Records, File No. 811.04418/228.

[53] *Congressional Record*, 75 Congress, 1 session (1937), pp. 337, 611; Hull, *Memoirs*, p. 507; transcript of meeting of Senate Foreign Relations Committee, February 13, 1937, pp. 1–2, Senate Foreign Relations Committee Files, 75 Congress.

[54] Transcript of meeting of Senate Foreign Relations Committee, February 13, 1937, pp. 1–46, Senate Foreign Relations Committee Files, 75 Congress.

[55] *Washington Post*, February 27, 1937; *Congressional Record*, 75 Congress, 1 session (1937), p. 1798.

[56] *Congressional Record*, 75 Congress, 1 session (1937), p. 1807; Moore to Roosevelt, March 4, 1937, Roosevelt Papers, Official File 1561.

[57] Hull, *Memoirs*, pp. 508–9; Roosevelt to Joseph T. Robinson, April 20, 1937, Roosevelt Papers, President's Secretary's File, Neutrality Folder; *Washington Post*, April 29, 1937.

[58] *Washington Post*, April 29, 1937; *Congressional Record*, 75 Congress, 1 session (1937), pp. 3954–57.

[59] *Congressional Record*, 75 Congress, 1 session (1937), p. 3962; Hull, *Memoirs*, p. 509; Hull to Roosevelt, April 30, 1937, Roosevelt Papers, President's Secretary's File, Neutrality Folder; *Washington Post*, May 2, 1937; print of S. J. Res. 51, Nye Papers.

[60] *Congressional Record*, 75 Congress, 1 session (1937), p. 4264; *Baltimore Sun*, May 11, 1937; Sumner Welles to Pittman, May 27, 1937, Papers Supporting Senate Bills and Resolutions, 75 Congress, S. 2370.

[61] Nye to Walter Lippmann, April 26, 1939, Nye Papers.

[62] Hull, *Memoirs*, pp. 556–58; Herbert Feis, *The Road to Pearl Harbor* (Princeton: Princeton University Press, 1950), pp. 10–11.

[63] *Congressional Record*, 75 Congress, 1 session (1937), Appendix, pp. 2187, 2257–58; *New York Times*, August 15, 1937.

[64] *Congressional Record*, 75 Congress, 1 session (1937), pp. 8585–86. The author had interviews and conversations with many people in North Dakota in March 1960 – some who knew Nye and many who did not. Almost without exception discussion of Nye with them included, on their own initiative, favorable mention of Nye's prediction in this speech.

[65] Hull, *Memoirs*, pp. 544–46; *New York Times*, October 8, 1937.

[66] *New York Times*, December 14, 1937, April 30, 1938.

[67] *Griggs County Sentinel-Courier*, December 11, 1924.

[68] Samuel I. Rosenman, ed., *The Public Papers and Addresses of Franklin D. Roosevelt* (13 vols.; New York, 1938–50), 1938 vol. (*The Continuing Struggle for Liberalism*), pp. 36–37; Hull, *Memoirs*, pp. 563–64; *Congressional Digest*, XVII (February 1938), pp. 37–41.

[69] *Congressional Record*, 75 Congress, 3 session (1938), pp. 2410–11.

[70] United States Senate, *Hearings before Subcommittee of the Judiciary Committee*, 76 Congress, 1 session, on S. J. Res. 84 (Washington, D.C.: Government Printing Office, 1939), pp. 127–28.

[71] Hull, *Memoirs*, pp. 563–64; *Congressional Digest*, XVII (February 1938), p. 64; Harry H. Woodring to Carl A. Hatch, June 9, 1939, Papers Supporting Senate Bills and Resolutions, 76 Congress, S. J. Res. 84; *Congressional Record*, 75 Congress, 3 session (1938), p. 278; Roscoe Baker, *The American Legion and American Foreign Policy* (New York: Bookman Associates, 1954), pp. 160–62; *New York Times*, August 23, 1938.

[72] Detzer, *Appointment on the Hill*; Robert Edwin Bowers, "The American Peace Movement, 1933–41" (Unpublished Ph.D. dissertation, Department of History, University of Wisconsin, 1949). The Roosevelt Papers, Nye Papers, Department of State Records, and Munitions Investigating Committee Records all contain many letters, resolutions, and petitions on neutrality and peace proposals from leaders and units of the various pacifist organizations.

Chapter 8. Armaments and Disarmament

[1] *Griggs County Sentinel-Courier*, December 22, 1921.

[2] Gerald P. Nye, "My Christian Church in the Nation" (Typed copy of an address delivered before the Women's Missionary Federation International Convention, Grand Rapids, Michigan, October 28, 1954), Nye Papers.

[3] *Congressional Record*, 72 Congress, 1 session (1932), p. 9691.

[4] Print of S. 4054, 75 Congress, 3 session, Nye Papers.

[5] *Congressional Record*, 70 Congress, 2 session (1929), p. 2594.

[6] *Ibid.*, 75 Congress, 3 session (1938), pp. 5528, 5571–81; United States Senate, *Hearings before the Special Committee Investigating the Munitions Industry* (74 Congress, 2 session, Washington, D.C.: Government Printing Office, 1934–37), p. 12,033.

[7] United States Senate, *Hearings before the Special Committee Investigating the Munitions Industry* (74 Congress, 2 session, Washington, D.C.: Government Printing Office, 1934–37), p. 12,033; *Congressional Record*, 75 Congress, 3 session (1938), p. 5850; *St. Louis Globe-Democrat*, January 15, 1939.

[8] *Fargo Forum*, February 3, 1942.

[9] *Congressional Record*, 75 Congress, 3 session (1938), p. 5574.

[10] *St. Louis Globe-Democrat*, January 15, 1939.

[11] *New York Times*, May 11, 1940; Nye to G. W. S. Musgrave, May 30, 1940, Nye Papers.

[12] *Congressional Record*, 70 Congress, 2 session (1929), p. 2594.

[13] *Ibid.*, 73 Congress, 2 session (1934), pp. 3780, 6458.

[14] *Ibid.*, 72 Congress, 1 session (1932), p. 9690.

[15] *Ibid.*, p. 9688; 74 Congress, 1 session (1935), p. 3191.

[16] *Ibid.*, 74 Congress, 2 session (1936), p. 6809; *ibid.*, 74 Congress, 1 session (1935), p. 11,127; *New York Times*, July 25, 1935; Roscoe Baker, *The American Legion and American Foreign Policy* (New York: Bookman Associates, 1954), pp. 125–26. Representative Paul J. Kvale was elected on a Farmer-Labor party ticket in Minnesota and was a product of the agrarian reform sentiment in the upper Mississippi valley just as Nye was.

[17] *Griggs County Sentinel-Courier*, November 17, 1921.

[18] *Congressional Record*, 73 Congress, 2 session (1934), p. 3782; *Hearings before the Special Committee Investigating the Munitions Industry*, Part 9, p. 2161; *Congressional Record*, 74 Congress, 2 session (1936), p. 7433.

[19] *Congressional Record*, 75 Congress, 3 session (1938), p. 5578.

[20] *Ibid.*, 72 Congress, 1 session (1932), p. 9691.

[21] *Ibid.*, 73 Congress, 2 session (1934), p. 3780.

[22] *Ibid.*, 74 Congress, 1 session (1935), p. 3192.

[23] *Ibid.*, 75 Congress, 3 session (1938), Appendix, p. 238.

[24] *Ibid.*, 70 Congress, 2 session (1929), p. 2599; *ibid.*, 73 Congress, 2 session (1934), p. 6458.

[25] *Ibid.*, 73 Congress, 2 session (1934), p. 6458.

[26] *Ibid.*, p. 3781.

[27] *Ibid.*, 75 Congress, 3 session (1938), p. 5841; *ibid.*, 75 Congress, 1 session (1937), Appendix, p. 121.

[28] *Ibid.*, 74 Congress, 2 session (1936), pp. 6801–2.

[29] *Ibid.*, 75 Congress, 3 session (1938), p. 5840.

[30] *Ibid.*, 74 Congress, 2 session (1936), pp. 6801–3.

[31] *Ibid.*, p. 6802.

[32] *Ibid.*, 75 Congress, 1 session (1937), pp. 6141–45.

[33] *Ibid.*, 75 Congress, 3 session (1938), pp. 5571, 5827.

[34] *Ibid.*, 77 Congress, 1 session (1941), pp. A1603–5.

[35] *Ibid.*, 75 Congress, 3 session (1938), p. 8341.

Chapter 9. Political Struggles and Transition

[1] *Congressional Record*, 74 Congress, 1 session (1935), pp. 3194–97, 11,842–56; *New York Times*, April 25, 1935; Arthur M. Schlesinger, Jr., *The Age of Roosevelt: The Politics of Upheaval* (Boston: Houghton Mifflin Company, 1960), pp. 19–20.

[2] *Congressional Record*, 74 Congress, 1 session (1935), pp. 7681, 9650; *New York Times*, June 22, 1935.

[3] Elliott Roosevelt, ed., *F. D. R.: His Personal Letters, 1928–1945* (2 vols.; New York: Duell, Sloan and Pearce, 1950), I, 452–53.

[4] *New York Times*, March 24, 1935, June 9, 1935; *McKenzie County Farmer*, January 2, 1936; *Devils Lake Journal*, May 1, 1936; *Topeka Daily Capital*, June 1, 1936; interview with Gerald P. Nye, July 20, 1959.

[5] *Washington Daily News*, June 13, 1936; *New York Times*, June 13, 1936.

[6] *New York Times*, July 7, 1935.

[7] *Devils Lake Journal*, August 10, 1935.

[8] *New York Times*, March 12, 1936, April 6, 1936.

[9] *Star* (Washington, D.C.), July 10, 1936.

[10] Gerald P. Nye to Franklin D. Roosevelt, July 17, 1936, Roosevelt to Nye, July 21, 1936, Roosevelt Papers, Official File 987.

[11] Harold L. Ickes, *The Secret Diary of Harold L. Ickes: The First Thousand Days, 1933–1936* (New York: Simon and Schuster, 1953), pp. 655–56, 661; interview with Nye, August 4, 1959.

[12] Samuel I. Rosenman, comp., *The Public Papers and Addresses of Franklin D. Roosevelt* (13 vols.; New York, 1938–50), 1936 vol. (*The People Approve*), pp. 285–92; Cordell Hull, *The Memoirs of Cordell Hull* (2 vols.; New York: Macmillan Company, 1948), pp. 479–80.

[13] Ickes, *First Thousand Days*, pp. 662–63, 665; telegrams Roosevelt to Nye, August 17, 1936, Nye to Roosevelt, August 17, 1936, Ambrose O'Connell to Marvin H. McIntyre, August 20, 1936, Roosevelt Papers, President's Personal

File 1614; *Fargo Forum*, August 20, 1936; interview with Nye, August 4, 1959; *Fargo Forum*, September 6, 1936; *New York Times*, October 2, 1936.

[14] *Ibid.*, October 8, 1936; *Devils Lake Journal*, October 9, 1936; Ickes, *First Thousand Days*, pp. 691–92; *News-Week*, VIII (October 17, 1936), pp. 15–16; *Time*, XXVIII (October 19, 1936), pp. 20–21. The key documents on Elliott Roosevelt's role in this episode are in the Nye Papers.

[15] Ickes, *First Thousand Days*, p. 698; Harold L. Ickes, *The Secret Diary of Harold L. Ickes: The Inside Struggle, 1936–1939* (New York: Simon and Schuster, 1954), p. 10; *New York Times*, October 2, 1936; *Des Moines Tribune*, October 9, 1936; Jesse S. Raphael to Harry Slattery, September 29, 1936, President's Personal File 1820, Roosevelt to Henrik Shipstead, November 4, 1936, President's Personal File 2863, Roosevelt Papers; interview with Nye, August 4, 1959.

[16] H. A. Mackoff to Nye, July 15, 1936, Official File 987, Roosevelt Papers. This file also contains copies of other letters or telegrams to Nye describing the drought conditions in North Dakota.

[17] See various items in Official File 987, Roosevelt Papers; *New York Times*, October 14, 1936; Nye to State Department, December 26, 1935, File No. 611.423 Potatoes/70, Nye to Cordell Hull, April 1, 1936, File No. 611.423 Dairy Products /19, Department of State Records.

[18] *New York Times*, March 15, 1936; *Jamestown Sun*, April 2, 1936; Jacob Krier to Nye, July 1, 1936, Nye Papers; John M. Holzworth, *The Fighting Governor: The Story of William Langer and the State of North Dakota* (Chicago: Pointer Press, 1938), pp. 91–101; Thomas Hall, *Compilation of Election Returns: National and State, 1930–1944* [Bismarck, 1945].

[19] *New York Times*, October 14, 1936; *Bismarck Tribune*, October 28, 1936; Holzworth, *Fighting Governor*, p. 101.

[20] Hall, *Compilation of Election Returns, 1930–1944.*

[21] Walter Johnson, *1600 Pennsylvania Avenue: Presidents and the People, 1929–1959* (Boston: Little, Brown and Company, 1960), pp. 91–92; Samuel Lubell, *The Future of American Politics* (2nd ed. rev.; New York: Doubleday and Company, 1956), pp. 41–54; Earle D. Ross, *Iowa Agriculture: An Historical Survey* (Iowa City: State Historical Society of Iowa, 1951), p. 176; Edgar Eugene Robinson, *They Voted For Roosevelt: The Presidential Vote, 1932–1944* (Stanford: Stanford University Press, 1947), pp. 8–9, 20–21.

[22] *New York Times*, February 6, 1937; J. R. to Roosevelt, February 19, 1937, President's Secretary's File, Roosevelt Papers; interview with Nye, July 20, 1959. Unlike many leaders of the Farmers' Union, Thatcher was distinctly pro-New Deal. This faction in the organization was not in control in the first half of the 1930's but gained ascendancy before the end of the decade. Nye's views were more like those who had lost control of the organization by the end of the decade. Nye believed that the White House had asked Thatcher to try to persuade him not to oppose the court packing bill.

[23] *Congressional Record*, 75 Congress, 1 session (1937), Appendix, pp. 311–14; *New York Times*, February 22, 1937.

[24] Telegram from A. F. Whitney to Nye, February 24, 1937, Daniel J. Tobin to Nye, February 26, 1937, Nye Papers; Ickes, *Inside Struggle*, pp. 125, 129, 135.

[25] *Congressional Record*, 75 Congress, 1 session (1937), p. 7381; Alfred H. Kelly and Winfred A. Harbison, *The American Constitution: Its Origins and Development* (New York: W. W. Norton and Company, 1948), pp. 751–54.

[26] Ickes, *Inside Struggle*, p. 196.

[27] *New York Times*, July 23, 1937; *Congressional Record*, 75 Congress, 1 session (1937), pp. 7734–39; *Fargo Forum*, August 1, 1937.

[28] *Congressional Record*, 75 Congress, 2 session (1937), pp. 1235–39; Gerald P. Nye, *The Farmer and the New Farm Bill* (print of speeches by Nye, December

10, 1937, and April 9, 1938, Washington, D.C.: Government Printing Office, 1938); mimeographed text of radio address by Nye over KFYR, Bismarck, North Dakota, October 5, 1937, Nye Papers.

[29] Nye, *The Farmer and the New Farm Bill*, pp. 4, 13–16.

[30] *Star* (Washington, D.C.), January 7, 1937; *Griggs County Sentinel-Courier*, March 24, 1938; *Nation*, CXLVI (May 7, 1938), p. 543; *Christian Science Monitor*, May 11, 1938; *Fargo Forum*, June 12, 1938, June 14, 1938; "Duel in North Dakota," *Newsweek*, XI (June 27, 1938), p. 12.

[31] National Non-Partisan Committee for the Re-election of Senator Nye, *Senator Gerald P. Nye: Will He Go Back?* (n.p., [1938]), Nye Papers.

[32] *New York Sunday News*, June 25, 1938; *Fargo Forum*, June 26, 1938; *Nation*, CXLVI (May 7, 1938), p. 543.

[33] Hall, *Compilation of Election Returns, 1930–1944.*

[34] *The Leader* (North Dakota), August 11, 1938; *Bismarck Tribune*, September 29, 1938.

[35] *Bismarck Tribune*, August 6, 1938; Howard I. Henry to James A. Farley, October 31, 1938, James D. Robertson to Farley, December 12, 1938, Henry Hammerly to Farley, December 12, 1938, Charles H. Tolan to Farley, December 22, 1938, S. G. Nagel to Farley, December 23, 1938, S. J. Umber to Farley, January 17, 1939, Official File 300, Roosevelt Papers.

[36] *Nye-Lemke Record* (n.p., [1938]), Nye Papers; Nye to Hannah B. Haaland, August 22, 1938, Nye Papers; *Star* (Washington, D.C.), October 19, 1938.

[37] *Bismarck Tribune*, October 17, 1938, October 22, 1938; *Fargo Forum*, October 1, 1938, September 28, 1938; *Nye-Lemke Record*, Nye Papers; Nagel to Farley, December 23, 1938, Official File 300, Roosevelt Papers.

[38] *Star* (Washington, D.C.), October 19, 1938; *Fargo Forum*, November 4, 1938.

[39] Hall, *Compilation of Election Returns, 1930–1944*; *Fargo Forum*, November 13, 1938; and previously cited letters to Farley in Official File 300, Roosevelt Papers.

Chapter 10. The Advent of Foreign War

[1] Samuel I. Rosenman, comp., *The Public Papers and Addresses of Franklin D. Roosevelt* (13 vols.; New York, 1938–50), 1939 vol. (*War – And Neutrality*), pp. 1–12, 70–74.

[2] *St. Louis Globe-Democrat*, January 15, 1939; *Congressional Record*, 76 Congress, 1 session (1939), Appendix, pp. 282–83; Gerald P. Nye, "Should America's Defense Frontier Extend beyond the American Continents? – Con," *Congressional Digest*, XVIII (March 1939), pp. 88–89.

[3] *New York Times*, January 28, 1939, February 2, 1939; Basil Rauch, *Roosevelt from Munich to Pearl Harbor* (New York: Creative Age Press, 1950), pp. 112–13.

[4] Transcript of "Conference with the Senate Military Affairs Committee, Executive Office of the White House, January 31, 1939, 12.45 P.M.," Roosevelt Papers, President's Personal File 1-P.

[5] *Congressional Record*, 76 Congress, 1 session (1939), p. 1010.

[6] Rauch, *Roosevelt*, p. 113; transcript of Franklin D. Roosevelt's Press Conferences, February 3, 17, 1939, Roosevelt Papers.

[7] Interviews with Gerald P. Nye, August 27, 1956, August 26, 1958, and July 20, 1959.

[8] This analysis is based on an examination of numerous items in the Roosevelt Papers, but see particularly President's Personal File 70, 200B, 866, 897, 977, 2489, 3338, 5457, 6650; and Robert E. Sherwood, *Roosevelt and Hopkins: An Intimate History* (New York: Harper and Brothers, 1948), p. 165. Most of these business conservatives opposed Roosevelt in the election of 1940 – but not his foreign policies. If the G.O.P. had nominated a western "isolationist" in place of

Willkie, it is reasonable to suppose that many conservative interventionist businessmen and publications would have backed Roosevelt for re-election.

[9] The historian cannot be certain of the soundness of his analysis of emotional and psychological bases for individual actions and attitudes. This paragraph was written after several years of research on Nye and Roosevelt – including a summer doing research in the Roosevelt Papers, several weeks of research in the Nye manuscripts, and numerous conversations and visits with the senator. Convenient and useful accounts relating psychological theories to foreign policy attitudes are Bernard Fensterwald, Jr., "The Anatomy of American 'Isolationism' and Expansionism. II," *Journal of Conflict Resolution*, II (December 1958), pp. 280–307; and Vernon Van Dyke, *International Politics* (New York: Appleton-Century-Crofts, 1957), pp. 131–52. For reference to Nye's vacation in March see Gerald W. Movius to John A. Hastings, March 14, 1939, Nye Papers; *Bismarck Tribune*, March 15, 1939.

[10] *Congressional Record*, 76 Congress, 1 session (1939), Appendix, pp. 648–50; *New York Sun*, February 18, 1939.

[11] *Congressional Record*, 76 Congress, 1 session (1939), pp. 2003–5, 2197–2203.

[12] Rosenman, *Public Papers and Addresses of Franklin D. Roosevelt*, 1939 vol., pp. 3–4.

[13] Wayne S. Cole, "Senator Key Pittman and American Neutrality Policies, 1933–1940," *Mississippi Valley Historical Review*, XLVI (March 1960), p. 657; Cordell Hull, *The Memoirs of Cordell Hull* (2 vols.; New York: Macmillan Company, 1948), pp. 612–14.

[14] Cole, "Pittman and American Neutrality Policies," *Mississippi Valley Historical Review*, p. 658; Hull, *Memoirs*, pp. 613–14, 641–42; *Congressional Record*, 76 Congress, 1 session (1939), Appendix, p. 1318; and *Text of Legislation Relating to Neutrality, Peace, and Our Foreign Policy Pending in the Committee on Foreign Relations, United States Senate* (Washington, D.C.: Government Printing Office, March 31, 1939).

[15] Cole, "Pittman and American Neutrality," *Mississippi Valley Historical Review*, p. 658; Hull, *Memoirs*, pp. 643–53.

[16] *Congressional Record*, 76 Congress, 1 session (1939), Appendix, pp. 1317–19, 2435, 3362–63; *ibid.*, 76 Congress, 1 session (1939), pp. 4729–33; Nye to Walter Lippmann, April 26, 1939, Nye to Clarence E. Parr, May 8, 1939, Nye Papers.

[17] *Philadelphia Record*, July 7, 1939; *Washington Times Herald*, July 12, 1939; undated item in Foreign Relations Committee Files, 75th Congress.

[18] *Congressional Record*, 76 Congress, 1 session (1939), pp. 10399–10407.

[19] *Ibid.*, 76 Congress, 2 session (1939), Appendix, pp. 89–91.

[20] *Ibid.*, 76 Congress, 1 session (1939), Appendix, p. 2435; Gerald P. Nye, "Alien-Imperialism – and America," *Vital Speeches of the Day*, V (July 1, 1939), pp. 574–75.

[21] *Congressional Record*, 76 Congress, 1 session (1939), p. 10401.

[22] *Minneapolis Tribune*, August 19, 1939; Gerald P. Nye, "Save American Neutrality," *Vital Speeches of the Day*, V (September 15, 1939), p. 724; *Denver Post*, August 30, 1939; Nye to C. E. Backman, July 25, 1939, Nye Papers.

[23] *New York Times*, October 8, 1939, August 28, 1940; *Congressional Record*, 76 Congress, 3 session (1940), pp. 8793–97.

[24] Rosenman, *Public Papers and Addresses of Franklin D. Roosevelt*, 1939 vol., p. 518.

[25] Cole, "Pittman and American Neutrality Policies," *Mississippi Valley Historical Review*, pp. 659–60; Hull, *Memoirs*, I, pp. 693–97; Key Pittman, "The Embargo Should Be Repealed," *Vital Speeches of the Day*, VI (October 15, 1939), p. 20.

[26] *Washington Times Herald*, September 12, 1939; *New York Times*, September 26, 1939; telegram from Gerald W. Movius to Associated Press, Bismarck, North Dakota, September 13, 1939, Movius to Nye, January 14, 1941, Nye to Mrs. Bennett Champ Clark, January 14, 1941, Nye Papers.

[27] *Congressional Record*, 76 Congress, 2 session (1939), Appendix, pp. 83–85; *ibid.*, 76 Congress, 2 session (1939), pp. 113–14, 360–83.

[28] *Ibid.*, Appendix, pp. 83–85; *Chicago Daily Times*, September 15, 1939.

[29] Memorandum by Joseph C. Green, September 19, 1939, Department of State Records, File No. 811.04418/696; *Devils Lake Journal*, September 25, 1939.

[30] Elliott Roosevelt, ed., *F. D. R.: His Personal Letters, 1928–1945* (2 vols.; New York: Duell, Sloan and Pearce, 1950), pp. 921–46; Walter Johnson, *The Battle against Isolation* (Chicago: University of Chicago Press, 1944), pp. 31–54.

[31] *Congressional Record*, 76 Congress, 2 session (1939), pp. 747–54, 775–76, 846–56, 1024–27; Tom Connally, *My Name Is Tom Connally* (New York: Thomas Y. Crowell Company, 1954), pp. 230–31; *Devils Lake Journal*, November 14, 1939; *New York Times*, March 16, 1940, March 17, 1940.

[32] *Cincinnati Post*, November 30, 1939; *New York Times*, January 11, 1940; *Bismarck Tribune*, January 24, 1940.

[33] *Star* (Washington, D.C.), December 7, 1934; *New York Times*, January 25, 1940, February 9, 1940; *Congressional Record*, 76 Congress, 3 session (1940), p. 1207; Eleanor E. Dennison, *The Senate Foreign Relations Committee* (Stanford: Stanford University Press, 1942), pp. 192–95; Cole, "Pittman and American Neutrality," *Mississippi Valley Historical Review*, pp. 647–48; *Newsweek*, XVI (November 25, 1940), pp. 16–17; America First Committee Bulletin No. 396, July 8, 1941, America First Committee Papers, Hoover Library, Stanford, California; interview with Nye, July 20, 1959. The author has done research in the records of the Foreign Relations Committee in National Archives for 1933 through 1945.

[34] *New York Times Magazine*, January 14, 1940, pp. 1–2.

[35] John Koehn to Nye, April 24, 1940, Nye to Jacob S. Quanbeck, April 26, 1940, unaddressed and unsigned letter, April 26, 1940, undated clipping from *Grand Forks Herald*, Nye Papers; interview with Nye, July 20, 1959.

[36] *Congressional Record*, 76 Congress, 3 session (1940), pp. 8790–91, 9313–16.

[37] *Ibid.*, pp. 10804–20.

[38] *New York Times*, August 26, 1940, September 2, 1940.

[39] *Ibid.*, June 9, 1935; interview with Nye, July 20, 1959; *Star* (Washington, D.C.), August 12, 1939; *Washington Times Herald*, October 18, 1939; *Congressional Record*, 76 Congress, 2 session (1939), Appendix, pp. 89–91; Nye to Rose Fogarty, March 25, 1939, John Cheshire to S. W. Hooper, March 27, 1939, Nye Papers.

[40] *Washington Times Herald*, October 18, 1939; Gerald W. Movius to P. N. Whisnant, October 24, 1939, Movius to William R. Ransom, November 13, 1939, Movius to John W. Smith, November 13, 1939, November 18, 1939, Nye Papers; interview with Nye, July 20, 1959.

[41] *New York Times*, January 10, 1940, April 1, 1940, April 7, 1940; Donald Bruce Johnson, *The Republican Party and Wendell Willkie* (Urbana: University of Illinois Press, 1960), pp. 61–108.

[42] *New York Times*, January 10, 1940; *Time*, XXXV (April 15, 1940), pp. 21–22, and (June 24, 1940), pp. 15–16; Arthur M. Schlesinger, Jr., *The Age of Roosevelt: The Politics of Upheaval* (Boston: Houghton Mifflin Company, 1960), pp. 136–42.

[43] *Congressional Record*, 76 Congress, 3 session (1940), pp. 8790–98; *New York Times*, June 22, 1940.

[44] Gerald P. Nye, "No Third Term, No War" (Mimeographed text of address over Mutual Broadcasting System, Chicago, November 2, 1940), Nye Papers.

[45] Shelby J. Light to Nye, November 4, 1940, Nye Papers.
[46] *Richland County Farmers Globe*, December 3, 1940; Thomas Hall, *Compilation of Election Returns National and State, 1930–1944* ([Bismarck], 1945); Walter Johnson, *1600 Pennsylvania Avenue: Presidents and the People, 1929–1959* (Boston: Little, Brown and Company, 1960), pp. 91–92; Wilfred E. Binkley, *American Political Parties: Their Natural History* (New York: Alfred A. Knopf, 1947), pp. 383–86; Samuel Lubell, *The Future of American Politics* (2nd ed. rev.; New York: Doubleday and Company, 1956), pp. 54–60.
[47] *Fargo Forum*, February 27, 1940; *Jamestown Sun*, March 14, 1940; *New York Times*, February 27, 1940, March 14, 1940.
[48] *New York Times*, November 10, 1940, November 28, 1940, December 15, 1940, December 22, 1940; *Bangor* (Maine) *Daily News*, December 3, 1941; conversations with Mrs. Marguerite Nye, July and August 1959.

Chapter 11. America First

[1] Walter Johnson, *The Battle against Isolation* (Chicago: University of Chicago Press, 1944), pp. 59–223; Richard Austin Thompson, "The Committee to Defend America" (Unpublished M.S. thesis, Department of History, University of Wisconsin, 1953), *passim*; Franklin D. Roosevelt to William Allen White, December 14, 1939, White to Roosevelt, December 22, 1939, and other items in President's Personal File 1196, Thomas W. Lamont to Roosevelt, May 15, 1940, President's Personal File 70, F. H. LaGuardia to White, December 26, 1940, President's Personal File 1376, Lamont to Roosevelt, January 3, 1941, and materials dated April 15, 1941, and May 1, 1941, Official File 4230, Roosevelt Papers.
[2] Johnson, *Battle against Isolation*, pp. 223–27; Henry L. Stimson and McGeorge Bundy, *On Active Service in Peace and War* (New York: Harper and Brothers, 1948), pp. 364–76; numerous items in Official File 4461, Roosevelt Papers.
[3] Wayne S. Cole, *America First: The Battle against Intervention, 1940–1941* (Madison: University of Wisconsin Press, 1953), pp. 10–26, 71–79; undated telegram from R. Douglas Stuart, Jr., and Potter Stewart to Gerald P. Nye, and telegram from Nye to Stuart, October 26, 1939, General Robert E. Wood Papers, Chicago, Illinois.
[4] Cole, *America First*, pp. 26–31; Wayne S. Cole, "America First and the South, 1940–1941," *Journal of Southern History*, XXII (February 1956), pp. 36–47.
[5] Cole, *America First*, *passim*, but see particularly pp. 15–16, 36–41, 89–100, 104–30.
[6] Minutes of a meeting of the America First national committee, Chicago, Illinois, October 25, 1940, Stuart to William R. Castle, October 24, 1940, America First Committee Papers, Hoover Library, Stanford, California; Stuart to Nye, November 22, 1940, Nye to Stuart, December 7, 1940, Robert L. Bliss to Nye, December 11, 1940, Gerald W. Movius to Bliss, December 23, 1940, Movius to Nye, January 14, 1941, Nye to Mrs. Bennett Champ Clark, January 14, 1941, Nye Papers.
[7] Winston S. Churchill, *Their Finest Hour* (Boston: Houghton Mifflin Company, 1949), pp. 557–09; Robert E. Sherwood, *Roosevelt and Hopkins: An Intimate History* (New York: Harper and Brothers, 1948), pp. 221–29; William L. Langer and S. Everett Gleason, *The Undeclared War, 1940–1941* (New York: Harper and Brothers, 1953), pp. 225–54.
[8] *New York Times*, November 26, 28, 1940, December 22, 1940.
[9] *Ibid.*, February 1, 2, 21, 1941; *Congressional Record*, 77 Congress, 1 session (1941), pp. 1108–21, 1363–70, 1406–36, 1722–35, 2082–96, A1333–39; *Hearings before the Committee on Foreign Relations, United States Senate*, 77 Congress,

1 session, on S. 275 (Washington, D.C.: Government Printing Office, 1941), p. 905; Nye to Anna M. Lauers, February 14, 1941, Nye Papers; mimeographed text of address by Nye at America First rally, New York City, February 20, 1941, America First Papers; Tom Connally, *My Name Is Tom Connally* (New York: Thomas Y. Crowell, 1954), p. 244.

[10] *New York Times*, February 21, 1941; Cole, *America First*, pp. 43–49; daily memos to Rudolph Forster tabulating letters, cards, and petitions received at the White House for and against lend-lease, Official File 4193, Roosevelt Papers.

[11] Johnson, *Battle against Isolation*, pp. 206–9; Hadley Cantril, ed., *Public Opinion, 1935–1946* (Princeton: Princeton University Press, 1951), pp. 409–10; *Congressional Record*, 77 Congress, 1 session (1941), pp. 2082, 2097–98, 2507–9, 8201–2.

[12] Minutes of America First executive committee meetings, March 28, 1941, April 10, 1941, Wood Papers; Nye to Crawford A. Peffer, March 28, 1941, Joseph R. Boldt, Jr., to Nye, May 7, 1941, Nye to Richard A. Moore, September 15, 1941, Peffer to Nye, November 22, 1941, M. R. Page Hufty to Nye, December 11, 1941, Nye Papers; Robert J. Lavell to Moore, July 11, 1941, Moore to Fred Allhoff, August 23, 1941, Mrs. Mark Mitchell to Hufty, September 20, 1941, Hufty to Mrs. Mitchell, September 23, 1941, Elizabeth Landa to Helen Lamont, November 10, 1941, America First Papers; *Chicago Tribune*, March 29, 1941, June 14, 1941, July 23, 1941; *Bangor* (Maine) *Daily News*, December 3, 1941. By way of illustration of the expenses of Senator and Mrs. Nye that were paid for by America First: the committee paid him $827.91 on October 17, 1941, for expenses when he addressed meetings in Rochester, New York; Cincinnati, Ohio; Dayton, Ohio; Cleveland, Ohio; Brooklyn, New York; Newark, New Jersey; Boston, Massachusetts; Long Island, New York; Bridgeport, Connecticut; and Hoopeston, Illinois. For their expenses in addressing meetings in Waterbury, Connecticut, and in Princeton, New Jersey, Nye received a check for $137.52 from America First. These were typical. Moore to Nye, October 17, 1941, William S. Foulis to Nye, November 8, 1941, America First Papers.

[13] Katrina McCormick to Nye, June 30, 1941, Nye to McCormick, July 3, 1941, Nye Papers.

[14] Nye to Leon Thomson, October 25, 1939, Nye to Louie Fife, May 27, 1941, Nye to Edward J. Ryan, October 17, 1941, Nye Papers; Emil J. Ruckert to New York America First Committee, September 24, 1941, America First Papers.

[15] *Congressional Record*, 77 Congress, 1 session (1941), p. 4589; Stuart to Wood, June 13, 1941, America First Papers; minutes of America First national committee meeting, Chicago, October 20, 1941, Wood Papers; Cordell Hull to Walter F. George, June 19, 1941, Roland Young to E. W. Sheets, September 4, 1941, Tom Connally to Robert F. Campbell, December 3, 1941, Papers Supporting Senate Bills and Resolutions, 77 Congress, S. Res. 124; *Chicago Tribune*, October 21, 1941.

[16] Langer and Gleason, *Undeclared War*, pp. 570–74; Cole, *America First*, pp. 100–3; Gerald P. Nye, "No A.E.F. – We Must Not Go Hunting for War," *Vital Speeches of the Day*, VII (August 15, 1941), pp. 650–52; *Chicago Tribune*, July 20, 1941; *New York Times*, July 20, 1941; Nye to J. Austin White, July 31, 1941, Nye Papers.

[17] Cole, *America First*, pp. 56–59; Report of Ruth Sarles, March 17–April 19, 1941, Hufty to Stuart, June 24, 1941, Sarles to Stuart, June 26, 1941, mimeographed America First news release, June 28, 1941, America First Papers; *Chicago Tribune*, June 30, 1941; Walter F. George to Hull, April 16, 1941, Hull to George, May 7, 1941, File No. 740.00111A/403, Department of State Records.

[18] Mimeographed text of address by Nye at an America First rally, New York

City, February 20, 1941, America First Papers; *New York Times*, February 21, 1941, May 7, 1941.

[19] *New York Herald Tribune*, September 8, 1929; *Congressional Record*, 73 Congress, 2 session (1934), p. 12340.

[20] Cole, *America First*, p. 140; Johnson, *Battle against Isolation*, p. 153; telegram from Harry and Jack Warner to Roosevelt, May 16, 1940, radiogram from Frank Capra and Robert Riskin to Roosevelt, June 11, 1940, telegram from Constance Bennett to Roosevelt, December 30, 1940, President's Personal File 200B, Darryl F. Zanuck to Stephen Early, March 5, 1941, Zanuck to Sheridan Downey, March 5, 1941, Official File 4193, Roosevelt Papers; William T. Dodson to Benson Inge, June 2, 1941, America First Papers.

[21] *Congressional Record*, 77 Congress, 1 session (1941), p. 6565; Nye to Clark, August 1, 1941, Papers Supporting Senate Bills and Resolutions, 77 Congress, S. Res. 152.

[22] Gerald P. Nye, *Our Madness Increases as Our Emergency Shrinks* (Washington, D.C.: Government Printing Office, 1941); Gerald P. Nye, "War Propaganda – Our Madness Increases as Our Emergency Shrinks," *Vital Speeches of the Day*, VII (September 15, 1941), pp. 720–23.

[23] Burton K. Wheeler to D. Worth Clark, August 5, 1941, John T. Flynn to Wheeler, August 6, 1941, Bennett Champ Clark to A. W. Wells, August 12, 1941, Papers Supporting Senate Bills and Resolutions, 77 Congress, S. Res. 152; Robert E. Wood to John L. Wheeler, August 11, 1941, Wood Papers; Cole, *America First*, pp. 140–41.

[24] Cole, *America First*, pp. 104–16.

[25] Donald S. Strong, *Organized Anti-Semitism in America: The Rise of Group Prejudice during the Decade, 1930–40* (Washington, D.C.: American Council on Public Affairs, 1941), p. 19.

[26] *Congressional Record*, 77 Congress, 1 session (1941), pp. 7627–30.

[27] *Pittsburgh Press*, February 22, 1933; text of address by Nye before National Jewish Congress, May 21, 1933, Nye Papers; *New York Times*, November 26, 1938; *Congressional Record*, 76 Congress, 3 session (1940), pp. 10805–6.

[28] *New York Times*, April 25, 1935; *Congressional Record*, 74 Congress, 1 session (1935), p. 3195; Nye to Robert Wagner, March 14, 1939, Nye to Harry Fein, May 6, 1939, Nye to S. E. Paletz and others, May 22, 1939, Gerald P. Winrod to Nye, September 15, 1939, James True to Nye, April 30, 1940, Nye to True, May 3, 1940, press release from Committee of 1,000,000, February 14, 1941, Nye to Gerald L. K. Smith, February 19, 1941, telegram from Stephen S. Wise to Nye, May 20, 1941, Nye to Wise, May 21, 1941, Smith to Nye, July 9, 1941, Nye to Harry Lashkowitz, August 29, 1941, Nye Papers.

[29] Nye to William Stern, August 29, 1941, Nye Papers.

[30] *Congressional Record*, 77 Congress, 1 session (1941), pp. 7627–30; carbon copy of a statement by Nye before Interstate Commerce Subcommittee, September 9, 1941, Nye Papers.

[31] Cole, *America First*, p. 141; *Washington Post*, September 28, 1941; Bennett Champ Clark to C. E. Lay, November 22, 1941, D. Worth Clark to Burton K. Wheeler, December 18, 1941, Papers Supporting Senate Bills and Resolutions, 77 Congress, S. Res. 152.

[32] *Chicago Tribune*, September 12, 1941; *Des Moines Register*, September 12, 1941; Cole, *America First*, pp. 141–54; Kenneth S. Davis, *The Hero: Charles A. Lindbergh and the American Dream* (Garden City, N.Y.: Doubleday and Company, 1959), pp. 411–15.

[33] Carbon copy of undated article reporting interview of Nye for the *American Israelite*, Nye to Richard Scheiner, September 16, 1941, Nye to Martin Loewenberg, September 29, 1941, Nye to Irving Amdur, October 7, 1941, Nye to Joseph

A. Luther, October 8, 1941, Nye to Taylor Caldwell, October 16, 1941, Nye Papers; *Democrat Chronicle* (Rochester, New York), September 18, 1941; *PM* (New York), September 18, 1941; *Des Moines Register*, September 21, 1941; *Washington Post*, September 21, 1941; *New York Herald Tribune*, September 23, 1941.

[34] Nye to Theodore H. Hoffmann, July 19, 1941, Hoffmann to Nye, August 28, 1941, Nye Papers; *Congressional Record*, 77 Congress, 1 session (1941), pp. 7626–27.

[35] Russel Mack to Nye, September 24, 1941, Richard G. Benson to Nye, September 24, 1941, Mrs. J. B. O'Donnell to Nye, September 23, 1941, George Sweet to Nye, September 24, 1941, Fred Kreeger to Nye, September 22, 1941, Nye Papers. These were just a few out of hundreds of similar letters and cards in the Nye Papers.

[36] Friends of Democracy, Inc., *The America First Committee – The Nazi Transmission Belt* (New York, n.d.); *PM* (New York), September 18, 19, 1941; *Film Bulletin*, VIII (September 20, 1941), pp. 3–4; *Congressional Record*, 77 Congress, 1 session (1941), pp. 7625, A4813; A. Liddon Graham to "Dear Member," September 20, 1941, Charles Emde to "Dear Mr. Publisher," September 20, 1941, undated special release for weekly newspapers from Fight for Freedom, Inc., George Gordon Battle to "Dear Friend," October 1941, Nye Papers.

[37] Sidney Ross to Nye, September 24, 1941, unsigned letter to Nye, September 23, 1941, telegram Henry W. Hobson to Nye, October 1, 1941, Nye Papers; Harry Wolf to America First Committee, October 21, 1941, America First Papers. There are many other similar letters to Nye and America First in these manuscript collections.

[38] *Bismarck Tribune*, November 13, 1939.

[39] Langer and Gleason, *Undeclared War*, pp. 422–35, 442–50; Cole, *America First*, pp. 155–57; daily memos to Rudolph Forster tabulating cards, letters, and petitions received at the White House for and against convoys, Official File 4193, Hull to Roosevelt, April 29, 1941, President's Secretary's File, Roosevelt Papers; Ruth Sarles to Kendrick Lee, April 20, 1941, April 21, 1941, April 27, 1941, May 4, 1941, May 11, 1941, Sarles to Stuart, May 18, 1941, May 24, 1941, America First Papers; *Congressional Record*, 77 Congress, 1 session (1941), p. 3374; Elliott Roosevelt, ed., *F. D. R.: His Personal Letters, 1928–1945* (2 vols.; New York: Duell, Sloan and Pearce, 1950), p. 1158; Stuart to Lindbergh, May 13, 1941, Wood to Charles W. Tobey, May 13, 1941, telegram Tobey to Wood, May 15, 1941, Wood Papers; Gerald P. Nye, "This Is Our Critical Hour – We Are Being Blitzkrieged into War," *Vital Speeches of the Day*, VII (May 15, 1941), pp. 453–55.

[40] Langer and Gleason, *Undeclared War*, pp. 427–34, 452–54, 575–80; Cole, *America First*, pp. 157–58; *Chicago Herald-American*, April 12, 1941; *New York Times*, July 20, 1941; Gerald P. Nye, "No Convoys: No War" (Mimeographed text of radio address over the Mutual network, May 8, 1941), America First Papers.

[41] Langer and Gleason, *Undeclared War*, pp. 456–58, 519–20; Cole, *America First*, p. 158; *Killdeer Herald* (North Dakota), June 19, 1941; *Cincinnati Times-Star*, June 16, 1941.

[42] *New York Journal American*, April 20, 1941; unidentified newspaper clipping, May 1941, America First Papers.

[43] Langer and Gleason, *Undeclared War*, pp. 743–44, 756; Cole, *America First*, p. 159.

[44] Samuel I. Rosenman, comp., *The Public Papers and Addresses of Franklin D. Roosevelt* (13 vols.; New York, 1938–50), 1941 vol. (*The Call to Battle Stations*), pp. 384–92.

[45] Cole, *America First*, pp. 159–62; *Democrat Chronicle* (Rochester, New York), September 18, 1941; *Washington Post*, October 18, 1941.

[46] Rosenman, *Public Papers and Addresses of Franklin D. Roosevelt*, 1941 vol., pp. 406–11.

[47] Cole, *America First*, pp. 162–66; *Congressional Record*, 77 Congress, 1 session (1941), pp. 8305–14.

[48] *Congressional Record*, 77 Congress, 1 session (1941), p. 8680; Langer and Gleason, *Undeclared War*, pp. 757–59; *Public Opinion Quarterly*, VI (Spring 1942), p. 162.

[49] Cole, *America First*, pp. 165–66; Nye to Millard C. Dorntge, November 22, 1941, Nye Papers.

[50] Nye to Clarence E. Parr, May 8, 1939, Nye Papers; *Fargo Forum*, November 21, 1941; *New York Times*, November 21, 1941.

[51] *Pittsburgh Press*, December 8, 1941.

[52] *Ibid.*; *Pittsburgh Sun Telegraph*, December 8, 1941; John B. Gordon to Nye, December 9, 1941, Nye to Gordon, January 7, 1942, undated account of Pittsburgh America First meeting in Nye's handwriting apparently written a few days after the meeting, Nye Papers; M. E. Armbruster to Page Hufty, December 11, 1941, undated clipping from *Pittsburgh Press*, James L. Fallon to Gordon, February 6, 1942, America First Papers; *Congressional Record*, 77 Congress, 2 session (1942), p. 8574; interview with Nye, July 20, 1959.

[53] *Pittsburgh Press*, December 8, 1941; *Washington Post*, December 8, 1941; Cole, *America First*, pp. 193–94.

[54] Memorandum in Nye's handwriting, Nye Papers; *Fargo Forum*, December 10, 1941.

[55] Nye to William S. Foulis, December 10, 1941, Nye to Hufty, December 16, 1941, Nye Papers; Cole, *America First*, pp. 194–95.

[56] Stuart to Nye, January 7, 1942, Nye Papers.

[57] Nye to Hufty, December 16, 1941, Nye to Foulis, December 23, 1941, Nye to Stuart, January 19, 1942, Nye Papers; *Fargo Forum*, August 27, 1942; *Congressional Record*, 78 Congress, 1 session (1943), p. 9084.

Chapter 12. The Lonely Road

[1] Conversations with Mrs. Marguerite Nye, August 7 and 8, 1959.

[2] *Congressional Record*, 77 Congress, 2 session (1942), pp. 709–12, 1125, 7574–84; *New York Times*, January 11, 1942, February 8, 1942, February 10, 1942.

[3] *Congressional Record*, 77 Congress, 2 session (1942), p. 8659.

[4] *Ibid.*, 78 Congress, 1 session (1943), pp. 1600–4; Roland Young, *Congressional Politics in the Second World War* (New York: Columbia University Press, 1956), pp. 70–74.

[5] Young, *Congressional Politics*, pp. 70–74; *Congressional Record*, 78 Congress, 1 session (1943), pp. 8147–48.

[6] *Congressional Record*, 78 Congress, 1 session (1943), pp. 5634–35, 6902–6, 7164–65; *Devils Lake Journal* (North Dakota), February 26, 1942; Nye to Glenn Talbott, June 16, 1943, Nye Papers.

[7] *New York Times*, July 12, 1942; *Congressional Record*, 77 Congress, 2 session (1942), pp. A4189–91; *PM* (New York), February 2, 1943; Nye to Alexander H. Uhl, January 28, 1943, and enclosed copy of revised interview statement, Nye Papers. The article in *PM* omitted the first portion of the interview as enclosed with Nye's letter.

[8] *PM*, February 2, 1943.

[9] *Congressional Record*, 78 Congress, 1 session (1943), Appendix, pp. A2553–56.

[10] Ruhl J. Bartlett, ed., *The Record of American Diplomacy* (New York: Alfred A. Knopf, 1947), pp. 675–76; Elliott Roosevelt, ed., *F. D. R.: His Personal Letters, 1928–1945* (2 vols.; New York: Duell, Sloan and Pearce, 1950), II, 1467; Young, *Congressional Politics*, p. 192. The five who voted against the resolution were Hiram

Johnson, William Langer, Robert R. Reynolds, Henrik Shipstead, and Burton K. Wheeler.

[11] *Congressional Record*, 78 Congress, 1 session (1943), pp. 9082–91.

[12] Ralph Townsend to Nye, April 6, 1942, Nye to Joseph Y. Reeves, April 11, 1942, Nye Papers; *New York Times*, January 29, 1942, March 28, 1942.

[13] *New York Times*, January 5, 1943; *Congressional Record*, 78 Congress, 1 session (1943), pp. 167–69; O. John Rogge, *The Official German Report: Nazi Penetration, 1924–1942; Pan-Arabism, 1939–Today* (New York, London: Thomas Yoseloff, 1961), p. 155.

[14] Rogge, *The Official German Report*, pp. 152–74; *New York Times*, December 1, 1944.

[15] *Grand Forks Herald* (North Dakota), June 22, 1944; *New York Times*, July 26, 1944; Nye to Francis Biddle, [June 22, 1944], Nye Papers. This letter is in Nye's handwriting and may have been a first draft of a letter sent. It is also possible that any letter sent may have had somewhat different content. This draft, however, provides a vivid statement of the senator's first reaction to the radio news report of the story.

[16] *Devils Lake Journal*, January 3, 1941; *Bismarck Tribune*, March 28, 1942; United States Senate, 77 Congress, 2 session, Committee on Privileges and Elections, *Senator from North Dakota*, Senate Report 1010 (Washington, D.C.: Government Printing Office, 1942); Nye to T. T. Fuglestad, January 30, 1941, Nye to C. E. Verry, October 15, 1941, Nye to John H. Voorhees, November 25, 1941, Nye Papers.

[17] *Fargo Forum*, January 2, 1944; *Chicago Sun*, May 18, 1944; *Fargo Forum*, June 17, 1944; *Time*, June 19, 1944. The one charge by Stambaugh against Nye in this quotation was based on an interview of Nye by eight or ten newspaper correspondents in the senator's hotel room in Chicago on November 17, 1943. Nye insisted he was misquoted by the newsmen and said he had commented, in answer to a question, that fascism was not "more essentially aggressive and militaristic than have been other forms of government we have known in this world." According to Nye he also told the newsmen: "If Germany and Italy want that form of government, then under our policy of self-determination they should have fascism. It is hard for me to believe that the people of Germany and Italy would tolerate more of it after what fascism had brought to them. Maybe the United Nations will have to afford safeguards that will insure the people of Germany and Italy an honest chance to express their choice in reaching their determination." *Congressional Record*, 78 Congress, 1 session (1943), pp. 10133–34.

[18] *Fargo Forum*, January 2, 1944, May 28, 1944; *Minot Daily News*, January 10, 1944; *Griggs County Sentinel-Courier*, June 22, 1944; *Time*, June 19, 1944; John Roy Carlson, *Under Cover: My Four Years in the Nazi Underworld of America* (Cleveland and New York: World Publishing Company, 1943); *Congressional Record*, 78 Congress, 2 session (1944), Appendix, p. A1965; D. K. N. to Grace Tully, March 9, 1944, Official File 300, Roosevelt Papers; press release text of radio address by Gerald P. Nye, April 18, 1944, Nye Papers; interviews with Math Dahl, March 1, 1960, J. C. Goll, March 5, 1960, Gerald P. Nye, July 20, 1959. On September 12, 1944, Nye told the Senate that in September 1943, a former member of the Department of Justice who was "very close to the White House," Joseph B. Keenan, urged Fay DeWitt, a World War I veteran from Minot, to run for senator in the primary against Nye and promised to finance DeWitt's campaign to the extent of $110,000. According to Nye, Senator Langer introduced Keenan to DeWitt. Nye said DeWitt was told that if he lost in a three-way race, "he would be taken care of, appointed United States marshal, for instance." When DeWitt rejected the offer he was allegedly told that he was "making a mistake in not accepting the proposition, that there could be a guaranty that some serviceman would be in the race for the United States

Senate." Nye introduced statements and affidavits to support his account. Senator Langer then took the floor and denounced "as entirely false the statement that Mr. Joseph B. Keenan ever offered anybody a single dollar to be a candidate against the senior Senator from North Dakota in the coming election." He admitted, however, being at the conversation between Keenan and DeWitt. *Congressional Record,* 78 Congress, 2 session (1944), pp. 7669–76.

[19] *Minot Daily News,* January 10, 1944; *Fargo Forum,* March 19, 1944; *Chicago Tribune,* June 18, 1944; *Griggs County Sentinel-Courier,* June 22, 1944; Edwin S. Webster, Jr., to Nye, November 3, 1943, Nye to Webster, November 8, 1943, November 29, 1943, Nye to Howard A. Smith, December 18, 1943, Gerald W. Movius to editor of *Grand Forks Herald,* January 21, 1944, press release of text of radio address by Nye in North Dakota, April 18, 1944, P. L. Foss to Nye, June 27, 1944, Nye Papers.

[20] Press release of text of radio address by Nye, April 18, 1944, and mimeographed text of address by Nye on "What Has Nye Done for North Dakota?" May 24, 1944, Nye Papers.

[21] *Chicago Tribune,* February 14, 1944; *Chicago Sun,* May 18, 1944.

[22] This was Nye's explanation in an interview on August 17, 1959.

[23] Thomas Hall, Secretary of State, *Compilation of Election Returns: National and State, 1930–1944* ([Bismarck], 1945); *Fargo Forum,* July 2, 1944; Nye to "Dear Friend," July 5, 1944, Nye Papers.

[24] *Which Way North Dakota* (n.p., n.d.). This printed pamphlet in the Nye Papers does not identify the author or publisher except as "A group of citizens of all parties interested in the future of their nation."

[25] This conclusion was reached by the author after interviewing and visiting with many people in Bismarck, North Dakota, in March 1960.

[26] Printed copy of radio address by Nye in North Dakota, October 18, 1944, Nye Papers.

[27] *Bismarck Tribune,* August 28, 1944, September 5, 1944; *Fargo Forum,* September 1, 1944; Hall, *Compilation of Election Returns*; interviews with Math Dahl, March 1, 1960, J. C. Goll, March 5, 1960, Gerald P. Nye, July 20, 1959; Loren R. Gajewski to Nye, November 10, 1944, Josephine Efteland, November 9, 1944, Nye to Milton Young, November 14, 1944, Nye to Fred Aandahl, November 21, 1944, Nye Papers.

[28] *Congressional Record,* 78 Congress, 2 session (1944), pp. 9683–89; *New York Times,* December 21, 1944.

[29] *New York Times,* December 20, 21, 1944, January 10, 1945.

[30] Gerald L. K. Smith to Nye, November 10, 1944, Nye to Smith, November 17, 1944, Nye Papers.

[31] Nye to Milton Young, November 14, 1944, undated clipping from *Griggs County Sentinel-Courier* of early 1945, Nye Papers; Alton G. Sorlie to author, September 23, 1960; interviews with Math Dahl, March 1, 1960, J. C. Goll, March 5, 1960.

[32] Undated, unidentified newspaper clippings of articles by John O'Donnell, datelined Washington, D.C., March 8, 22, Nye Papers; Fred G. Aandahl to the author, September 15, 1961.

[33] Nye to Fred Aandahl, November 21, 1944, Aandahl to Nye, November 24, 1944, Harry M. Anderson to Nye, January 24, 1946, Nye Papers; *New York Times,* March 14, 1946.

[34] Nye to "Dear Friend," March 21, 1946, R. R. Robinson to Nye, March 27, 1946, S. A. Reko to Nye, March 29, 1946, Albert Lundberg to Nye, April 2, 1946, Theodore Swendseid to Nye, April 3, 1946, Nye to Merwin K. Hart, May 18, 1946, Vera Sessler to Nye, undated, Nye to Harold Trownsell, May 19, 1946, statement signed by George Schonberger, Asher Anderson, and George Olson, May 20, 1946, undated handwritten card listing financial supporters of Nye's campaign in 1946,

Nye Papers; *New York Times*, March 7, 1946, April 17, 1946, April 26, 1946, June 23, 1946.

[35] Griggs County Committee for Nye, *Griggs-for-Nye News* (Cooperstown, n.d.; this is a one-page printed copy of a radio address by Nye on May 6, 1946, opening his campaign), Nye Papers; Nye to Bob Dugan, June 8, 1946, Nye Papers.

[36] Nye to Bob Dugan, June 8, 1946, Nye Papers; Griggs County Committee for Nye, *Griggs-for-Nye News*, Nye Papers.

[37] Nye to Hart, May 18, 1946, Nye to Joseph Pew, May 19, 1946, Nye to Burton K. Wheeler, May 19, 1946, Nye Papers; *New York Times*, June 26, 27, 28, 1946.

[38] Nye to author, August 8, 1956, April 2, 1959, December 19, 1960; interviews with Nye, July 20, 1959, Mrs. Nye, August 7, 8, 1959.

[39] *New York Times*, April 15, 1960; Nye to author, December 19, 1960.

[40] Based on numerous conversations with Senator and Mrs. Nye in July and August 1959.

[41] Interview with Nye, August 17, 1959.

[42] *Ibid.*

[43] *Ibid.*; copy of address by Nye before Tall Cedars of Lebanon, Atlantic City Convention, May 21, 1959, Nye Papers; *New York Times*, September 7, 1953.

[44] Interview with Nye, August 17, 1959; copy of address by Nye, May 21, 1959, Nye Papers; Citizens Foreign Aid Committee, *Foreign Aid and You: A First Report* (Washington, D.C., 1959).

[45] Interview with Nye, August 17, 1959, and other conversations with him.

[46] *Ibid.*

Chapter 13. The Decline of Agrarian Isolationism

[1] Samuel Lubell, "Who Votes Isolationist and Why," *Harper's Magazine*, CCII (April 1951), p. 36.

[2] United States Bureau of the Census, *Historical Statistics of the United States, Colonial Times to 1957* (Washington, D.C.: Government Printing Office, 1960), pp. 9, 538, 547–51, 563–66; Merrill Jensen, *The New Nation: A History of the United States during the Confederation, 1781–1789* (New York: Alfred A. Knopf, 1950), pp. 194–240; Herman E. Krooss, *American Economic Development* (Englewood Cliffs, N.J.: Prentice-Hall, 1955), pp. 118–21, 225–27, 303–4, 327–28, 371–401.

[3] Bureau of the Census, *Historical Statistics*, p. 9; United States Department of Commerce, Bureau of the Census, *United States Census of Population, 1960: Number of Inhabitants, United States Summary* (Washington, D.C.: Government Printing Office, 1961), pp. xii–xvii, S24–S35; *Des Moines Sunday Register*, August 13, 1961.

[4] Bureau of the Census, *Historical Statistics*, pp. 537–48, 565; Krooss, *American Economic Development*, pp. 387–95; *Congressional Quarterly Weekly Report*, XIX (June 30, 1961), p. 1171.

[5] Earle D. Ross, "Agriculture in Our Economic History," *Agricultural History*, XXII (April 1948), pp. 65–69; Earle D. Ross, "The Role of the Farmer in American Life," *Current History*, XXXI (September 1956), pp. 129–33; Vernon Carstensen, "The Changing Nature of the American Farm," *Current History*, XXXI (September 1956), pp. 134–38; Mervin G. Smith, director, and Carlton F. Christian, ed., *Adjustments in Agriculture – A National Basebook* (Ames, Iowa: Iowa State University Press, 1961), *passim.*

[6] Samuel Lubell, *The Future of American Politics* (2nd ed. rev.; New York: Doubleday and Company, Anchor Books, 1956), pp. 29–60; Walter Johnson, *1600 Pennsylvania Avenue: Presidents and the People, 1929–1959* (Boston: Little, Brown and Company, 1960), pp. 76–92; Edgar Eugene Robinson, *They Voted for Roosevelt: The Presidential Vote, 1932–1944* (Stanford: Stanford University Press,

1947), pp. 8–40; Donald Bruce Johnson, *The Republican Party and Wendell Willkie* (Urbana: University of Illinois Press, 1960), pp. 61–108; Arthur M. Schlesinger, Jr., *The Politics of Upheaval* (Boston: Houghton Mifflin Company, 1960), pp. 407–43; Ross B. Talbot, "The Declining Political Importance of Farmers," *Successful Farming*, LIX (May 1961), pp. 42, 90–91; *Des Moines Sunday Register*, July 2, 1961; *Des Moines Tribune*, November 9, 1960.

[7] *Congressional Record*, 76 Congress, 3 session (1940), pp. 4001–6.

[8] *Des Moines Sunday Register*, March 26, 1961; *Des Moines Tribune*, November 10, 1960; *Daily Cardinal* (Madison, Wis.), August 20, 1957.

BIBLIOGRAPHICAL NOTE AND ACKNOWLEDGMENTS

Bibliographical Note

THIS STUDY is based largely on primary sources — manuscript, printed, and oral. The footnotes indicate in detail the sources for specific information. This bibliographical note is designed to show in broader terms the principal materials used.

Manuscripts were essential for this study. Despite the valuable data they included, Nye's own letters (both in his papers and in other collections) were less revealing and enlightening than had been hoped. His personality, views, and activities generally came through less vividly in his letters than they did in his editorials, speeches, and press interviews. Nevertheless, the Gerald P. Nye Papers in the senator's home in Chevy Chase, Maryland, were of central importance. The collection is by no means complete, but Nye's staff appears to have tried to preserve important items when it arranged to move his files out of the Senate Office Building in 1944–45. Senator Nye gave me unrestricted access to these previously unused materials. In the National Archives, Washington, D.C., I did research on Nye in the files of the Senate Committee Investigating the Munitions Industry, the Senate Foreign Relations Committee, the Department of State, and in Papers Supporting Senate Bills and Resolutions. The Roosevelt Papers in the Franklin D. Roosevelt Library, Hyde Park, New York, were extremely useful. The America First Committee Papers in the Hoover Library, Stanford, California; the R. Douglas Stuart, Jr., Papers that I used in California; and the General Robert E. Wood Papers that I used in Chicago were essential for studying Nye's role in the America First movement. I found a few items of value to the project in the papers of Senators Key Pittman, George W. Norris, and Tom Connally, in the Library of Congress, Washington, D.C.

Newspapers were particularly useful in studying Nye – both before and during his Senate career. The files of the *Wittenberg Enterprise* (1893–1914), in the Wisconsin State Historical Society Library, Madison, Wisconsin, were invaluable for studying his father's views, the environment in which Gerald was reared, and his activities as a boy and young man. Gerald P. Nye was a prolific editorial writer during his fifteen years as a newspaper editor. Scattered clippings from the Hortonville, Wisconsin, *Weekly Review* in the Nye papers revealed his views and activities in his first editorial position. The files of the *Creston Daily Plain Dealer* for 1915 in the custody of E. J. Van Nostrand, Creston, Iowa, provided a vivid portrait of Nye's views on domestic and foreign affairs before American entry into World War I. I also used the files of the *Fryburg Pioneer* (1916–19), and the *Griggs County Sentinel-Courier* (1919–25), in the North Dakota State Historical Society Library, at Bismarck, North Dakota. These gave a full and colorful account of Nye's views and activities during his decade in North Dakota. The Nye Papers in Chevy Chase contain thirty-four scrapbooks filled with newspaper clippings from all over the United States covering his career in the United States Senate. The fact that the senator expressed his views so freely, candidly, and often impulsively in response to questions from newsmen makes these clippings unusually illuminating. The America First Papers in the Hoover Library include many newspaper clippings from all parts of the country covering his role in that movement. Of course, periodicals also provided useful data on his Senate and post-Senate career.

The *Congressional Record*, both in its daily record and in its appendixes and extensions of remarks, is an invaluable source on Nye's activities and views during his years in the Senate. He spoke often and at length on a wide range of topics and many of these statements are available in the *Record*. The hearings and reports of Senate committees on which he served are also useful – particularly the thirty-nine volumes of hearings and documents and the seven volumes of reports of the Senate Committee Investigating the Munitions Industry. The published volumes of the Department of State, *Foreign Relations of the United States: Diplomatic Papers*, contain relevant documents. Numerous published memoirs, diaries, and secondary accounts also had valuable material on the subject. These are cited in the footnotes, but the accounts by Cordell Hull, Tom Connally, and Harold L. Ickes, as well as the studies by Arthur M. Schlesinger, Jr., and by William L. Langer and S. Everett Gleason were particularly useful.

Finally, I obtained much information and enhanced my understanding through interviews and correspondence with persons who knew Nye or were active in the events. Of special importance were the many conversations and interviews I had with Senator Nye in 1956, 1958, and 1959. In the course of my research and interviewing I visited many of the places where Nye had lived or been active, including Hortonville and Wittenberg, Wisconsin; Creston, Iowa; Bismarck and Fargo, North Dakota.

Acknowledgments

I AM GRATEFUL to Senator and Mrs. Gerald P. Nye for their generous cooperation and help. Senator Nye made his papers available to me for research without any restrictions. He spent many hours patiently answering my questions and discussing his career. His candor, helpfulness, and respect for my intellectual freedom in the project could serve as models for other public figures. Mrs. Nye, too, graciously and helpfully contributed to my knowledge of her husband and his career. Their warm hospitality and tolerance of disruptions caused by my comings and goings as I used the materials in their home greatly exceeded my expectations. They did not read the manuscript in advance of publication, however, and the interpretations and conclusions in this study are entirely my own.

Many who knew Nye (both friends and foes) enhanced my knowledge and understanding of him through interviews and letters. Interviews and conversations with Math Dahl, Luther England, J. C. Goll, Mrs. Henry Hanson, Anton Lavik, Ray Peterson, Mr. and Mrs. Arthur R. Schmidt, Mrs. Schwebs, Walter Trohan, and others provided useful information, as did letters from Fred G. Aandahl, Homer T. Bone, Elmer W. Cart, Stephen Raushenbush, and Alton G. Sorlie.

I am indebted for aid and encouragement from several scholars. Professor Richard S. Kirkendall of the University of Missouri read the entire manuscript and gave me the benefit of suggestions rooted in his extensive research and knowledge of agricultural, political, and intellectual patterns in the Roosevelt era. Professor Ross B. Talbot of Iowa State University also read and criticized the entire study and I drew on his knowledge of agricultural politics, farm organizations, and North Dakota farm politics. He also made available to me useful materials in his possession on North Dakota farm politics. Professor Emeritus Earle D. Ross of Iowa State University read the whole study and his perceptive suggestions reflected his vast knowledge of agricultural history. The constructive criticisms of these three scholars greatly improved the quality of the book; it probably would have been further improved if I had followed more of their suggestions. Professor Walter Johnson of the University of Chicago encouraged me in the project and helped stimulate my thinking on the significance of agrarian radicalism as a base for American isolationism. Professor William B. Hesseltine of the University of Wisconsin, and W. Robert Parks, vice president for academic affairs at Iowa State University, both gave me needed support and encouragement. I owe a special intellectual, professional, and personal debt to Fred Harvey Harrington, president of the University of Wisconsin, for his continuing aid and encouragement.

Numerous librarians and archivists, the unsung heroes of historical research, have extended to me the same generous courtesies and informed professional assistance that scholars have learned to take for granted. Among those whose aid made my task easier and more pleasant were Robert W. Orr, John C. McNee, and Mrs. Mildred E. McHone of the Iowa State University Library; Herman Kahn, Robert L. Jacoby, Louise Evans, J. V. Deyo, William J. Nichols, and Carl Spicer of the Franklin D. Roosevelt Library; Philip T. McLean and John Caswell of the Hoover Library; Miss Margaret Rose of the Library of the State Historical Society of North Dakota; Mrs. Esther Nelson of the Wisconsin State Historical Society Library; and Watson G. Caudill and others of the National Archives. Dr. E. Taylor Parks gave me the same helpful cooperation in the use of Department of State files that he extends to other scholars. E. J. Van Nostrand, publisher of the *Creston News Advertiser,* generously permitted me to do research in his files of the *Creston Daily Plain Dealer.*

Grants from the American Philosophical Society made possible part of the research and much of the writing of this volume.

The staff of the University of Minnesota Press was very helpful in guiding the book through publication. My wife, Virginia Rae Cole, assisted in typing research notes in the Roosevelt and Nye papers. She also read the entire manuscript, helped with proofreading, and patiently tolerated my preoccupation with the project. Our son, Thomas Roy Cole, despite an insatiable curiosity on other matters, demonstrated little interest in the preparation of this book during the first two years of his life — but he helped to make it all worth the effort.

W. S. C.

Ames, Iowa
June 1962

INDEX

Index

Index

Index

Index

Index